Barbed-wire, Barricades & Miss Becker

T G O'Dell

Introduction

This book started life as just a few lines for our family history records. In January 2004 my wife, Kate, and I had visited Australia on holiday and met up with my cousin who had lived there for many years. I was riveted when she told us some of what had happened to her and her brothers 60-odd years before. When I returned to the UK, I began to research the various aspects of her story and became totally absorbed. I was also fascinated by the stories of others who were caught up in the appalling mess of internment in the UK during the Second World War. As I learnt, I knew I wanted to make sure that future generations of our family would know about it. In particular, I hope that my grandchildren, Thaya, Isla, Harry, Eoife, Sienna and Kolbie, will read this when they are older and understand that history is not just a dry collection of dates and facts: it is about real, breathing and feeling people, their lives and their sufferings.

The basis of the story I was told was that, on the outbreak of World War Two, Ruby was interned on the Isle of Man and her brothers were put on the ship "Arandora Star" and this was torpedoed on its way to Canada. They were rescued, returned to the UK and, almost immediately, put on the notorious ship "Dunera" to endure passage to Australia.

So, having put down the broad outline, I started to research the various aspects of her tale. Like most fascinating stories, the more I looked into it the more compelling it all became.

After a while, I realised that it would make an incredible book if only someone would write it. It was only some time later that I thought I might give it a try. Having never before had the time nor inclination to write a novel, my initial attempts were fun but all over the place. But, gradually, it started to have a life of its own. Dialogue became easier as personalities formed. Strangely, I couldn't wait to find out what happened next.

In Alistair MacLean's collection of short stories "The Lonely Sea" published in 1985 there is a chapter on "The Arandora Star" and I would urge anyone who is interested to get hold of a copy if you can. It makes fascinating but chilling (that's not meant to be a pun) reading.

In turning fact into this fictionalised form, I have taken the basic facts and added bits and pieces of others' experiences together with a considerable amount of imagination to try and link it all together. Therefore, any errors and omissions are down to me and I apologise to everyone for that. If anyone is offended, I am truly sorry. It was not my intention.

Finally, I am eternally indebted to Anne-Marie Rogers for her diligence in proof-reading this book as well as correcting my schoolboy German. I can't thank you enough, Anne-Marie.

I hope you enjoy reading it as much as I enjoyed writing it.

T.

Chapter 1

January 29th 2007

Ruby just had this feeling. She'd woken up with it going round and round in her head but still couldn't put her finger on precisely what it was that was making her feel uneasy. She didn't feel unwell: a few aches and twinges maybe but that was normal, expected even at her age. It was more of a fear, no, expectation that something different, out of the ordinary, was about to happen. An excitement. By the time she'd eaten her toast and home-made marmalade, she'd convinced herself that today was the day when all the horses that she picked out of the paper would romp first passed the post. Wouldn't that be something for the rest of the racing syndicate down at the Oakpark Seniors Centre where she went on Mondays, Wednesdays and Fridays.

She'd woken with a start. A noise had startled her. She must have dozed off over the paper. Always happened these days. Must be getting old. Someone was coming up the path.

The man had unlatched the gate and paused, jealously admiring the huge electric-blue hydrangeas in the corner of the garden. Although he wouldn't know a rose from a rhododendron, his mother had always loved hydrangeas and coming here always took him back to his childhood. The woman was seated in a wicker-work garden chair, shading under a mature fruit tree that cast its dappled shade over most of the stone patio which adjoined the bungalow.

"G'day, Missus. Sorry if I woke yer" he announced. "I've got something for you this morning." He passed her a couple of letters, bills by the look of them, and a rather large, flat parcel which, intriguingly, was tied up with string.

"Looks interesting!" he commented.

The woman half-smiled half-yawned. "Yes, doesn't it". She started to unwrap it but her arthritic fingers just weren't up to loosening the knots in the string.

"Hang on Missus" said the man, as he patted his trouser pockets, "I've got a knife somewhere." Finding it, he offered the knife to the woman but she countered by offering him the parcel instead.

"Would you do it? I don't like sharp knives."

With the string easily severed, the postman handed back the still-wrapped parcel. The woman peeled open the brown paper and found an envelope sitting on top of another wrapped parcel.

"Curiouser and curiouser" said the woman as she opened the envelope, finding a hand-written letter on blue writing paper inside.

"You alright now Missus?" said the postman. "Only I've got to get a move on."

"What!" exclaimed the woman, who was now engrossed in the letter. "Oh, yes. And thank you for your help."

"No worries. Mind how you go" called the postman as he let himself out of the gate. The woman could hear him whistling as he walked down the road towards her neighbours. She had known something was going to happen. Shame about the horses. She turned back to the letter.

"Dear Ruby,

Forgive me for addressing you by your Christian name but I only have the attached to go on. I hope this reaches you.

I found the enclosed in a pile of old pictures and books in a flea market in Ashwood, here in Melbourne, the other day.

Most of it was the usual junk that people get rid of from time to time – you must know the sort of thing. Anyway, as I said, the enclosed was in amongst all this stuff and the more I looked at it, the more intrigued I became.

I had the strangest feeling that there were so many memories tied up in it that I thought I would just post it back to the address on the letter and allow providence to take care of the rest. If it never got back to you, well, it wasn't meant to be.

I hope I've done the right thing – that I haven't opened old sores. Please forgive me if I have. If not, then just put it down to fate.

Yours sincerely,

Mary Frobisher."

PS. If you feel like letting this nosey parker out of her misery about what the tokens were all about, perhaps you could give me a ring. If not, well, best wishes.

Ruby gingerly opened the package. No string this time. It was a picture frame and she recognised it immediately although she hadn't seen it for what must be at least twenty years. It was a framed letter to her with three cardboard tokens stuck to it at the bottom and had been in a box in her smallest bedroom for a long time. In fact she had thought it was still there. She almost knew the contents by heart.

"Dearest Ruby,

Guess what? I saw Shirley on the television yesterday. Something about the Australian Parliament – didn't catch the beginning so don't know what it was all about, sorry. You must be ever so proud of her.

How are things in Oz? Hot and sunny I'll bet. Not like here. It just never stops raining – well it seems like that anyway. The forecasters reckon things are going to improve next week but they never seem to get it right. I think I'll just stick to the seaweed.

The Hotel's doing pretty well. We've been concentrating on the Italian market (Get me! You can tell I went to Marketing Evening Classes). You'd be amazed at the amount of Italians who want to see where Grandpapa spent the War and with Rico in the kitchen, we can provide a real home-from-home for them. He's in his element. Shouting and hollering at everyone. Typical Italians! But, you know, he still makes those little hairs on the back of my neck stick up. He sends his love by the way.

Anyway, I found loads of these Service Exchange Tokens the other day and as they made me think of all the good times we had together, I thought I'd send some to you hoping they did the same for you.

Do you remember that day we got hold of the teaching skeleton from Dandy Hill Hospital and sneaked it into that horrible Mitzi Muller's bed. Christ, I thought she was going to have a heart attack when she got into bed. Even better that it was so dark that night. Can you imagine it?

She was all fur coat and no knickers, that one. She didn't stay long after that, did she? Moved up to The Stanley Hotel with the rest of the prossies, I seem to remember. Did you know (I only found this out years later) that there were about 150 of them there in the end? It still makes me laugh when I remember it.

Anyway, got to rush as we've got another load coming in soon. Take care and do write soon.

Love

Tilly"

Ruby smiled at the letter and reached for her hankie to wipe away the moisture that had appeared in the corner of her left eye. Some happy times. Strange when you think that there were so many reasons why the memories should have been anything but. It had been wartime, her Mother's country at war with her Father's; she'd been away from her home, her family and under the constant threat that something even worse would happen to her. But, perhaps for the first time in her life, she had been free. Free to do what she liked and, within reason, when she liked. All responsibilities taken away from her. Yet she hadn't been free at all - living on an island in the middle of the Irish Sea. Surrounded by barriers and barbed-wire and guarded by policemen.

But that was the point. In a way, those barriers and guards had kept the rotten, dangerous world out just as much as they kept the women in.

She remembered that they were bored most of the time, especially in the early days – always trying to think up things to do that would earn them extra money. Although they hadn't starved – far from it when you think of the suffering and deprivation that was being endured on the mainland– extra money was always useful when it came to getting the luxuries that had made life that little bit more bearable, like those bloody sunglasses. "I wonder what ever happened to them" she said to herself.

And then came the same twinge of guilt that she had often felt over the sixty or so years since those days. Guilt that she had been safe, secure, fed and free to enjoy whatever was around her. Not a choice her Mum and her siblings had had.

And guilt about the other things.

The wind suddenly blew up and she looked at the sky. It had suddenly gone cloudy and it looked like rain was on the way. In all the years she had lived in Melbourne, she was always amazed how changeable the weather was and how quickly it happened, too. She picked up her reading glasses from the little table at the side of her chair and, together with Mary Frobisher's letter, the picture frame containing Tilly's and the newspaper, she walked slowly into her bungalow.

Having put the kettle on, she took the letters through to the Lounge and reached for the phone. She knew from the area code that it was somewhere nearby in Melbourne.

"Is that Mrs Frobisher?" said Ruby when the phone was answered. "My name's Ruby Morrison. You kindly sent my letter in the picture frame back to me and I just wished to thank you."

"Oh! Yes" said Mary Frobisher. "Sorry, I'm quite shocked. I never expected to hear from you. To be honest, I never expected that it would ever find you."

"You mean you thought I might be dead" Ruby chuckled.

"Well, maybe the thought had crossed my mind" admitted Mary.

"Don't worry" said Ruby. "I might be in my nineties but I'm not ready for that journey yet. Anyway, thank you again for returning the letter. It was very thoughtful of you to go to so much effort. I'm very grateful."

"You're most welcome" said Mary. "As I think I said in my letter, it intrigued me. I just couldn't understand what those cardboard squares were and why they were so important. My mind did all sorts of imaginings but the only thing I could think of was that they are some sort of money system – you know like the Africans using cowrie shells."

"Well, how perceptive of you" said Ruby. "You're right. They were used as a form of money, but in a million years I don't think you would guess where they were used."

Mary immediately took up the challenge and said "Well, I know they were in English, but if you say that I'd never guess then England is going to be out. And here in Australia's too obvious." She was quiet for only a couple of moments and then replied "How about Gibraltar?"

"That's really quite clever" said Ruby. "And in some ways quite close. But it's not Gibraltar. Look, how would you like to come round for tea sometime and I can tell you about it if you're so interested. At least it would give me a chance to thank you properly."

"Oh, thank you but please don't think I'm being nosey!" exclaimed Mary, worried that she had appeared to be exactly that. "My son is always telling me to stop getting involved in things that don't concern me. I'm just......... I'm really not ...." she stopped, took a deep breath and said "I'd love to. If it won't put you to too much trouble."

"Well that's settled then. How about next Tuesday at 3 o'clock?"

Mary Frobisher was not at all like Ruby had imagined – much younger – late 50's she would guess – and birdlike – about five feet tall and very slim with short wavy auburn hair.

Ruby Morrison, on the other hand, was not at all like Mary had imagined – tallish, about 5 feet 7 inches, and very upright. In fact Mary at first thought that the woman who had answered the door was a daughter or a friend. This woman did not look to be in her eighties let alone into her nineties.

They sat in the Lounge with the tea and biscuits that Ruby had arranged on the ornate oriental mahogany coffee table that matched other furniture in the room. Photo frames of various children and weddings littered the room – all placed very precisely. There was not a hint of dust on any of them, Mary noticed. Either she had a very conscientious cleaning lady or Ruby was remarkably fit.

The tea poured and the biscuits offered but declined ("As you can see" Mary had said, "I don't have much of an appetite these days"), Ruby asked if she had had to come far.

"Not at all" answered her guest, "I live in Mount Waverley, near the Golf Course, so it wasn't difficult at all to get here". Then she added "What about you? Have you always lived here?"

"Well" she said, then paused to take a sip of her tea, "I came to Melbourne from England after the War, after my husband died and I've lived here" - she looked around the room - "since it was built in the 70's. A long time!"

"It's a lovely place you've got. I can see why you've never moved" said Mary, trying to keep the conversation away from anything that she felt might upset her new friend or, indeed, herself as she too had been widowed the previous year when her husband had died of a sudden and massive heart attack. ("I kept telling him he needed to take a holiday.")

"So please tell me about the letter and the tokens" she said. "I'm just dying to know."

Ruby smiled. "I suppose I've kept you hanging on long enough" she said. She thought for a moment or two while she sipped her tea again and then she said "Let me start by giving you a bit of background. Although I was born in London during the First World War, I'm only half English. My mother was English, but my father was German. He died just a few months after I was born and my mother remarried – to my father's best friend. He was also German. As the years went by they had three boys and a girl. We all went to a German school in the east end of London. We mostly spoke in German within the family although my mother never really mastered it and usually spoke to us in English.

"But although we children were brought up being bi-lingual, our home was London and England. Never Germany. We were happy there, doing the things that all the other children did in the 1920's. But, as you can imagine, things began to change in the 1930's. When Hitler came to power, people in England began to think that we were somehow connected to the Nazis. The newspapers began talking about "German 5th Columnists" and this got worse as rumours that another war was coming started to circulate.

"Ironically, at the same time, thousands of Germans were fleeing to Britain to escape anti-Semitism in Germany. I read somewhere that at the outbreak of the war in September 1939, there were 75,000 people of Germanic origin, Austrians as well as Germans, living in Britain and that about 60,000 of them were Jews who had escaped the Nazis in 1939 alone.

"Well, when the war broke out it was decided that all those of German or Austrian origin, male and female, had to be registered. We had to go before an Enemy Alien Tribunal. Even though it was only just down the road, it was awful. We felt like criminals. They asked us where we lived, what jobs we did, when we were last in Germany, all that sort of stuff. Well, it was daft because we had never even been to Germany. Because we were just ordinary people, my brothers and I were put into Category "B" like the vast majority of those who went before the Tribunal. This meant that although we were free to return to our homes and our jobs, our loyalty to England was in some way suspect. We didn't understand at the time, but now I think they just didn't really know what to do with us all."

"What about your sister…. Eh, I mean half-sister?"

"Oh, Dot was too young. Only in her early teens. Anyway, we got through that and for a while things returned to normal. We went out to work. Just did the things we had always done. The war didn't seem to be as bad as people had said it was going to be and we all thought it was a storm in a tea-cup. You know, over by Christmas! But it wasn't and in early 1940 German forces invaded Belgium and Holland.

"Well, I think that was too close for comfort for the British authorities and they decided to intern all those who had been registered who were between 16 and 60 years of age – all of them, regardless. That meant my brothers and me.

"A day or so afterwards, four policemen came to our house and told us to pack a few essentials and then they took us away. Just like that! We didn't even have time to say goodbye to our mother because she was out at work. I just scribbled a quick note on the back of an envelope and that was it."

Mary sat riveted to the sofa, as Ruby got up to make another pot of tea. Was there just the hint of a limp as she walked across the lounge to the kitchen?

"Where did they take you?" shouted Mary as Ruby put the kettle on.

"Holloway Prison" replied Ruby impassively.

"No! They never!" gasped Mary. "Seems a bit harsh and over the top. Why, did they think you were a spy or something?"

The hairs on the back of Ruby's neck stood up, but her voice didn't betray the disquiet she suddenly felt. "I've no idea. Just some sort of crazy over-reaction, I suppose."

"What was it like – in Holloway?"

"It was horrid" said Ruby. "And they took the boys to Ascot Racecourse where they put them into the old stables. But at least they were together."

Ruby returned with a fresh pot of tea and, as she proceeded to pour, Mary asked "Were you put in the cells?"

"Oh yes. But they weren't locked except at night and, although it was on a separate wing from all the convicts, we were confined to that wing."

"How long were you there for?" asked Mary, having changed her mind and now nibbling a biscuit.

"Just a couple of days as far as I remember. The worse thing was that we just didn't know what was going to happen to us. We didn't know if we were going to be kept there for the duration of the war or, even worse, deported to Germany. But early one morning, they came for us and put us on a train to Liverpool and then stuck us on a boat to the Isle of Man where we were interned."

"Ahh!" exclaimed Mary, "so that's where the letter came from."

"That's right" said Ruby, who was now aware that she was suddenly feeling quite drained. "And it was while we were on the island that we used the tokens, which were taken from old Cornflake packets, to buy things we needed."

"How intriguing" said Mary, realising that her host was looking noticeably paler. "Well thank you so much for explaining it all to me. I'm absolutely shocked that they could have treated you so badly. Look, I hope you don't mind but I really need to make a move, otherwise I'm going to hit the rush-hour traffic". So saying she got to her feet and took her cup and the tea-pot through to the kitchen. "Can I wash up for you?" she asked.

"No, leave it" replied Ruby, getting to her feet. "I'll do it later."

As Mary walked to the front door she said "Thank you so much for inviting me here. Perhaps we can meet up again some time?"

"Yes, that would be nice" said Ruby. "I don't get many visitors these days."

After Mary had driven away, Ruby sat back into her favourite chair and closed her eyes. She was aware that she hadn't told Mary the full story, far from it, but some things were best left alone. The feelings of guilt and humiliation were still there after all this time. And she knew that she didn't know all of the facts, anyway. Probably just as well.

Chapter 2

May 1940

It was four o'clock in the afternoon. The heavy knock on the front door came just twenty seconds after Ruby had sat down. She had just got home after completing the morning part of her job "in service" and doing some shopping in the local market. "Just enough time for a nice cup of tea" she had said to the goldfish in its jam jar on the mantelpiece.

She had about fifteen minutes before she had to start back to do the early evening chores at the home of her employer, Mr. Mendelsohn, whom she knew was something to do with banking in the City. She really liked Mr Mendelsohn. He always seemed to have a little smile for her and often asked how her mother was. She knew that he had known her step-father and that they always passed the time of day on the rare occasions that they had met in the street. The boys would be home from their shifts at the munitions factory any minute. Time enough for them to tidy the house before their mother got home at six o'clock.

"God this place is a mess" said Ruby to the fish, although it didn't seem to be bothered one way or another. Wearily she got up from the chair and went to the door. There were four policemen standing there.

"What's happened?" she said, the alarm bells ringing in her head. "Is it Mum…… or the boys….or Dot?"

"Are you Ruby Becker?" said the oldest policeman.

"Yes. That's me." And then it dawned on her. Oh God! She'd thought they wouldn't come for her but they had. "Oh God!" she said out loud.

"Ruby Becker, we have a detention warrant in your name issued under the Emergency Powers Act. You are required to come with us."

Ruby thought she was going to faint.

"We have similar warrants for Karl Darling, Peter Darling and Johann Darling also at this address" added the policeman.

"They're my brothers" said Ruby weakly as she looked down the street to see if the boys were coming. "But they're not home from work yet." It was then that she noticed that quite a large crowd of people, friends and strangers alike, were standing in the street and in doorways watching what was going on. The arrival of the police in the street always created a spectacle.

She was going to shout out something but she couldn't think what to say and besides, her voice seemed to have died in the back of her throat. All she could do was look around at the faces that were looking back at her. Some smiled supportively. Some looked to their feet when she made eye contact with them. Others, strangers, shouted horrible things at her only to be rounded on by yet others, people she knew by sight only, people who she was astonished to find supporting her and her family.

In the end, she turned away, the tears welling up, and, with legs that felt like jelly, went back into the kitchen followed by two of the policemen. Ruby stood with her back towards the men and tried to control herself. She blew her nose on her handkerchief and then turned round. "What happens now......eh....?" she queried.

"Hammond, Miss. Sergeant Hammond. By rights we should have been here early this morning, but the police station got hit last night so you could say we've been a bit busy. Still nobody was hurt, thank God. Right, now you need to get a few essentials packed into a small suitcase or bag. I have to tell you that the journey could last two or three days." Then he added "You know the sort of thing, I'm sure, Miss. For what it's worth, I would suggest you make sure you've got lots of thin layers – to keep you warm and plenty of...eh....unmentionables, if you know what I mean."

"I think I understand, Sergeant. Thank you."

"But first we have to search the house" said the other policeman with open enthusiasm.

"Whatever for" asked Ruby, alarmed.

"Regulations, Miss" the Sergeant replied.

"Yeah" sneered his colleague. "Just in case you've got two-way wirelesses, cameras and secret code books stashed away."

"That will do, Johnson" snapped Sergeant Hammond. "When I want your opinion, I'll tell you what it is. In the meantime, keep your trap shut and get on and search the house. Get Stephenson to help you."

"Yes Sergeant". Johnson stood to attention but Ruby didn't miss the brief smirk on his face as the Sergeant turned to her.

"Right! Come on now, Miss. How about putting the kettle on? You can think about what you need to take while they do what they have to. Oh, Johnson?" he shouted.

Johnson's face appeared round the door. "Yes Sarge?"

"I'm watching you, so mind you keep it tidy."

"Yes, Sarge."

The search took all of thirty minutes, during which time Ruby sat in the kitchen, her mind racing with a thousand questions. What to take? What would they do to her? What did they know? Where would they take her? How long would she be away?

"What about my Mum?" said Ruby. "We can't leave before she gets home."

"Need her to hold your hand, do yer?" said a sneering Johnson, appearing at the door at that precise moment.

"Have you finished?" barked Hammond.

"Yes, Sarge. And surprise, surprise we found this under one of the beds in the small bedroom." He handed a small black leather suitcase to his superior. "It's locked."

"Is this yours, Miss?" asked Hammond.

"Yes. Well no, it belongs to my boyfriend. He asked me to look after it while he went home to see his parents" replied Ruby. She thought she might faint or be sick, or both.

"I see. Do you have a key?"

"No, I don't" she lied. "Dieter didn't leave one."

"Then I'm afraid we will have to prize it open. Johnson?" He handed the case to Johnson who took out a pocket-knife.

"No" gasped Ruby. "You'll ruin it and Dieter will be furious. He doesn't like other people touching his things."

"Sorry, Miss. Get on with it, Johnson" said Hammond.

With a deft twist of the blade, each clasp sprang open. Hammond opened the lid. Inside were a number of blue folders each with a different address written in the top left-hand corner. Inside every folder were photographs of a different building, each of which looked like a warehouse, together with a description relating to size, age, address, number of floors etc. There was also a street map of London and a small notebook which contained page after page of squiggles and dots.

"There you are" cried Johnson. "It's a bloody code book."

"Shut up, Johnson" said Hammond, turning to Ruby. "Do you know what this stuff is, Miss?"

"The folders must have something to do with Dieter's work" she said, trying to keep calm. "He works for a firm that buys and sells property. The notebook must be his personal jottings, so to speak. He knows this sort of shorthand, he calls it, and he's teaching me, although I can't seem to do it very well." She knew she was beginning to babble – nerves. She remembered Dieter saying it was always best to say as little as possible and keep it simple.

"Told yer" said Johnson. "Bloody Nazi spies, both of 'em. We should shoot…."

"I told you to shut your trap" shouted Hammond. "Go and stand outside and don't let me hear you say another word - to anyone. You hear?"

"Yes, Sergeant" he said as he went out of the room whistling Colonel Bogey.

"JOHNSON!" shouted the Sergeant and the whistling abruptly stopped. "Right, Miss. I'm afraid we'll have to take this with us and see what the Powers-That-Be have to say about it. Now I suggest you get your things together."

Upstairs, Ruby found that all three bedrooms had been completely ransacked. In tears, she went into her mother's room first, righted the bed and mattress, refolded all her underwear and jumpers and hung up the dresses and skirts and the two coats that were strewn over the bed and on the floor. The picture of her father and stepfather that was taken when they were lads together, lay under the last coat that she picked up. Its glass was smashed. Hurriedly, she got a brush and swept the shards into an old newspaper and put this in the bottom of her own small wardrobe. "Maybe she won't notice" she said to herself. Her own room, which she shared with her sister, and that of the boys were in the same state, although she did think that the boys' room looked much as it always did.

With both rooms put back into some sort of order, Ruby was absent mindedly packing a small suitcase when she heard shouting from downstairs.

"Ruby! Wo bist du?" It was Charlie, the eldest of her three half-brothers.

Ruby rushed down the stairs and hugged him, then Jonny and lastly Pete, who asked "Was ist los?"

"They've come for us all" she said. Then addressing all of her brothers, she said "We must speak English, not German, otherwise they will think that we have something to hide."

The brothers looked at each other as if one of them might know what to do and take charge. But it was Ruby, whose mind was now coming to terms with everything that was happening, who explained that they had to pack and go with the police. She looked at the Sergeant. "Please can we wait for our Mother to come home?"

"I'm afraid not, Miss" he said. "I wish I could say yes but we're already hours late. As I told you earlier, we should have been here first thing this morning. My orders are that we move as soon as the four of you are packed. If your Mum comes home before then, fair enough."

"We can't just go without seeing Mutti" said Jonny, the eighteen year old youngest brother. "She'll go spare if she comes home to find that we've just disappeared?"

"I'm sorry, son" said the Sergeant. "There's nothing I can do. Let's hope your Mum finishes early today."

But she didn't.

Ruby finished her packing and then helped the boys do their's. Charlie had suggested to Sergeant Hammond that the boys could use just one large suitcase and was horrified to be told that, as they might not be going to the same places, they should each have their own bag or case.

"Would it at least be alright if we left out mother a note?" asked Ruby.

"I don't see why you shouldn't" replied Sergeant Hammond, who was anxious to make a move. "But, show it to me when you've done it and make it quick! We've got to get a move on."

Ruby looked around for something suitable to write on but could only find the envelope that her mother kept the rent-book in. Hurriedly, she scribbled a note telling her what had happened and that she loved her. Each of the boys added his own message and then Ruby stood the envelope against the Daddies brown sauce bottle on the kitchen table.

Outside, the crowd had grown, but there was no animosity any more. Instead, someone shouted "Good Luck, lads. Good Luck, Ruby" and everyone started cheering. Taff Morgan, who ran the local football team that the boys all played for, shouted "Keep yourselves fit, lads. We've got to get back to the top of the league as soon as we can start playing again."

Charlie smiled at him. "We might be a bit late, Mr Morgan, but we'll do our best."

All four, together with the Sergeant and two of his constables (Ruby was pleased to see that Johnson was told to go in the front cab with the driver), were helped into the back of the black police van, bearing the words "Metropolitan Police" on the side.

No one spoke for a while and then Pete said "Don't worry, Ruby. No matter what happens, we'll come through this. Things may not ever be the same again, but I'm sure that we'll be fine."

Ruby smiled at her half–brother who sometimes was more like a forty year old than someone half that age. She reached across and gripped his hand. "Yes, I know. We'll be fine." But she doubted things would be fine at all. They didn't know what she did.

Just at the moment the "Black Maria" was being driven away, Lily Darling was getting off the Number 37 bus that had stopped at the bottom of her road. She noticed immediately that there seemed to be an unusual number of people milling around the dark coloured van that was just driving away in the opposite direction. As she carried her bags towards her home, she was approached by her friend Molly James, who was hurrying down the road towards her. Molly's eyes were all red and she looked frightful.

"Hello Molly, Love. You alright?" said Lily, smiling at her friend.

"Oh, Lily. I've bin watchin' fer yer. It's awful. They've bin for the boys and Ruby."

All colour drained from Lily's face as the realisation of what Molly was saying hit her. "Oh God!" she cried as she dropped her bags and ran the fifty or so yards to her home.

Her next-door neighbours on both sides, Annie Barker and Lizzie Watson, were gossiping across her front door. As Lily ran the last few yards, Lizzie said "The coppers 'av taken 'em, Lily."

Lily didn't say anything but rushed through the unlocked door. The two neighbours looked at each other and then, joined by a breathless Molly James carrying the bags that had been dropped, they followed Lily into the house.

Annie shouted "Where are you, Lily?"

There was no answer but they knew she'd be in the kitchen.

Lily was leaning against the kitchen table holding the envelope. Tears were flowing freely down her face and her nose was running. As the uncontrollable sobbing came, Molly took her hanky out of her sleeve and gave it to Lily. Then she put an arm round her and held her.

"It'll be alright, love. They'll be fine. They'll be back before you know. You just see if I'm not right. They'll be alright."

"You'll be alright" said Sergeant Hammond, looking at each of the frightened and confused siblings in turn. "Just do as you're told, stay out of trouble and keep your heads down. This'll all blow over."

"But we're not spies or anything!" said Charlie. "We might be half-German but that don't make us Nazis. We're Londoners. We've been 'ere all our lives. All of us!"

"I know, son. It's all bloody stupid" said Hammond. "Yesterday we had to take a nurse in from one of them big hospitals in the City. Bathing a patient, she was, and we couldn't even wait for her to finish. Had to leave the patient in the bath, didn't we, just with a little nursing cadet, not much bigger than a kid herself." Then he added "There's no way she's a spy. Just a nurse who happens to have a German dad. Poor little bugger, if you'll pardon my French, Miss."

Less than fifteen minutes later the engine of the police van was switched off. The siblings looked fearfully at each other and at the policemen. Then the doors at the back of the van opened and the policemen climbed down the steps.

"Just sit tight" said the Sergeant, turning back to his charges.
"I need to go and find out what's happening. I'll be back in a
couple of ticks."

Leaving Ruby and the boys in the van and making sure he
took Johnson with him while the other two policemen waited
nearby, Sergeant Hammond walked off with the suitcase under
his arm.

"Wo bringen sie uns hin? (Where are they taking us?)"
whispered Jonny.

"Wo immer sie Euch hinbringen, haltet zusammen und passt
aufeinanderauf. (Wherever they take you, just stick together and
look after each other)" said Ruby.

"What do you mean?" asked Pete. "Wherever they take
you….. it's wherever they take us. We're all together."

"I don't think I'll be going to the same place, somehow" said
Ruby. Then, to stifle the outburst from each of her brothers, she
raised her hands and added "But listen to me. It's important that
you write to Mutti. Whatever happens, you must write to her as
often as you can to let her know where you are and that you're
safe. D'you hear me?"

At that moment Sergeant Hammond arrived with three
soldiers. "Right, Miss. You're to go with these soldiers. The rest
of you are coming with me. Best of luck, Miss."

"Go on" urged Ruby, with the most convincing smile she
could manage. "It'll be alright. Just remember to write to Mutti."
With a last hug, they all clambered down clutching their bags and
gas masks.

While the boys followed the policemen, Ruby was escorted in
the opposite direction and through a double-door into a large
room. As she walked she tried to breathe deeply and relax. At
one end of the room sat an army officer behind an enormous
mahogany desk. He was flanked by two other men; both in dark
civilian suits. Ruby was ushered towards the desk where she
stood and looked at each of the men and then at the suitcase,
Dieter's suitcase, on the desk. The officer asked her to confirm
her name and address and then he asked about Dieter, the suitcase
and its contents.

"What is your boyfriend's full name?"

"Dieter Manfred Spitz" replied Ruby.

"Age?"

"Mine or his?" asked Ruby, truthfully confused.

"Don't play games with me, young lady" said the officer, angrily. "His."

"Eh….twenty-seven, I think" said Ruby, feeling her cheeks blush.

"What is his address in England?" Ruby told him.

"What can you tell us about these folders? I would advise you that it is in your best interests to tell us the truth."

Ruby told him the same thing as she had told Sergeant Hammond.

"We are not idiots, Miss Becker. Please do not treat us as such. Do you know what is kept in these warehouses?"

"No" said Ruby, keeping her eyes fixed on the poster on the wall behind the desk. It was a picture of Winston Churchill with the words LET US GO FORWARD TOGETHER.

"What about this notebook? What does this page mean?" The officer handed Ruby the notebook open at a page that had several English names such as Houndsditch and Bellingham underlined in red.

"I don't know, sir."

"You told the Police Sergeant that you were being taught this code by Spitz."

"It's not a code, it's shorthand" exclaimed Ruby.

"We've had our people look at it. It's not any form of shorthand we've ever seen. What does that page say?"

"I don't know. I'm sorry, I'm not very good at it."

"Well I suggest you try. You are in serious trouble Miss Becker. Very serious indeed."

Ruby looked again at the page and tried desperately to remember what she had been taught. Say as little as possible and keep it simple.

"I think that squiggle there means Strasse or street in English."

"Ah. So it is in German?"

"Yes, I think it was always in German. Dieter said he preferred to write in German."

"What else does it say?"

Ruby pulled out what words she thought they would be satisfied with and then said "I don't know any more. I really don't."

"Of course you do. Tell us the truth and it will go better for you. Continue to lie to us like this, we will have no alternative but to seek the most severe sentence."

"I can't read it. I don't have a clue what it's about." She burst into tears.

Despite Ruby's protestations of innocence, the questioning continued for another half an hour and by the end of it Ruby was sobbing uncontrollably. As she blew her nose on a now soggy hanky, one of the men in suits said "I don't believe a word you have said this afternoon. You have been wasting our time, Miss Becker. We know all about Herr Spitz. We have had our eye on him for a long time and whether you help us or not, we will find out what this all means." He leaned back and rang a bell on the wall behind him. A soldier immediately opened a door behind Ruby.

"Take this woman out and hold her in the outer office" said the Officer.

An hour and a half of sitting on a hard wooden bench later, Ruby was told she was to be reclassified to that of a Category "A" Internee, which meant that she was now considered to be a potential threat to national security and could be held indefinitely. With a soldier holding each arm to restrain her and another carrying her own suitcase and gas mask case, she was taken out into the same courtyard where she had arrived earlier with her brothers. The "Black Maria" had been replaced by an Army lorry, painted in camouflage greens and browns.

At its side were a group of women and soldiers. Ruby was immediately ushered up the lorry's steps at the back. She was followed by three women who were obviously a mother with two quite grown-up daughters. They sat in the middle of the bench-seat on the opposite side to Ruby. A slim woman with long blonde hair, about the same age as Ruby, climbed in next, smiled at Ruby and sat beside her. The next, a rather plump woman slightly older than Ruby, with her hair tied back in braids, went to sit beside the blonde.

"No" said one of the soldiers pointing to the opposite side from Ruby. "You go over there, beside those three."

"I vill not seet der" she said in a thick German accent. Looking directly at the mother, she added "I do not seet vith dat Jewish filth."

"You sit where I tell you!" shouted the soldier, about to prod her with his rifle.

"I vill not!"

"It's alright" said the blonde. "I'll sit there" and, she got up and sat opposite Ruby.

With the plump woman sitting next to Ruby and the last woman to get on the truck sitting beyond her, two soldiers tossed a succession of cases and bags onto the floor of the vehicle, climbed in, released the straps which held the canvass rear curtain up in a roll and sat down, one on each side beside the exit. The remaining soldier folded the steps up and then walked round to the cab where he joined the driver. The lorry was started up and, with a crash of gears, it began its journey.

In the gloomy half-light offered by a tiny skylight and the thin gaps at the side of the rear curtain, Ruby looked at the faces of those opposite through her swollen red eyes. The soldier, who must have been no older than her brothers, leered at her and seemed to be undressing her with his eyes. The dark haired girl on his right, who was about eighteen or nineteen Ruby thought, sobbed into her handkerchief as she was comforted by her mother who had her arm round her shoulder saying "Shhh. Shhh." The mother herself was a small woman dressed in a black coat which came down to her ankles. She just stared forlornly at the ceiling as if she were trying to pretend it was all just a nightmare. The other daughter, obviously slightly the elder of the two, just stared straight ahead. Although staring directly at Ruby, she showed no sign that she was seeing anything except the tears that were flowing from her own raw, red eyes.

As Ruby made eye contact with the final occupant of the seat, the blonde girl smiled and winked. Then, inclining her head slightly in the direction of the plump woman with braids next to Ruby, she surreptitiously sat up straighter and put her index finger above her top lip, imitating a Hitler moustache. Ruby couldn't help but smile back. She understood. Nazi.

"I saw dat!" shouted the braid woman, glowering at the blonde. "I saw vot you did. You vill get your.... how you say it? ......cumtuppence ven ze glorious Third Reich ist in control of dis pathetic country."

The blonde just giggled and said "It's uppance, Fräulein. Not tuppence. Comeuppance." With that she winked again at Ruby and pretended to polish her nails on her sleeve, leaving the braid woman to fume.

The rest of the journey, conducted in complete silence from thereon, took twenty minutes. When the lorry finally stopped and the rear curtain rolled up again, the women could see they were in the courtyard of a huge forbidding Victorian building with an enormous studded gate in front of them. The soldiers clambered down followed by the mother and daughters, and then the woman who Ruby had not yet had chance to see much of. The blonde and the braid woman went to make their exit at the same time, but the blonde waved her arm and said "After you, Tuppence!" The braid woman scowled at her, but hurried out.

"Bitch!" said the blonde under her breath so that only Ruby could hear.

"Don't upset her too much" replied Ruby softly. "She might make trouble for you."

"I'm not scared of her or her type" said the blonde.

"Come on, you two" shouted one of the soldiers. "We ain't got all day."

"Right, Ladies" he said when all had disembarked. "Welcome to Holloway Prison. Your new home."

The Jewish mother fainted.

Chapter 3

The boys sat in silence, looking out of the back of the open truck, lost in their own fears and apprehension. What was going to happen to them? At the moment, the future seemed a very dark place.

They had each been interrogated separately, in different rooms but at the same time. When they had finished with Pete, he was taken back to the waiting room to find that both of his brothers were already there.

"Bloody Hell, Pete" said Jonny. "What kept you so long?"

"You alright, mate?" asked Charlie. "You look as white as a sheet."

"I'm fine" said Pete, with a tired smile, but he was lost in his own thoughts.

As they were bounced and flung around the inside of the vehicle which was crawling its way through the bomb-damaged, debris-blocked London streets, they were astonished at the sheer scale of the carnage. In some areas it seemed that not a single building was left intact. In one small side-road, they watched with macabre fascination as the side of an old factory, all that remained after a direct hit in the night, was demolished by a large crane swinging a huge weight into the brickwork. Amid the noise and the dust, it was like watching a huge long-necked dinosaur feeding off giant trees.

After almost an hour, it was obvious that they were coming out of the city. The tall buildings of London gave way to two storey ones in anonymous provincial towns and villages, each with its long queues of exhausted, grey-faced people trying to live their lives as best they could and patiently hoping that the few shops that had produce to sell wouldn't run out before they got to the front. And then they were into wide stretches of peaceful, timeless countryside, with numerous teams of horses silently ploughing in the fields, seeming to give lie to the devastation that was being inflicted elsewhere.

Eventually, with the late afternoon sunshine slanting through a forest of pine trees, the truck stopped. They could hear men talking and then what sounded like a squeaking gate being opened. As they started moving again, the boys could see soldiers moving a barrier back into position across a gap in a high fence which was topped with coils of barbed-wire. Other soldiers, armed with rifles, continued to patrol the area. Wherever this was, the natives didn't look friendly.

"Where are we?" asked Pete.

"Wherever we are, I hope you Nazi traitors stay here to rot" snarled the soldier who was seated opposite him and he spat at Pete's feet.

"You bastard!" cried Pete, leaping to his feet and raising his clenched fists to the soldier. Fortunately, Charlie caught his arm and prevented the blow reaching its target.

"Sit down!" shouted the other soldier, raising his rifle.

Pete just looked at him, wondering what would happen if he did land a blow. Would they shoot him?

"Now!" shouted the soldier, pointing the rifle directly at Pete's chest.

"Sit down, Pete" said Charlie calmly as he pulled his brother's arm. "He's not worth getting shot for."

Pete allowed himself to be pulled onto the seat, but continued to stare contemptibly at the soldier who had spat at him.

When the lorry stopped again, the back of the truck was let down and the boys were ordered out. They were escorted to a low windowless building with its green door barricaded with a pile of sandbags. Here they were ordered to strip off all their clothes and stand naked while a medical orderly examined them and soldiers examined the contents of their cases. Having satisfied themselves that there was nothing that could be used to escape or to communicate with the outside world, the soldiers handed the clothes back to the embarrassed, naked men who quickly got dressed.

"You are prisoners but you will not be kept in cells." They were being addressed by an army officer in a peaked cap. He had a handle-bar moustache which he twiddled continuously. "You are free to go more or less wherever you like within the compound, but you are not allowed beyond the fenced perimeter. Should you do so, you are at certain risk of being shot. Do you understand or do you want the written instructions which we have in German?"

"We understand" replied Charlie sullenly.

"Excellent!" said the officer, continuing with his induction. "This is a transit camp. You will be moved from here soon, although I have no precise information as to when that might be. You will receive food and water and all the exercise you care to take." He paused to smile, then cleared his throat and said "Right, any questions?" He paused again, waiting and then continued "No? Fair enough. You will each be given a mattress, blankets, soap and a tin plate and mug together with details of where you will be billeted. Sergeant, will you sort that out?"

"Yes Sir!"

"Oh, one final thing" said the officer, "There is a curfew from nine o'clock in the evening until six o'clock in the morning. Do not leave your billet between these times. Understood?"

Ten minutes later the boys found themselves in what must have been an old stable block. There was still the unmistakably bittersweet smell of animals. Bundles of straw were piled up at the far end of the block to form a sort of privacy screen around several large, old oil cans with rough wooden slats across them for sitting on. The stench was enough to tell the boys exactly what they were used for.

"The emptying will be done by all of you" said the Sergeant. "The others'll tell you how it works. The roster is pinned over there on that beam. Make sure you put your names on it and do your bit when your turn comes around. Failure to carry out your duties will put you straight into the Punishment Hut – and you don't want to be in there. So take my advice, do you're jobs and stay out of trouble."

"Home sweet home" said Pete.

"Ain't it just" replied Jonny looking quizzically at the four large posters of Bertram Mills' Circus which strangely adorned the walls either side of the entrance. "And there was me expecting The Ritz."

"Stick your mattresses down in there" said the Sergeant, pointing to an empty stall "and then I'll show you the wash house and where you get your grub. Then you're on your own."

Having been shown the wash house – "I'm afraid it's cold water only at the moment, Gentlemen" the soldier had delighted in telling them – they were taken to the Mess Hall which, rather incongruously, did in fact look like it had always been some sort of restaurant or canteen. Unfortunately, the food offered was somewhat less inspirational than the surroundings.

"What do you reckon the meat is in this stew?" whispered Pete.

"Well you know all the animals that they must have had in these stables…….?" grinned Jonny.

Pete looked back at the plate with its green-tinged fat congealing in front of him. He couldn't eat another mouthful and pushed his plate away.

And so it was in the growing gloom of early evening, that the boys wandered wearily back towards their stable block between lines of large khaki tents from which came voices in German, English, Yiddish and Italian – all seemingly mixed up together. Beyond the tents, workmen and soldiers involved in erecting about two dozen wooden huts, were packing away their tools and paintbrushes for the night.

"Accommodation for future guests" said Jonny.

"Ain't they the lucky ones?" said Charlie.

Back in their stall, they threw themselves onto their straw-filled mattresses, each trying to get his head around the day's events.

"Where the bloody hell do you think we are?" asked Jonny.

"Christ knows" replied Charlie, yawning.

"Ascot" came a voice from the next stall over. "To be precise, Gentlemen, you're in Bertram Mills Circus' Winter Quarters on Ascot Racecourse. And a right load of bollocks it is too!"

The boys grinned at each other and then stood and leant over the side wall of the stall so they could see the owner of the voice which seemed somehow familiar.

"Well, bugger me" said Pete. "Look who it ain't!"

"Manny Goldfarb" said Jonny. "How long you bin 'ere?"

"Couple of days" replied Manny. "I was wondering if you lot would be picked up as well."

"This afternoon" answered Charlie. "Bastards picked us and Ruby up when we got home from work. Didn't even have chance to say goodbye to Mum."

"Bleedin' coppers" agreed Manny. "At least me mum was there when the coppers came for me. Bleedin' woke us up at 6 o'clock in the bleedin' mornin'".

"So what are we supposed to do now?" asked Jonny.

"Nothin'" answered Manny, coming round into the boys' stall, "apart from doin' yer turn at emptyin' the cans with the little brown noses in back there. Yer just wait 'til they move us somewhere else and they will – tomorrow, next week, next bleedin' year for all I know. They'll come and in the meantime" and he looked around him to make sure no one was listening "you stay close to me and if I ain't around, you stay away from the Nazi-boys and you stay away from the Yids. Do you 'ear me?"

"But you're a Yi……. Jewish, Manny" said Jonny.

Manny quickly rounded on Jonny but kept his voice low. "I'm only half Jewish and I ain't no Yid. Not like these ones they've got in 'ere. They're strict they are. Only just escaped to England themselves, ain't they. Most of 'em don't even speak English. Got out before old Adolf had a go at 'em, good and proper. I feel sorry for 'em, mind. Moved from pillar to post, they've been; treated worse than the bleedin' animals what was in these stalls. But if you get involved with 'em, you'll get the Black Shirts coming down on yer backs. So keep to yourselves." The boys just looked at each other as if to reassure themselves that they would be fine if they just stuck together.

Aware that the stable block was filling up with other internees prior to the curfew at nine o'clock, Manny changed the subject to something less contentious. "This place has only just been opened. They're still tryin' to get everything organised. So at the moment it's like Fred Karno's bleedin' Army – absolute bloody chaos. The Army doesn't seem to know when people are arrivin', or when they're goin' for that matter. Everything seems to happen on the spur of the moment. Yesterday, one lot was halfway through 'avin' some grub when the soldiers marched in and took them off in a lorry. Not so much as an 'ow's yer father. Some others were taken from the shower block. Wringin' wet they were. Bloody mad they were too– the lot of 'em."

"Where were they being taken" asked Charlie.

"Dunno" said Manny "but I've 'eard rumours. Liverpool, the docks and then on to Canada!"

"Canada! Bloody Hell!" exclaimed Jonny. "I 'ope that's not where we're goin' to end up. It's bloody miles away. Do they play football in Canada?"

"Ain't got a clue, mate" replied Manny. "Too bloody cold, I reckon."

"I think we've got relations in Canada somewhere" said Charlie. "That'd be a turn up for the book, wouldn't it"?

"Be great, wouldn't it" grinned Jonny. "Us lot just turning up and knocking on the door one day."

"Right, my bed's calling" yawned Manny, rising to his feet. "Tomorrow's another day! Just remember what I said: keep away from the Nazis and the Yids."

With that they all sorted out their mattresses and settled down. It was strange that now, as the most awful day of the boys' lives was coming to an end and darkness was falling, the sounds and the smells around them seemed to become so much more pronounced. The odour of animals seemed to have faded only to be superseded by the sickening mixture of human excrement, tobacco smoke and body odour. And cutting through this aromatic concoction came the sounds: snoring, coughing, farting, talking and even laughing all laid on a bed of fear and expectation.

"D'you think Mutti, Ruby and Dot are alright?" said Jonny, more to himself than anyone.

"They're tough" said Charlie. "They'll survive." Then he laughed. "Mutti'll probably enjoy the peace and quiet and not having us to tidy up after."

"Where d'you think they've taken Ruby?" asked Jonny.

"Dunno. But she'll be alright. Y'know what Ruby's like. She'll soon have them runnin' around after her."

"Yeah, I suppose. I wonder what tomorrow's gonna be like?"

"I bloody 'ope it's better than today" replied Charlie, noticing that Pete was already asleep.

"Can't be any worse" added Jonny.

"I wonder what tomorrow's going to be like. I hope it's better than today. Can't be any worse. Can it?"

"Eh. Sorry. I was thinking about something. What did you say?"

"No I'm sorry. Should have realised you'd be worried about your Mum. I just said that I wondered what tomorrow would be like."

"I was just thinking about the way people act differently when they're scared?"

"Do you suppose they'll keep us here for long? Do you think they'll have us stitching mail-bags? Christ! My needlework's rubbish. All my bags'll burst" she laughed. And then Ruby started to laugh at her cellmate's laughing. The tears of laughter, however, quickly turned to those of despair as the two new friends tried to stifle their tears in embarrassment.

Earlier, with the Jewish mother having been revived, the women had been escorted through various courtyards and locked gates until they arrived at a building about a hundred yards long. On each side of the concrete floor were open-doored cells. At each end and in the middle were broad metal staircases leading up to a similar arrangement on the first floor. This was repeated on a second floor and then again on a third. Heavy-duty nets were strung across the open space on the top three floors to prevent falls, both accidental and intentional.

The Internment Wing was a part of Holloway Prison which had been set aside for female internees. Although its main entry doors were locked, each individual cell was left unlocked during the daytime. Lock-down, as Ruby quickly found out it was called, was at nine o'clock in the evening until seven o'clock in the morning when they would be free to wander within the Wing.

The new arrivals had been allocated to cells. The mother and her daughters had been given the largest one available which had enabled the soldiers to get an extra bed into it. Initially Tuppence was to share with Ruby, but after the blonde girl had managed to whisper something to one of the soldiers, Ruby was ordered to share with the blonde and Tuppence shared with the quiet woman who was on their lorry. It was the latter who was puzzling Ruby because she looked so calm and self-possessed.

"What did you say to the soldier?" asked Ruby when she and the blonde were in their cell.

"You don't want to know" came the laughing reply. "I just hope I don't meet him after the War. You didn't want to share with Tuppence, did you?"

"No fear!" Then Ruby added "My name's Ruby, Ruby Becker."

"Matilde Nussbaum. But everyone calls me Tilly, thank God."

To her surprise and delight, Ruby quickly learned that Tilly too was a Category "A" Internee.

"Christ knows why" Tilly had said. "The old duffer on the Enemy Alien Tribunal spent more time looking at my bust than he did asking me questions. In the end he said that he wasn't convinced that I wasn't spying for the Nazis. I think he just wanted to put me over his knee and spank me and because he couldn't he took it out on me."

Ruby smiled. The thought that this categorisation business was such an obvious farce made her feel distinctly less pessimistic about the future.

Tilly was talking about her parents, both German, who had died in a coach crash when she was a baby and that she had been brought up by her paternal grandparents in Watford. Her grandfather was a piano-tuner who had come over from Hamburg in 1910 with his wife and their fifteen year old son, Tilly's father, to seek work and escape from conscription.

"The really sad thing is, I don't have any memories of my parents" added Tilly, sombrely.

Ruby didn't quite know what to say but she never got the chance as Tilly quickly said "But my grandparents are wonderful. I just hope they'll be alright without me."

"Come on!" said Ruby, jumping up from her bed where she had been sitting, "we need to cheer ourselves up. Let's go and explore before they lock everything up. We might even find people we know."

And in a way they did, for around the very next corner they were confronted by Tuppence, flanked by three other, equally earnest, young women.

"I haf friends here, ja. You better keep looking over your shoulders. Ve vouldn't vant sometink to happen mit you. Verstehst du?"

"I understand, you nasty racist bitch" said Tilly raising her finger to point at Tuppence. "But get this clear, you and your pathetic Nazi friends are not going to bully me or my friends. Now," and she brought her head so close to Tuppence's that their noses were almost touching, "verstehst du?" The two just stared, menacingly, into each other's eyes; neither giving way.

"Oi! What's goin' on up there?" shouted a soldier from the floor below as he started running towards the stairway. The spell having been broken, Ruby was able to drag Tilly away.

"We've got to stand up to them, Ruby" Tilly said, still worked up and now openly shaking. "Her and all those other small-minded Nazi cows who think they are so superior, they know nothing. My grandparents…" Then she looked around her. "No, not here. I'll tell you when we get back to our cell."

So, with still ten minutes to go before lock-down, Ruby and Tilly were back in their cell; neither had the appetite for any more adventures today.

As Ruby brushed her teeth, Tilly told her all about her grandparents: how, even though they were both in their seventies and weren't Jewish, they used their meagre life-savings to act as guarantors for Jewish people to come to England to escape the increased anti-Semitism in Germany and Austria. Those that did manage to get here were helped to find food, shelter and jobs. "Loads of musicians, scientists, writers. And their families. Scholars of every subject you could think of. These are really clever people, Ruby. They are open minded and are looking to push the boundaries of knowledge far beyond anything we could even imagine. Not like those bigots back there who only want power and don't mind who suffers in the process. Makes me sick."

Ruby felt sick too but for a different reason. "Not in here, I hope" she said with a toothpaste-covered mask.

Tilly laughed. "Oh we are going to be such good friends, you and me" she said. "I can feel it."

Chapter 4

It wasn't one of the coldest May nights there had ever been in Ascot, but, with the thin mattresses offering little insulation from the cold concrete floor of the stable block, Charlie and Jonny had had a miserable night. They had ended up huddling together with both their mattresses in a double layer beneath them and their combined blankets above them. This had worked reasonably well but every time one of them moved, the other lost his bit of the blanket. It ended up as being a constant tug of war. In the end, as dawn was breaking, they decided to admit defeat and get up and join in the card game that had just started up at the other end of the block.

Not so Pete. It was always said in the family that he could sleep on a clothes-line if he chose to and tonight had proved to be no different. However, at the moment, his was no peaceful slumber. He was being attacked by a huge, red octopus wearing pink and yellow pyjama trousers. Each of its enormous pyjama-clad tentacles was wrapped around his body and was pulling him inexorably towards a huge, beaked mouth that was snapping viciously, trying to take its first bite of his flesh. The more he struggled, the tighter he was held. There was no escape. He was about to die the most horrible, painful of deaths – eaten alive, mouthful by mouthful. He watched with detached fascination as the beak came closer and closer. But just as the beak was about to destroy any chance of Pete ever becoming a father, he felt himself suddenly become free and, with one kick, he was soaring up to the surface of the ocean. Suddenly, like a firework, he was bursting through into the air. He was now flying like a bird on a warm, sunny, new day. He had survived. He was alive and his wedding tackle was still intact. Myrna would be pleased.

He opened his eyes and saw that a large wall clock above the door was showing twenty-five past six. For a second or two he had absolutely no idea where he was. Then, just as the memories began flooding back, he became aware that he was itching from head to foot. He looked down the front of his shirt to find that he was covered in red blotches and half a dozen tiny reddish-brown stripy beetles, about an eighth of an inch long, were crawling slowly across his chest. "Ergh!" he shouted as he hurriedly stripped off his clothes. Naked, he could see that his groin, thighs and legs were also covered in the same sort of red blotches. Every one of them itched like mad. He scratched each one furiously but this only made them itch more: some even started to bleed.

The commotion attracted an audience and soon the raucous cheering reached the card game. Puzzled, the players folded their cards and wandered in the direction of the impromptu entertainment. Charlie and Jonny were astonished to find their brother, their naked brother, apparently pretending to be a Sioux Indian warrior complete with yelps and war paint.

"Don't just stand there grinning, you two" cried Pete. "Do something."

"What do you want us to do?" asked Charlie.

"I don't know! Anything! I'm being eaten alive here."

Still grinning, Charlie and Jonny went over to their brother but were horrified to discover that the warpaint was in fact blood.

"Lummee, Pete" said Jonny. "Look at the mess you've made of yourself. You're bleedin' all over the place."

"I can't help it. These things are itching like crazy."

"Here, let me have a butchers" said Manny, coming over to get a closer view. Then he started laughing. "I know what this is. Me Gran used to call 'em "Breakfast, Dinner and Tea" cos they usually take three bites out of yer before they're full."

"For fuck sake, Manny" cried Pete. "I don't need a fucking lecture. Just tell me what they are."

Manny grinned. "They're bed bugs."

With that announcement, the whole block cheered and laughed.

"Well three bloody cheers for your Gran" said a decidedly pissed-off Pete. "Was she always such a smart arse or did she show you something useful like how to get rid of them and how to stop this awful itching? I'm going fucking mad 'ere."

"Well" said a smug looking Manny, "as a matter of fact she did." Then he paused.

"Well go on!" shouted Pete. "What are yer waitin' for, written permission from His Majesty?"

"What you've gotta do is work up a sweat and then the salt'll get into the bites and kill 'em off."

"Like this" and Pete began running furiously on the spot and then doing press-ups.

"No, that's no good" said Manny. "You've gotta 'ave the fresh air on your skin to dry the sweat off straight away. That way the salt's much more concentrate."

"You mean I've got to run about out there with nothing on at half past six in the morning?" The anguish on Pete's face was pitiful. "You're avin' me on, aren't you?"

"Nope" replied Manny. "It's the only way."

"Oh Christ" said Pete, still furiously scratching. "Oh, fuck!" With that he took a deep breath, ran to the stable door, threw it open and charged off across the yard, passing the partially-built new huts, and into the empty field opposite, accompanied by the shouts and cheers of encouragement from the stable block.

"Seems a strange sort of cure for your Granny to come up with, Manny" said Charlie as they watched his brother career around the field like a horse being chased by a swarm of bees.

"She didn't" replied Manny with a grin from ear to ear. "I just made it up, didn't I. Bloody good though, eh?"

Charlie and Manny had tears streaming down their faces by the time they were joined by Jonny.

"What's up with you two?"

"It's a wind up" spluttered Charlie. "Manny's 'avin' Pete on. That's not his Granny's cure. Manny just made it up."

"You bastard" said Jonny, angry at the deception, but another glance at Pete running around the old racecourse in his birthday suit was too much for him and the three of them collapsed into rib-aching laughter.

"Sir!" shouted the Corporal as he burst into his Commanding Officer's sleeping quarters. "There's a naked man running around in the field and he's covered in blood."

The officer had been asleep, but immediately sat bolt upright.

"What did you say?"

"One of the prisoners is running around in the field, naked."

"Bloody foreigners" said the Officer, leaping to his feet and quickly pulling his uniform over his striped pyjamas. Then, charging towards the door, he said "Think they can bring their filthy habits over here. I'll show these buggers that in England, we save that sort of thing for the bedroom…..with the lights off…. and then only on special occasions."

By now, the whole of the Camp had turned out to watch the show. As the fire alarm bells were wound up, those who had just started working on the new huts stood on the half-finished roofs. Poised on the edge of the field and with bayonets fixed to their rifles were twenty or so nervous looking soldiers. Others, awakened by the cacophony, scrambled to their colleagues' assistance, pulling on their tunics as they ran.

"Let me through!" shouted the officer as he approached the raucous crowd, which must have numbered several hundred by this time. "Move out of the way!" Like the parting of the seas, a way miraculously cleared and the officer strode to the front with all the dignity he could muster. "Where is he?"

"Over there, Sir" said a Sergeant, who was exceedingly glad that his CO had arrived to take charge of what he thought looked like becoming a riot. "Over by the perimeter fence."

The officer looked in the direction that his Sergeant was pointing and saw the naked man running for all he was worth up and down the old racetrack. "Get him into my office, Sergeant."

"Yes, Sir"

"Now!" shouted the CO and turned on his heels and strode purposefully back through the crowd. "And get these men back to their billets!"

The crowd, however, were in no mood to comply and their cheering doubled as they watched the Sergeant's posse of six soldiers hurtle across the field towards the internee who was now engaged in a series of press-ups. The farce was compounded by the fact that having set off in one direction after their quarry, the soldiers had to abruptly change course as Pete leapt to his feet and ran the opposite way. In doing so, one soldier tripped up another and the collision brought down two more. The crowd roared with derision.

But by now Pete was exhausted and no match for the soldiers. Without too much trouble, one of them managed a flying rugby-tackle and brought him to the ground, whereupon more soldiers were able to pile in on top of him.

"Enter" shouted the officer when a puffing, red-faced Sergeant knocked on his door.

"We got him, Sir."

A sweating, muddy Pete, wrapped in a blanket, was brought up to the front of the officer's desk.

"Speak English?"

"Yes" panted Pete.

"Name?"

"Darling."

The CO's face coloured up like a beetroot. "Are you taking the fucking piss out of me?" he shouted.

"No. That's my name. Peter Darling."

"Mmm" said the not-totally convinced officer, giving a slight cough. "And what the bloody hell do you think you were doing out there?"

"Getting' rid of bed bugs."

"I beg your pardon?"

Pete did his best to explain to the increasingly sceptical Commanding Officer.

"You are taking the piss!" he said.

"No I'm not" countered Pete indignantly. "That's what I was told. It's the only way to stop the bites itching."

"I've had enough of this nonsense. Sergeant, take this man to the Punishment Hut. He will stay there for forty-eight hours." Then he added "and stick him under a cold shower for ten minutes. That should cool his ardour."

"Yes Sir!" said the Sergeant, saluting.

"Oh, and Sergeant!"

"Yes Sir?"

"Get the Medical Officer to have a look at him."

"Yes Sir."

Just as the door was about to shut, the officer shouted "and Sergeant!"

"Yes Sir?" said the Sergeant peering round the door.

"Burn that man's blankets and mattress. I don't want those Red Cross buggers on my neck any more than they are already."

"Yes Sir."

Despite the best efforts of the soldiers to disperse the crowd of internees, there was still a sizeable number waiting for Pete as he was escorted out of the officer's office. A loud cheer went up and Charlie and Jonny pushed to the front.

"You alright, Pete?" shouted Jonny.

Seeing his two brothers, Pete shouted "I'm fine. Tell Manny thanks. It seems to have worked. I'm not itchin' any more, just knackered."

"Where are they takin' you?" shouted Charlie.

"Punishment Hut" shouted Pete. "Forty-eight hours!"

"Bloody Hell" said Manny when Charlie was able to talk to him after his brother had been taken away. "I'm a bloody genius. Never dreamed it would actually do any good."

"What's the Punishment Hut like?" asked Jonny.

"Not brilliant" answered Manny. "But better than what we've got. Pete'll actually be sleeping in a bed for the next two nights and he won't have to fight for a shower either. But there's sod all to do, just like the rest of us."

As Pete was escorted through the door of the Punishment Hut, he found himself immediately in front of a desk at which a Corporal was sorting through various forms.

"Right, Corporal" ordered the Sergeant. "Get him booked in, then."

When all the paperwork was completed and the cold shower taken, Pete was shown into his cell. Bliss – a bed, a sink and a toilet. This was The Ritz. Pete looked through the four-inch wide window on the back wall. "This'll do me for a couple of days" he thought to himself.

Then, from the next cell "I always like looking at the oak trees in May" said a quietly-spoken male voice.

Pete gave his answer in shock.

Tilly was re-reading the letter she had written to her grandparents. "Oh, bother!" she said.

"What?" said Ruby.

"I've missed out the "f" in performance" replied Tilly.

"Eh?" said Ruby, who was engrossed in writing her own letter.

"I said there's no "f" in performance."

"Well there's no need to swear" said Ruby, without taking her eyes from the page.

"Pardon?" asked Tilly.

"You're welcome" said Ruby absent-mindedly.

Tilly looked at her cellmate, not having a clue what she was talking about. She repeated the conversation in her mind. Then it dawned on her and she burst out laughing. "You soppy sod" she said and threw a pillow at Ruby.

"What?" asked Ruby, looking up.

The day continued as it had started with Tilly and Ruby staying in their cells, deciding that wandering around was asking for trouble. Around eleven o'clock, they were ordered into the exercise yard and there, together with the other internees, mostly Germans and Austrians, they marched around the yard. Traditional German songs were soon being rendered to the sky and both Ruby and Tilly, having recognised some of them, were able to join in. However, once Tuppence and the rest of the extremists took over the song selection, it took on a more nationalistic and sinister edge. The two girls, together with most of the others present, stayed silent and away from any confrontation.

As soon as the exercise period was over, they were able to go straight to the canteen for their meagre lunch of bread, cheese and a cup of tea.

"It doesn't get any better, does it?" said Ruby as she toyed with the small lump of cheese on her plate.

"It's an absolute disgrace, if you ask me" replied Tilly. "What if you don't like cheese!"

Ruby laughed. "Just have to ask the waiter for the menu and choose something else."

They both grinned at each other.

Back in their cell, the two girls were alternately laughing and crying as they talked about their respective homes and upbringings. For both of them it was as if they had known each other for years. Bringing back long forgotten, yet warm, memories in that high-ceilinged, bare room seemed so incongruous, so unreal, yet so necessary to both of them. But at the back of Ruby's mind was always the thought of what her relationship with Tilly would be like if her friend knew the truth about what she had done.

The afternoon seemed to just fly by and they were soon being ushered to get their remaining food of the day, which turned out to be bread, jam and a cup of tea.

"Real hôte cuisine" joked Ruby. "Do you think they send out to The Ritz for this?"

"Indubitably, my dear" replied Tilly, putting on a very affected upper class accent which left both girls in fits of giggles.

"How long do you think they'll keep us here?" asked Tilly some minutes later.

"I was just thinking the same thing" replied Ruby. "This is beginning to get so boring."

"I wonder if they'll keep us all together" pondered Tilly. "You know, like one big happy family" she added in an ironic tone.

Ruby laughed and then stopped abruptly. "I'd rather be with my own family" she said, now totally crestfallen and miserable.

"Well there's gratitude for you" said Tilly putting on an exaggeratedly miffed expression.

"No, I didn't mean that I was bored with you" said Ruby hurriedly. "I just meant…."

Tilly laughed. "Don't be daft. I know exactly what you meant and I feel that way too. We've just got to help each other through this." With that she jumped to her feet, grabbed Ruby and began dancing with her while singing "When the red red robin comes bob bob bobbing along." – much to the amusement of the rest of diners, some of whom began to clap in time to the tune. Even the guards seemed to enjoy this momentary diversion.

"QUIET!"

Ruby and Tilly dropped their arms to their sides and jumped apart. The clapping stopped instantly. All eyes went to the army officer who, with two other soldiers, was standing by the entrance to the canteen.

"Thank you" he said. "I have just been informed that some of you will be moved out of here tomorrow morning. Those of you who's names appear on this list must be packed and ready to move at 06.00 hours. Thank you." And with that he left the room followed by his escort.

"That was short and sweet" said Ruby, looking apprehensively at Tilly. They walked over to the notice which had been pinned to the door and eventually got close enough to read the names. Both of their's were there.

"It's a shame" said Ruby, with an ironic smirk. "I was just beginning to like this place."

"Where are they taking us now, do you think?" said Tilly.

"God knows" replied Ruby.

Chapter 5

In the half-light, Ruby lay on her bed staring above her, as she had since the lights had been turned off. All she could see was the underside of Tilly's bed. Somewhere in the far distance she had heard air-raid sirens followed, inevitably, by the drone of aircraft and then by explosions. Mercifully, these had now stopped and all she could hear was the sobbing of some poor frightened soul in a nearby cell. She wondered if any of the German planes were using information which she and Dieter had provided. She felt sick and wretched. There was no excuse for what she had been party to. This was the price for her stupidity. This was the real world.

She had earlier written a letter to her mother in which she had told her she was fine. She hadn't bothered to tell her where she was as it would have only upset her; besides, even if the Censors allowed it, which she doubted, tomorrow they would be somewhere else, so it was pointless going into details. And besides, she had no idea when she was going to get the opportunity to post it. She had told her about meeting Tilly and the things that they had got up to and what they had talked about. She thought that if her mother knew that the two of them had become such good friends, it might help to stop her worrying too much.

She thought about the boys. Were they alright? Were they still together and where? What about her sister, Dot? Was she still away at school or had she been allowed to come home to Mutti? But most of all she thought about Dieter and his suitcase. Why hadn't she just told him to find somewhere else to keep it? Apart from teaching her shorthand, which she never really got to grips with anyway, she didn't know a lot about the places they photographed. Had she been naïve? Of course she had, but that was no excuse. Although he'd certainly lied to her when he said no one would be killed because the buildings were warehouses, just used for storing Jewish-owned merchandise, she hadn't bothered to question how he could be so certain. Truth was she hadn't given it much thought at all: not the actual terror when the bombs started to fall, the not knowing which way to run. He'd tried to explain the basic strategy once by saying that if enough buildings could be destroyed, it would undermine the financial situation in the City of London and therefore make it more likely that the Government would not have the stomach for war. But she'd never once confronted him with the likely human cost of these raids. She'd been very much in love with him but did that justify her actions. Of course not. She was as guilty as the pilots who were flying the planes and dropping the bombs. No, more so because they were under orders – they had no choice. She had.

Now, having not seen him for weeks, she wasn't quite sure what she felt for Dieter. She certainly wasn't comfortable with the anti-Jewish stuff that Dieter had gone on and on about and she had told him so. But he had been adamant. "Wherever you look" he had said to her, "Jews have got their fingers in the pie. They always have to be the boss; always giving the orders and always taking the lion-share of the profits. Look at Germany in the last twenty years since the Great War and you'll see that it's the Jews that have prospered, no one else. While everyone else has become bankrupt in the worst economic depression the world has ever known, the Jews have been making a fortune. They're suffocating us, Ruby."

But Ruby didn't think this was true at all and she just couldn't see things like Dieter did. When she thought of Jewish people, she immediately thought of Mr Mendelsohn, a kind and clever man: someone she had always looked up to. He didn't deserve the things that Dieter was saying.

She turned onto her side, hoping that sleep would rescue her from her thoughts. She tried relaxing her mind by slowly tracing the wire that made up the springs in Tilly's bunk but all she could think about was when this nightmare would end.

"Are you awake?" came Tilly's voice from the bunk-bed above.

"Mmm-mm. Are you?"

"Just about. I could murder a cup of tea, though."

"Me too. What time do you think it is?"

"Well it's just started getting light outside so I'd reckon about 4-ish."

"Oh God! Only another two hours before we're off and I haven't had a wink of sleep at all yet."

"Worrying about your Mum?" yawned Tilly.

"Mmm" lied Ruby. "And Dorothea, the boys, you, me, the War, the plight of hedgehogs in East Anglia. You name it, I've been thinking about it."

"Well you're not going to do yourself any good if you don't get some sleep. Just try and relax. Count sheep. Or even better, count hedgehogs. They don't move so fast."

Ruby laughed and knew that Tilly's friendship and concern had broken the mood and she would now get some sleep. She closed her eyes and almost immediately felt that wonderful warm drifting feeling. Somewhere in the far distance she heard Tilly say "What's the matter with East Anglian hedgehogs anyway?" But it was too far away. Just too far away.

"Right you two. You've got twenty minutes to get yourselves sorted, packed and down by the gate." Whoever it was had unlocked the cell door but neither of the girls had heard a thing until he spoke. Ruby felt wretched, as if she had only just closed her eyes but she knew she must have managed to get some sleep.

Tilly yawned and said "I was just dreaming about tap-dancing hedgehogs. It was just like one of those Busby Berkeley films. You know, where they have the camera looking down and the dancers making fantastic patterns."

"You're amazing" laughed Ruby getting to her feet. "Come on, another chapter in our amazing adventure awaits."

At precisely six o'clock, Ruby and Tilly were at the main entrance to the Internment Wing. They were astonished to find at least two hundred women there before them, each with a little suitcase or bag plus their gas mask boxes slung round their neck. As more women hurriedly arrived, Ruby was disappointed to see that Tuppence and some of her cronies, including the quiet, strange one from the truck, were also awaiting departure. She nudged Tilly and cocked her head in their direction.

"Oh Bugger!" said Tilly.

"QUIET!" shouted a soldier standing by the entrance, a clip-board in his hand. "I want you all to come through this door and out to the transport which awaits you in the yard. As you pass me, each of you will show me your identity papers so that I can tick you off my list. Understood?"

No one answered but those at the front began to file past him.

"This is just like being at school again" Tilly said in Ruby's ear.

"Oh! Look over there" said Ruby, nudging her in the ribs. "That girl with the auburn hair. Isn't she that film star - what's-her-name?"

Suddenly a scream pierced the quiet conversations of those waiting their turn. For a second there was silence and all eyes were on the front of the queue, necks craned to get a better view. Then another scream. "NEIN. NEIN. Nicht meine Tochter. Nicht meine Tochter."

Standing on tiptoe, Ruby could see that it was the mother with the two daughters who was the one so upset. "It's that women from the truck. The mother with the daughters ... who came in with us."

Moments later, the crowd parted and the mother was being supported under the arms by two soldiers. "Mind yer backs!" said one of them. "She's only fainted."

Closely following behind was the younger daughter. As Ruby reached out her hand and touched the daughter's arm, the young girl looked up through her tears.

"What's happened? asked Ruby.

"My sister, she goes. We stay. Next time maybe we go." Then she was gone, after her mother.

"Bastards" said Tilly. "Don't they know what they're doing with people's lives?"

"Sounds like another wonderful piece of British bureaucracy" said Ruby. "Let's try and find the other daughter and see if we can help her."

"Good idea" said Ruby. "She'll need all the friends she can get, especially with that lot around" and she gestured in the direction of Tuppence, who was just going through the exit door.

In the courtyard, Ruby and Tilly found that about half a dozen assorted buses and coaches had been requisitioned to take them to their next destination.

"How many more times are they going to move us?" said Ruby.

They followed those in front of them and boarded an old red double-decker bus with a faded "London Transport" sign written along the side. They went up to the top deck using the outside stairs at the back.

"Would you just look at this?" said Tilly. "It must have come out of a museum."

"Pass down the bus, please" someone shouted. "Any more fares?" cried another, but the English humour was lost on most of the travellers and a morose silence quickly prevailed.

The convoy set out soon after Ruby and Tilly had found seats; one army lorry taking the lead and another following up at the rear. Two army motorcycles with sidecars squeezed into the column while two goggled policemen on motorcycles cleared the way through the streets. As they passed, bystanders stopped to watch the cavalcade.

"It's a bit like being Royalty" giggled Tilly and she started to wave in the same way she had seen the Queen and the Princesses do on the newsreels at the cinema, by just pivoting at the elbow. She turned and smiled at Ruby just at the instant a rotten tomato crashed against her window. She shrieked with fright. Looking out through the splattered fruit on the glass, she could see that some of the onlookers were shouting and jeering: some were waving their fists and one old man was even waving his walking stick.

"Oh! This is awful. Inside I'm just the same as them" she said. "I'm on their side."

"But they don't know that. Do they?" replied Ruby. "As far as they're concerned, we're all Nazi spies. And it's the newspapers that have stirred that up. They're the ones who are really to blame." Not totally true, thought Ruby, trying to put as much distance between herself and reality.

"They really hate us, don't they" said Tilly, with tears in her eyes.

"It's not us they hate" said Ruby, squeezing her friend's hand. "It's what they think we stand for, that's what they hate. They're scared. And I can't say I blame them."

Twenty minutes later, the column pulled into what Ruby instantly recognised as Euston Station even though all the signs identifying it as such had been removed for security reasons.

Without stopping, they were directed passed the area where taxis were still offloading fares into a vast cathedral-like space with a high arched roof: an area normally reserved for goods vehicles. Disembarkation proved to be a long-winded affair as those in each bus or coach were escorted in turn through the concourse to a waiting train.

When it came to their turn, Ruby clambered down the steps of the bus and onto the concrete floor. A young soldier had been detailed to assist any women who were finding the stairs difficult. As he had for everyone else, he offered Ruby his hand. "That's kind of you. Thank you" said Ruby, smiling at him. And then, on impulse, she said quietly "Do you know where we're going?" The young man blushed and looked around him, worried in case someone accused him of "fraternising with The Enemy". Then he looked back at Ruby. "I heard it was the Isle of Man" he whispered. Then much louder, for effect, he said "C'mon Miss. Get a move on."

The smells of the station, which Ruby fondly remembered from her childhood, now seemed to choke her. The Isle of Man..........why the Isle of Man? Ruby wasn't even sure she knew precisely where the Isle of Man was. Somewhere in the Irish Sea, she thought. Whatever, she knew it was hundreds of miles away. Suddenly, a jet of steam belched from the engine they were just passing. Ruby jumped and in doing so, dropped her case which hit the ground and burst open. Embarrassed that her most intimate belongings were on open view, she, with Tilly's assistance, scooped them up and stuffed them back into the case. She was just straightening when a voice cried out "Move to one side please! Move aside!"

A column of soldiers was coming in the opposite direction, escorting a group of men. In that instant, Ruby was convinced she would see her brothers. She concentrated on every face as it passed her. Then, incredibly, from their midst, Ruby did spot someone she knew.

"Mr Mendelsohn!" she shouted.

His grey, strained face turned towards her, searching for the owner of the voice. He looked at her with eyes that were both sad and embarrassed. "Ruby! Strange and unhappy times we live in, my dear. Take care of yourself. My best wishes to your mother." And he was gone.

"Who was that?" asked Tilly.

"Mr. Mendelsohn. I work....worked for him." At that moment Ruby felt as guilty as sin. "Oh Tilly! What is going to happen to us? The young soldier on the bus said we're going to the Isle of Man."

"Are we!" cried Tilly. "That's wonderful."

"Is it? Why?"

"I went there on holiday once, with a school friend and her family. It's lovely. Oh, that's the best news I've had in ages. You'll really love it, Ruby. You'll see."

The male internees having passed through, Ruby, Tilly and those behind them who had been held up, were escorted through the transfixed crowd to the commandeered train. On board were the hundreds of female internees who had been taken from temporary holding camps all over the south of England. As they passed along the corridor of the train, both Ruby and Tilly looked in each of the compartments, partly to determine where the Jewish woman's daughter was and partly to avoid Tuppence and her companions.

Six other women shared Ruby and Tilly's compartment. The most striking was sitting in the corner by the window, opposite Ruby. A woman in her mid-twenties, she had bright red hair, almost scarlet, and wore a dark astrakhan coat with a fox stole around her neck. Her fingernails were long and painted in the same shade of red as her hair. She wore red high-heeled shoes and had a thin gold bracelet around a nylon-covered ankle. This woman was captivating. Everyone seemed to snatch quick looks at her whenever she happened to glance out of the window.

It was when Ruby noticed the hint of a smile on her face as the woman gazed at the passing scenery, that she knew she was enjoying the attention. So Ruby held her gaze when she turned back to the carriage. She was rewarded with a smile but then, to Ruby's total embarrassment, the woman leant forward with a bejewelled hand extended. "Mitzi Muller" she said.

"Oh" said Ruby "Eh...Ruby Becker."

"Awfully dull and dirty in here" continued the redhead, attempting a middle-class English accent to replace a very definite German one. "Of course, when one usually travels first-class, one is bound to notice the difference in standards."

"I suppose one is" replied Ruby with a straight face and heard Tilly giggle beside her.

Mitzi Muller frowned at Tilly but then focussed back on Ruby. "I'm a dancer, you know" she said and looked around to the rest of the passengers to make sure that they were suitably impressed.

"Oh, that's nice" said Ruby, thinking she knew perfectly well how Miss Muller earned her living. "What sort of dancing do you do?"

"Well" said Mitzi with a slight hesitation. "I suppose you could call it contemporary, eh…. exotic."

Ruby was pretty sure what that meant too; she'd heard her brothers talk about "exotic dancers" but she wasn't going to let on. With the most innocent of expressions, she said "Is that like some sort of ballet?" She could feel Tilly shake with suppressed laughter beside her.

"Eh. Something of the sort, yes" replied Mitzi, who was wishing she hadn't started this at all. She turned to look out of the window again, trying to indicate to Ruby that the conversation was over.

"Oh I just love ballet." Ruby wasn't about to let her off the hook. "I used to go to lessons when I was little. I just loved wearing those frilly little tutus when we gave the parents a show. And the music……. Wonderful. Made me feel like I was a princess. Do you have to wear nice costumes?" Tilly groaned and crossed her arms in front of herself.

Mitzi coughed. "Well, not really. It's more….er… modern."

"Oh, I know!" Ruby had decided to go for the throat. "It's like with fans and things. My brothers told me about going to some place "Up West" once where the dancers wore nothing at all. And they had huge fans to cover themselves from the audience. And they weren't allowed to move."

Tilly exploded.

The dancer's face went the same colour as her hair and, with a cough, she rose to her feet. "I've just remembered that I have to find a friend on the train." She reached up into the luggage rack for a small leather suitcase and, wrapping her coat tightly in front of her, she sidled into the corridor, slamming the sliding door shut behind her. They could hear her arguing with the guards who were sprawled there.

"You're so cruel" said Tilly as she dabbed her now-reddened eyes.

"She deserved it" said Ruby. "Snooty Madam".

They were allowed to stretch their legs in some anonymous large station en route, but that really was no more than a long supervised wait in the queue for the Ladies toilet. In the end, the soldiers commandeered the adjacent Gents toilet to speed up the process, much to the annoyance of those gentlemen who were intent on using its facilities. "Bad enough allowing women to use it at all, but when they're Fifth Columnists it's beyond the pale. Wouldn't have been allowed in my day. Shoot the lot of 'em, I say. I shall be writing to my MP about this. Have no fear."

No sooner had they pulled out of the station and were into the surrounding countryside than the train screeched to a halt. Still no one in the carriage said a word. Tilly got up and released the leather strap that was holding the window closed. As the glass dropped down, she stuck her head out to see what was going on. "There's a herd of cows on the track" she cried. "The soldiers are shooing them away, but they look more scared of the cows than the cows do of them."

"Perhaps they'll shoot them" said Ruby. But five minutes later they were on their way again and twenty minutes after that everyone in the carriage was asleep.

Ruby was awakened by Tilly nudging her in the ribs. Grinning from ear to ear, she nodded her head towards the seat opposite. Ruby instantly saw the source of Tilly's amusement. A middle-aged woman, who until now had resolutely refused to acknowledge anyone else in the carriage apart from her haughty-looking companion at her side, was asleep with her head on her friend's shoulder. Her little pill-box hat had slipped sideways so that it now covered her exposed ear and her glasses were tilted sideways across her nose. But what had captivated Tilly, and now Ruby, was that her false-teeth were hanging halfway out of her mouth and she was dribbling down the front of her neighbour's velvet jacket.

This gruesome sight continued unabated for nearly twenty minutes: the dribble flowing like lava from Mount Etna; the wet patch on the jacket getting bigger with every passing second; the false-teeth hanging ever more precariously.

It was then that the real fun began.

Suddenly the train lurched to one side and screeched to a halt. The false-teeth dropped into their owner's lap and the lady with the saturated jacket awoke, becoming instantly aware of her own predicament.

"Eeeek" she screamed, waking her companion in the process. The sleeping woman jumped and this sent her false teeth flying across the compartment into the lap of the woman sitting next to Tilly.

Her screams could be heard in the next carriage.

Resolutely, Ruby and Tilly looked out of the window, refusing to acknowledge the pandemonium that was happening in their carriage. A couple of soldiers charged in, holding their rifles in front of them. Angry German voices competed with alarmed English ones. For the second time in the journey, the girls stifled their laughter until they were fit to burst.

"This is better than watching George Formby at the Odeon" Tilly managed to splutter before the pair of them collapsed with laughter.

By the time the train pulled into Lime Street Station in Liverpool, the journey had taken just over six hours. The exhausted and thirsty internees were gathered up in an adjacent freight depot and then, with a considerable amount of whistled signals from the soldiers, they were marched out of the dark station building into the blinding early afternoon sunshine and into Lime Street itself. The column, escorted on either side as well as front and back by soldiers with bayonets fixed to their rifles, was now set to endure yet another humiliation. Lining the street were hundreds of Liverpudlians. Most of them had come especially, determined to see what these Nazis looked like and to let them know what they thought of them.

At the top of the exit ramp from the station, seven-year old Billy Stephens waited impatiently with his mother. "When are the Nasties coming, Mam?"

"Hold your noise, Billy. They'll be here in a minute. Look, you can see the soldiers all getting ready."

Sure enough, the soldiers were organising themselves in ranks along the road. The crowd sensed something was about to happen and began to shout and scream their derision. The noise swelled into a roar the like of which was more typical of what used to come out of Anfield Football Ground just down the road; that is before the authorities had stopped all forms of mass entertainment. Then, amid shouted orders and whistles from the bustling army officers, the procession appeared. As they came up the slope, it was the heads of the leading soldiers that came into public view first.

The noise from the crowd around him became so loud that young Billy, who had been pushed to the front by his mother, held both hands tightly over his ears. But he couldn't see what the taller adults could see. Yes, now he could. Soldiers' heads, then the rest of them. Carrying rifles. Billy was petrified they were going to shoot him. He suddenly needed to go to the toilet. Desperately, he looked about for his mother but all he could see were other adults, shouting and screaming. He was scared out of his wits. He pressed his hands harder against his ears and clenched his eyes tight shut. Then, just when he thought he was going to have an accident in his trousers, he sensed something had changed. He opened his eyes and dropped his hands to his side. He looked up. Instead of the Nasties that he had been promised, hundreds of women were marching in front of him. You could have heard a pin drop, as he had heard his Granny say once, although despite trying many times since, he'd never succeeded in hearing anything.

Eerily, apart from the sobbing of distressed internees, some on the point of collapse, and the sound of hundreds of footsteps, there was silence. These were not the people that the crowd had expected. Where were the jack-booted Nazis that Mr Churchill had said were threatening the country? These were women, ordinary women: some of them old and sick, some of them heavily pregnant. All of them looking frightened and exhausted. Hundreds of them.

The silence spread as the crowd further along Victoria Street took in their first sightings of the procession. All the soldiers sensed this uneasiness in the crowd which had gone from animal aggression to shocked silence in a mere hundred yards. And now, as the column made its way down Victoria Street and onto The Strand alongside the River Mersey, some of the women in the crowd were dabbing their eyes and blowing their noses.

Trying to take her mind away from the misery and, ironically, the embarrassment that she felt around her, Ruby turned to Tilly. "Tell me more about the Isle of Man."

"Well it's ages since I was there so it might have changed."

"So what do you remember?" prompted Ruby anxiously.

Tilly recalled her holiday with enthusiasm, much to the delight, not only of Ruby, but to several others who were around them.

"Ist dat vere ve are going den - dis Island of Men?" asked one of them. Then she became frightened. "Vy are der no vimen on dis Island? Vot are dey doing mit us?"

Tilly laughed. "No, it's not the Island of Men; it's the Isle of Man. That's its name. The people who live there are called Manx."

All this was beyond the questioner's level of understanding of the English language and Tilly had to resort to giving a German translation. This had the effect of bringing even more people into the group and, as they walked down the road, Tilly soon found herself at the centre of a group of twenty or so women asking her to repeat this, or translate that, or explain something else. Ruby, now temporarily edged to one side, just smiled at the popularity that her new-found friend had gained. She knew that in these times it paid to have friends.

The trek of just over a mile took an hour and half to complete. Some didn't make it and were treated at the side of the road by eager first-aiders. Those who did could see their destination, held fast by giant hawsers in the Dock ahead of them. HMS Princess Josephine Charlotte, one of the early cross-channel ferries, had been in the Belgian Port of Ostend when the Low Countries had been invaded. She had taken on as many refugees as she could and sailed to Dover. When they'd disembarked, the ship had then been ordered to Liverpool.

Ruby and Tilly looked up at the ship with its two huge funnels framed against the milky afternoon sky. It seemed so serene and comforting, somehow safe from all the world's woes. That there were four lifeboats slung on each side seemed a somehow pointless decoration.

The women were crammed onto the ferry and left to make themselves as comfortable as they could. Most stayed in the fresh air, on either the main or the upper decks, but some sought the relatively more comfortable inside Lounge. Volunteers from the Salvation Army handed round cups of tea and offered biscuits. The escorting soldiers, although still wary of any unrest, took the opportunity to smoke and chat amongst themselves. Indeed, one could easily have mistaken the whole thing as being a typical voyage of holiday makers keen to enjoy themselves; apart, that is, for the overwhelming preponderance of women among the passengers.

Ten minutes after the gangplanks had been hauled aboard, and with a couple of blasts from her horn, the Princess Josephine Charlotte let go the hawsers and manoeuvred out into the river. The final part of the journey had begun. Next stop, The Isle of Man.

As the tidal surge of the River Mersey gave way to the gentle swell of the Irish Sea, Ruby left Tilly sharing her memories of her holiday on the island with half a dozen of the forty-five nurses on board from The German Hospital in Dalston, East London. Ruby climbed the steps up to the upper deck and wandered around the gangways, coming to terms with the extent of human misery that she saw there. Hundreds of tired, hungry and distressed women, most of them looking totally bewildered and shocked, had found whatever comfort they could and seemed to be in the process of escaping into the depths of their own minds in order to overcome their despair.

Ruby found herself standing as near the guardrail as she was allowed to and, childlike, she turned her head in the direction of her home and willed her thoughts to her mother. She thought about the last few days and wondered what her mother had been doing during that time. She wondered how she was coping, how she would survive financially without the money that Ruby and the boys brought into the house. And she wondered what they did to those found to be spying for the enemy.

For ages she watched a seagull battling against the breeze to stay abreast of the ship, waiting for any titbit that was thrown away. So effortless. Must be wonderful to be a bird, she thought: free to go wherever the fancy takes you; no constraints, no one imposing their will over yours.

"Hello."

Ruby jumped with surprise and spun round to find that she was face to face with the quiet woman from the ride into Holloway Prison.

"Oh!" she said. "It's you. Hello."

"Do you mind if I stand here for a while? I do so enjoy the sea. I used to live near Hamburg when I was young. Such fun we had."

Ruby didn't know what to say in reply but eventually said "I thought you would be with you friend."

"Hah!" said the woman. "You mean Hannah. The one your friend amusingly calls Tuppence. She is not my friend. I have no friends on this ship. I am here only until the paperwork is sorted out and then I will be able to go back to my book shop in Croydon. I am a prisoner but that is a mistake and will be sorted out quite quickly, I am sure. They think I am someone I am not."

"Mistaken identity?" said Ruby.

"Exactly. Mistaken identity."

"Who do they think you are, then?" asked Ruby.

"I don't know. They use my name, which is Annalise Braun by the way, but they seem to think I am some sort of foreign agent; that my bookshop is a centre for the Nazi underground."

"Oh God" thought Ruby but she said "Sounds awful."

"Yes it is. Well, I'm sure we will see more of each other when we get to the Island. Goodbye." And she walked off towards the bow of the ship.

"Goodbye" said Ruby. On the surface Annalise Braun seemed a genuinely friendly person but there was something about her that made Ruby uncomfortable.

"What's the matter with you?" It was Tilly. "Not feeling seasick, are you?"

Ruby laughed. "No, I'm fine. Just had a strange conversation with Annalise Braun. You know, that quiet woman who shared with Tuppence in Holloway. Her name's Hannah, by the way."

"I thought you just said it was Annalise."

"No, silly, Tuppence's name is really Hannah!"

"I think she looks more like a Tuppence than a Hannah, if you ask me. Come on" said Tilly, linking arms with Ruby. "Let's promenade and pretend we're on a Mediterranean Cruise. We can see if we can find that woman's daughter while we're at it."

Ruby laughed and they sauntered along the gangway, arm in arm, as if they hadn't a care in the world. But, in the back of her mind, Ruby was still thinking of Annalise Braun. She suddenly realised it was the eyes that had made her uncomfortable: cold and yet at the same time, vacant, almost lifeless. Was she really a spy? Is that what spies were supposed to look like? Is that what she looked like?

Having strolled round all of the upper deck in the gorgeous sunshine, they tried the main deck. Now in the shade, the temperature had dropped quite noticeably and so, even though both the girls had put their coats on, the saunter became a more purposeful walk. However, with both of the outside decks covered, there was still no sign of the young girl.

"You don't think she's jumped over the side, do you?" asked Tilly, who was beginning to get quite concerned.

"I don't see how she could have" said Ruby. "The soldiers might look fairly relaxed, but they've been on the alert since we came on board, especially if anyone gets too close to the rail. But there's one place we haven't looked. There!" and she pointed towards the small covered lounge area towards the front of the main deck.

"But that's where Tuppence and her mates are. I saw them go straight in there while we were still in Liverpool. Threw out almost everyone else in the process. She can't be in there."

"Well, she isn't anywhere else, is she? Come on. Let's go and see."

As they opened the door to the Lounge, all conversations stopped and nearly a hundred faces turned to look at the newcomers. Out of their midst, Tuppence stood and walked towards them.

"Vell. Vell. Und vot do you vant?" she sneered.

Ruby felt quite intimidated, but it was Tilly who spoke. "We are just looking for someone" she said in as determined yet calm a voice as she could muster. "But I don't think she is here after all."

"Who is dis person?" asked Tuppence, still with sneering smile.

"It doesn't matter" said Tilly, looking around the room at the hostile faces turned towards her. "She's not here."

"Hah!" cried Tuppence. "You are looking to be spying on us, Ja? You vant to tell your Englische soldier friends vot ve speak about, Ja?"

"No" interrupted Ruby. "We are not interested in what you've been saying. We were just looking for an old school friend of mine. We thought she might be here, but she's not. Sorry to disturb you." Then she grabbed Tilly's arm and propelled her back through the door, slamming it behind them and thereby shutting off most of the raucous laughter that followed.

"Bitches!" said Tilly when they were well away from the Lounge. "Who do they think they are? Well, they're not going to scare me. No Sir!"

"Well, they certainly scare me" said Ruby, with a weak smile.

Tilly looked at her friend, quizzically. Then she smiled. "Well, maybe just a little bit."

As their anxious fears about the Nazi women receded, they became increasingly concerned, worried even, for the Jewish girl. Deciding to retrace their steps, they each took an aisle of the main deck, but she was nowhere to be seen.

"Let's try the top deck again" said Ruby when they met in the stern. "Maybe she slipped passed us somehow." So, with each girl taking an aisle, they searched the upper deck again but they still came up empty handed.

"I'm beginning to think you may have been right, Tilly. But surely someone would have seen her if she jumped."

"Mmm" said Tilly, but her concentration was elsewhere. "Can you hear someone crying?"

"Oh yes. Just faintly."

They moved the few yards towards the guardrail where the sound appeared to be coming from. Then it stopped.

"There's no one here" said Tilly.

They both looked around. Indeed, there was no one within yards of them. Then the sobbing began again and Ruby and Tilly followed the sound down, below the line of the guardrails, to where one of the lifeboats was slung on its davits between decks.

"There!" cried Tilly pointing at the lifeboat. "She's in there!"

They both scrambled to reach the lifeboat's tarpaulin cover but quickly realised they couldn't do it on their own. Besides, if the soldiers saw any of the women messing about with the lifeboats, they would obviously think they were trying to escape. They might get shot. The girls had no choice but to tell one of the soldiers.

Events moved quickly after that. An army officer was summoned and a cordon established around the lifeboat. It didn't take long then for the lifeboat to be manoeuvred in towards the ship and the girl to be helped out onto the deck. Almost immediately she began screaming and crying out in incoherent German. The young officer called Ruby and Tilly over. "Do you understand what she's saying?"

"She's not making much sense at all" said Ruby "but she's just had to leave her mother and sister behind in Holloway Prison. She's bound to be upset."

"Look, can't we look after her? Get her to calm down a bit" asked Tilly.

The young officer was sympathetic, but he couldn't take the risk of leaving her unguarded. "I've got to find somewhere secure for her" he said. "Would you two ladies come with her? I think she needs some friendly faces around her who she can talk to. Would you do that?"

Without looking at each other, Ruby nodded and Tilly said "Of course."

So it was that, for the rest of the voyage, Ruby, Tilly and Amalia Beckmann sat in a locked room which doubled as a Medical Room and an occasional storeroom. Given a fresh cup of tea and someone to talk to and reassure her that she wasn't facing the future alone, Amalia eventually calmed down. Tilly went through her, by now, well-practiced presentation of her holiday in the Isle of Man and Amalia was soon dry-eyed and as happy as she could be, given the circumstances.

An hour or so later, and with there being no windows or port-holes to see out of, they could not see their new home coming into view, but they knew from the sounds of the engines and the shouts of the sailors and dockers that they had arrived.

After about half an hour, just when they had begun to think that they'd been forgotten, the door was opened and the officer came in. To Amalia he said "You look better, Miss." Then to Ruby and Tilly "Thank you. I appreciate your help. Now, on a more formal note, I'm afraid we need to hand this young lady over to the Medics, just to make sure she's fine. Will one of you please translate that to her." Tilly did.

"Right" said the young man. "If you grab you're things, we can get you all onto dry land" and he smiled at each of them. "I'm sure each of you will welcome that."

Their first sight of the Island, however, was a shock. Instead of the idyllic picture that had been painted by Tilly's memories, this was an island covered in barbed-wire and barricades.

"Oh God!" cried Tilly.

Chapter 6

Myrna Loy, the woman some called "The Queen of Hollywood" and with whom Pete was totally besotted, smiled seductively as she carried a small breakfast tray, covered in a crisp, white linen cloth, across the room. Dressed only in a tiny red satin dressing-gown, which revealed more than it concealed, and high-heeled red shoes, she gently put the tray on the sideboard and then turned to look at him. Her long eyelashes fluttered over her pale, blue-green eyes as she smiled again and crept up the bed. She nuzzled into his neck, smelling fresh and wonderful. "Wakey wakey, big boy" she said huskily. He couldn't smile wide enough. At this precise moment, happiness was definitely Pete-shaped.

"Wakey wakey. Here's your breakfast, Pete" Myrna purred in a deeper, rougher, London voice.

Pete groaned and opened his eyes as the soldier put the metal tray on the small table. "You bastard, Alf."

"What 'ave I done?" said Alf, the Private who had been on duty since yesterday evening. "I'm doin' you a favour, 'ere. What d'you fink this is? Bleedin' room service?"

"Oh, I'm sorry" groaned Pete. "Your timing's a bit out, that's all. I was 'avin' this gorgeous dream."

"Oh, I see" replied Alf with grin. "I thought you 'ad a strange look on yer face when I came in. Girlfriend?"

"No, even worse" said Pete. "Myrna Loy."

Alf sucked his teeth. "Ouch, mate. Now she can 'ave the top off my egg any time she wants it."

Pete laughed. "After me, you're first."

On the tray was a bowl containing what looked like porridge and a mug of tea. "Chef's speciality, today" said the soldier, grinning with unfettered enthusiasm. "Actually, it's not bad, though not as good as me Mum used to do us."

Pete groaned. "Cheers" he said. He had had the same breakfast yesterday and it was awful. He'd hated porridge for as long as he could remember. "What's 'appening? Anything?" he asked, rubbing his eyes and wondering what the chances were of getting back to Myrna.

"Not much" replied the soldier. "Load went out last night and a new lot're due in this afternoon. Other than that, nuffin'. Oh! I almost forgot. The Sarge says you can come out of 'ere at ten o'clock, after he's done the morning round."

"Cheers" said Pete and, then just as the soldier was going out the door, he said "'ere, Alf?"

"Yeah."

"Who was in the cell next to me when I first came in?"

Alf looked at him. "There weren't nobody in there, mate. No one at all." And with that he closed and locked the cell door after him.

In fact it was nearer eleven o'clock when the Sergeant came into the Punishment Hut. "Right, you" he said, pointing at Pete. "Get your bleedin' face out of my sight and if I ever clap eyes on you again, you'll wish I 'adn't."

Pete gathered his meagre belongings into his little brown cardboard case and, slinging his gas mask box round his neck, he stepped out of the door into the sunshine. The breeze, which was blowing across the fields into the Camp was fresh and smelt of horses mixed with the clean scent of the surrounding pine trees. Pete filled his lungs as if it was the first breath he had ever taken. He looked around him, noticing that three new lines of tents had been erected in the field where he had, only the day before yesterday, raced around like an idiot. The sound of hammering came from behind the Punishment Hut – presumably the new accommodation huts being put up. A dozen or so soldiers were reluctant participants in a series of physical jerks, lead by one of the Corporals. "C'mon you dozy sods! Get those fucking knees up! Highcr. Iligher. That's it. Pretend your gettin' yer leg over, Jamieson. Any of you not sweatin' at the end of this'll get fed to those Nazi-boys when they come in. They like a bit of tender English rump, so I hear. Don't they Bates?"

Pete laughed. It was good to see that it wasn't just the Internees that were treated like shit.

"What're you laughing at?" snarled the Corporal looking at him. "Piss off!"

Pete walked off in the direction of the stable block, still smiling. It was then that he noticed that apart from himself and the soldiers, there was almost no one else around. Three Orthodox Jews, with hair curled down from their temples and wearing yarmulke, were standing by one of the tents. Pete smiled at them, but they turned their backs on him and carried on with their conversation. "Please yourselves" he said and then turned away in a search for his brothers. He made his way across to the stable block, passing the old Elephant House, but found nothing. All the stalls were empty – no mattresses, no cases. Nothing. He went outside and walked back towards the lines of new tents. As he walked passed, and hearing nothing from inside them, he ventured a peak in a few. He found two which had mattresses laid on planks of wood and kit bags in a pile between them, but apart from these, the rest appeared empty. Where was everyone? Then he remembered Alf saying that some of the Internees had been moved out last night.

"But surely not all of them" he said to himself. He walked passed the remaining tents which, although brand new, were empty nonetheless. It was just as he was passing the last two tents in the line that he heard shouts from the field beyond. Looking up, he saw a group of men playing football with an old tennis ball. They were all in the same dark trousers but, whilst some wore black vests, the others, the younger ones, were bare-chested. Although the grass was far too long to allow any chance of a decent game to be played, it had been well and truly trampled by previous internees and so it was just about possible to stage some sort of competition. From the voices, it was apparent that they were all Germans.

As Pete watched, he realised that it was the comparatively older "Officers" against a younger and more athletic "Crew". The pitch was an equalising factor but, nevertheless, the young lads were winning hands down and their superiors had to resort to some very dubious tackles to stand any hope of staying in touch. Apart from an occasional glance in his direction, the men ignored him. He watched them for a few minutes - "Bloody useless, the lot of them" he thought then walked back towards the Mess Hall. He was just opening the door when he heard someone shouting at him.

"Where do you think your going?" It was the Sergeant.

Pete turned his head but kept hold of the handle. "Where is everyone?"

"All your little playmates were shipped out last night. So until the new holiday makers arrive this afternoon, you'll be pretty much on your little lonesome. Not goin' to cry, are you?"

Pete ignored the taunt. "Everyone's gone? Including my brothers?"

"Sorry" said the Sergeant, sarcastically "I was forgetting that English wasn't your native tongue."

Pete clenched his fists. He'd only just got out of the Punishment Hut and here he was an instant away from going back there, or maybe somewhere worse. He wondered how long he would get if he did stick one on this obnoxious pillock.

"In English," the Sergeant continued with his sarcasm "the word *everyone* means all, everybody, every one of your little traitor friends. Alle. Verstehen?"

"Yes, I understand, thank you" said Pete, forcing himself to smile as if he had received the best news ever. "Where have they gone?"

"Oh I'm afraid I can't divulge that sort of information, especially to you. Highly sensitive information, that is. In fact I've 'alf a mind to report you to the Intelligence Officers. Trying to obtain classified information is a serious offence. You'd be lucky to get anything less than ten years in The Scrubs."

"Piss off!" said Pete and walked away towards the open field, to the sound of the Sergeant's laughter. Towards the edge of the field there was a grassy bank which, in days gone past, would have been where some of the race goers would have stood to watch the horses at the start of their straight sprint up towards the Grandstand. Now it was empty and silent save for the occasional cry from the football game in the distance, the occasional hammering from the direction of the new huts or a shout from one of the guards over by the perimeter fence.

Pete lay on his back and idly watched the cotton-wool clouds drift and swirl in the blue sky above him. The morning sunshine was actually burning his cheeks, but it felt so comforting. For the first time in his life he was alone. He couldn't remember a time when at least one of his brothers, or his Mum or Ruby or Dot had not been within calling distance. He lay on the grass trying to remember such an occasion but couldn't. Half of him was scared stiff: not knowing what was to come or if he was doing the right thing. Yet the other part of him felt strangely liberated, grown up, an adult, free to make his own decisions, do what *he* thought was right. In a way, he didn't care where his brothers had gone and this made him feel guilty. But he knew he wasn't going to be able to choose where he was sent; they would just send him regardless. If that was the same place as his brothers, all well and good. If not, well, he would just have to make the best of things. He remembered his mother always used to say "It will all come right in the end."

"Perhaps it will" he said to a ladybird that had just landed on his arm. He thought about his mother, hoping she was coping. The ladybird crawled up his arm towards his elbow so he had to twist his wrist to watch its progress. "And what about Ruby?" he said. "She's too young to be treated like that. What damage could she have done to the country?" He thought about what he'd been asked to do. He couldn't get his head around the fact that they'd chosen him. Why him? Bloody stupid war. He sat up. "BLOODY WAR!" he shouted and then sank back into the grass. "What would Charlie do?" And then, as if suddenly the future was all mapped out for him, he thought "Try and get a cup of tea and something to eat, for a start. That's what he'd do." So he got up and ambled back across the field to the Mess Hall which now, fortunately, was open.

With a thick slice of bread and butter, a small lump of desiccated cheese and a cup of tea, Pete settled himself quietly in a corner. Alone. Alone that is until the German football players noisily filed in – officers first, Pete noticed. Some of them looked in his direction, but no one acknowledged him and all of them went to a table on the far side of the Hall: all except for the middle-aged officer who had come in after the others. Having picked up his plate of food and his mug of tea, he looked towards his comrades, but then walked over towards Pete.

In perfect English he said "Would you mind if I sat over here with you?"

"Please yourself, Mate" said Pete. Then he added with a smile "At least here it's a free country."

The Officer smiled but said nothing and sat down opposite him. "How come you are here, alone?" he said after taking a sip of the tea.

Seeing no harm in telling the story, Pete recounted his experience with the bedbugs and the "cure" which led him to be locked up. The officer was soon roaring with laughter; so much so that his colleagues had all turned to watch the encounter. "My name is Burfeind. Captain Otto Burfeind" and he offered his hand.

Pete looked at it and then clasped it. "Pete….Peter Darling" he said.

"Darling!" exclaimed Burfeind. "One of my men, who is still in Devon, is also named Darling. Maybe you are related."

"Maybe" said Pete. "My father came over from Germany just before the last war. Married my Mum, who's English. Lived here until he died a few years ago."

"Ah. That explains why you are being interned - because you have a German father."

"Mmm, maybe" said Pete, vaguely. "What about you and all them lot?" and he waved a hand in the direction of the crew.

Burfeind smiled at the way Pete was so dismissive of his men and then said "My colleagues and I work for a German shipping line which operates passenger vessels going from Hamburg to East Africa and back. When the War started we were on our return journey but we had to put into the port of Lobito, in Portuguese West Africa, for supplies. The Portuguese authorities there naturally decided to hold our vessel pending instructions from their superiors in Lisbon. Eventually, after weeks of doing nothing, we, all the remaining passengers and the crew, decided that we had had enough of their hospitality and we made a break for it, trying to get across the Atlantic to South America. We thought we had made it too, but then, after nearly a week at sea, we were found by the British cruiser HMS Neptune. In accordance with my orders, we evacuated our ship, the SS Adolf Woermann, and scuttled her. Fortunately, the Neptune took us all on board and brought us to England. We were all interned in Devon. Most of my crew are still there, but some of us were brought here yesterday evening. God knows why. So there you have it."

"But what if the Neptune hadn't picked you all up?"

"We might be on opposite sides, my friend, but there is still honour amongst seamen. There was never a doubt in my mind. And besides, I asked them before I scuttled the ship." Burfeind smiled and Pete laughed.

Pete was captivated by this ordinary-looking, round-faced man with a little snub nose and large ears. Never in his life had he met someone who had been so at ease with whatever life seemed to throw at him.

Having finished his tea, Captain Burfeind stood. "Goodbye, Herr Darling. I hope we will have the chance to chat again sometime."

"Eh. Yeah" said Pete. "Me too." As Burfeind returned to his crew, who, to a man, stood as he approached, Pete felt confused. The last thing he had expected was that he would actually like the man.

Around the middle of the afternoon, the new arrivals were brought into the Camp in a variety of buses and coaches. It reminded Pete of the first day at secondary school when all the terrified first-years arrived having heard grim stories that they would all be initiated by having their heads stuck down the toilet and the chain pulled. He had wandered over to watch the unloading; he had nothing else to do, and besides, there was always the chance that he might see someone he knew. He watched the succession of tired, bewildered faces trying to come to terms with how their lives had been turned upside down. For some, fleeing from repression and violence, it was yet one more step on the tortuous road through hell to the bright, new, tolerant future which they were certain lay somewhere before them. For others, who, like him, had never set foot outside England, this was the start of a life which they could never have dreamt of. Whatever they were thinking, Pete knew that nothing would ever be the same again. "Bloody war" he said again.

Then he noticed a frail old man with his arm in a sling being helped gingerly down the steps of a coach. His skin was thin and sallow, his cheeks sucked into whatever remained of his teeth. But what captivated Pete most was his eyes: haunted, wild, petrified eyes that plainly protested that they had seen too much unimaginable horror already without adding still more.

"Bloody, bastard war" Pete said. Then, embarrassed with himself for speaking out loud and for the emotion that had risen in him as he watched the old man, he turned and walked away. When he was round the corner of the next building, he put down his case and blew his nose on his grubby handkerchief. He smiled to himself as he thought of his mother's insistence that all their hankies had to be boiled in a special saucepan which, together with an old wooden spoon, she kept specifically for that purpose on the floor at the back of the pantry.

"What are you doing here, Darling?" The loud voice was the Sergeant's who had just come across from one of the other buildings. "Spying for the enemy, again?"

"No!" said Pete, indignantly. "I was just blowing my nose, that's all."

"Tell it to the marines" sneered the Sergeant. "You're trouble, you are. I can smell it on you."

"Oh piss off" said Pete and went to move away.

"STAY WHERE YOU ARE!" shouted the soldier, angrily. Some passing soldiers stopped and watched them.

Pete felt his face flushing with pure loathing and anger.

"As it 'appens" continued the Sergeant but in a much more measured tone, perhaps because he now had an audience, "I 'ave been sent to find you. I 'ave been told to ensure that you gather your belongings and then to escort you off the premises."

"You mean they're letting me go?" Pete beamed.

The Sergeant laughed. "Not a chance, Sunshine. You're on your way to somewhere much more fitting for the likes of you: somewhere where they know what to do with traitors and spies."

Pete dropped his case and aimed to punch the soldier's face in.

"Ah, Herr Darling." It was Captain Burfeind. "I am glad I have found you. You are coming with us, ja?"

"What do you mean? Where are you... we going?"

"Somewhere more suitable for us. Somewhere in the North, I think. You will be better off coming with us rather than staying here on your own. Don't you think?" and he looked pointedly from Pete to the Sergeant.

"I think you're probably right" said Pete with a smile, although a large part of him still wanted to smash his fist into the Sergeant's smarmy face.

So it was that two hours later Pete was seated in the exact same carriage of the train that his elder sister had travelled in only the day before. But, instead of having Tilly for company, he was sharing the carriage with seven Prisoners of War. Whilst four of the men were happily playing cards, the other three were sleeping, or at least trying to. No one talked to him so he looked out of the window too. He soon felt himself beginning to doze and welcomed the possibility of rejoining Myrna.

Unfortunately, she must have been busy elsewhere, because, when Pete awoke some hours later, he couldn't remember finding her. He opened his eyes. By now, all of the occupants of the carriage were awake and the card game had finished. Everyone was looking at him, smiling. "Was ist los?" he said.

Some of them exchanged glances and then the man opposite said, "Who is this Myrna?" Pete blushed and then grinned and all the German's laughed loudly. The armed soldiers in the corridor looked up nervously.

By the time the train pulled into Manchester's Exchange Station, Pete had become an unofficial member of the crew. He had recounted the bedbug story, which by now had been embellished ever so slightly to include the soldiers shooting over his head, and in return he had been told even more graphic details of the SS Adolf Woermann's escape disguised as a Portuguese ship, the Nyassa, and the chase around the South Atlantic by the British cruiser.

As the one internee and eleven Prisoners of War climbed down onto the platform, they were suddenly surrounded by what appeared to Pete to be a hundred nervous but eager soldiers, each pointing a rifle in his direction. One slight move in the wrong direction and we're going to be blasted to Kingdom Come, he thought. As if he had read his mind, Captain Burfeind, in German, ordered all his men to put their hands on their heads. Pete followed suit. This immediately seemed to defuse some of the tension, but more than one of the English soldiers must have thought it was his own fearless bravery which had won the day:

something to tell the rest of the lads when they were back in the NAFFI tonight.

The orders were given and, still with their hands on their heads and amid the abusive shouts from onlookers, the prisoners were marched to waiting Army lorries.

As the motorcycle outriders, who had cleared their route from the centre of Manchester out into the Lancastrian suburbs, deployed themselves on all of the access roads to the derelict cotton mill, Pete could see what looked like a large lake off to his right, presumably being fed by the river that seemed to snake around the back of the building. Cotton waste blew in the wind like snow.

"God Almighty!" said Pete as he took in the old, red-bricked building with its broken windows, its massive chimney and grey roof with its missing slates. As far as he could see, there were two chain-link perimeter fences surrounding the building, each topped with barbed-wire. Between the two fences, soldiers, carrying rifles and with fierce-looking dogs, were patrolling: each canine looking eager to be given the slightest opportunity to put "German prisoner" in its diet.

"Ja, Gott im Himmel!" agreed one of Captain Burfeind's crew who was standing next him.

They were ordered into the building, up the worn concrete steps, along dirty grey corridors and through a large double door into a room which had obviously contained some large machinery in the fairly recent past. The thick aromas of machine oil and unwashed bodies caught at the back of Pete's throat. There was a large patch of water on the concrete floor and, looking up, he could see a broken sky-light in the roof. Although the fine weather had given way to the series of short, sharp showers which had followed them all the way from Manchester, it wasn't cold outside. But in this living hell of a building, Pete could feel himself shiver and the hairs on his arms rise. The strip search, which quickly followed, did nothing to help matters.

With the search and the roll-call over, the prisoners were dismissed to explore their accommodation and join the rest of the poor unfortunates held in what was undoubtedly the worst of all of the Prisoner of War Camps in the UK, Warth Mill. The Ritz it wasn't: one bath tub to eighteen hundred people; only about a dozen water taps emitting freezing cold water; a similar number of stinking, filthy lavatories, some of them blocked and overflowing, and without the luxury of any form of paper to use; no mattresses to sleep on, just wooden boards for the lucky ones - the unfortunate remainder left to curl up on the floor in the corridors and sleep as best they could; and the rats, hundreds of them, scurrying along those self same corridors in their own life and death struggles to survive. The food provided was poor and inadequate and it was left to the prisoners themselves to organise its preparation and distribution.

Although, as an albeit honorary member of Captain Burfeind's crew, Pete was far more secure than if he had been here without knowing a sole, nevertheless this privileged position was only relative. It was still a stinking Hell, not fit for the rats let alone human beings.

"Bastard War." he said under his breath.

Chapter 7

At the same moment that Pete was trying desperately to come to terms with the nightmare of Warth Mills Prisoner of War Camp in Bury, less than thirty miles away Charlie and Jonny were enjoying a concert written by one of the internees and being played on a flute and two violins by three elderly Jewish men. Although they were more familiar with the works of Bix Beiderbecke, their father's favourite, both Charlie and, even more particularly, Jonny were enjoying the music. Jonny was fascinated by the way the instruments seemed to feed off each other just as they did on his father's records.

"I never knew classical music was like this" he said to his brother when the musicians had stopped for a few minutes break. "Good, ain't it? I always thought it was music for toffs."

"Mmm" said Charlie, not quite so enthusiastically. "Certainly better than nothing I suppose."

"Sort of takes your mind off things, as well" added Jonny, who was not going to let his brother's negativity ruin his enjoyment.

"Don't it just, my young friend" said Manny, who had just arrived at the house where the impromptu concert was being held.

"I thought you said you were going to play cards" said Charlie.

"Yeah, I was. But when I got there, I dunno, I just didn't feel like it so I went for a walk up the street to see what else was goin' on and then I came back 'ere."

"And?" asked Jonny.

"And what?"

"What is goin' on?" said Jonny in exasperation.

"Not much, really. A few lectures on things I never 'eared of and ain't got a clue about. You know, science and stuff. Some little old bloke reading poetry. Thought it was crap personally but there was quite a few listenin' who seemed to like it. Tears in their eyes, some of them 'ad."

"Yeah, I could never take to poems either" said Jonny. "The only one I ever remember is:

The boy stood on the burning deck

Whence all but he had fled;
The flame that lit the battle's wreck
Shone round him o'er the dead.

But I can't remember any more."

"I remember the next bit" said Charlie.
"The boy stood on the burning deck
His face was all a-quiver
He gave a cough, his leg fell off
And floated down the river."

That saw an end to their afternoon of culture.

This was their second day in their new camp at Huyton, on the outskirts of Liverpool. In fact, the Bluebell Estate, as it was known locally, was one of the biggest in the country and would eventually hold twenty-seven thousand internees and prisoners of war. On their arrival, the boys were astonished to discover that their new home was in fact centred on several streets of a half-finished council housing estate. These streets contained a mixture of houses and flats securely surrounded by high barbed wire fences. With twelve internees allocated to each house, conditions were extremely cramped and the air inside could not exactly be described as fragrant. However, as long as they kept themselves to themselves, there didn't seem to be too much aggravation from their fellow boarders, most of whom seemed to be elderly German Jews. But, if last night was anything to go by, their biggest problem would be getting some sleep. Amid the chest-tearing coughs of the sick, the heart-wrenching sobs of the frightened and bereaved and the vocalised nightmares of the poor souls who were forced to relive unimaginable horrors every time they closed their eyes, any peaceful sleep, when it came, was fleeting.

"I don't think even Pete could get an uninterrupted hour's sleep in here" Charlie had said after their first night. At the time, it had prompted a prolonged conversation about what might have happened to him. After some very fanciful suggestions including being personally rescued by Myrna Loy who had taken him off

to Los Angeles to be her sex slave, the general consensus was
that he had lost his temper when he had been released to find
Charlie, Jonny and Manny gone and had punched "that bastard
of a Sergeant". This had meant him being put back in the
Punishment Hut pending trial for assault. They each knew that
Pete's temper would be his undoing.

Under different circumstances, each of the lads could see that
this estate would be their mothers' dreams come true. Wide, open
roads instead of the dark back-to-backs; dry, not damp, houses,
some with little gardens in front of the house as well as at the
back; proper red tiles on the roof, not the broken black slates that
let the rain in even if there was only a shower. But best of all,
there was an inside toilet. "A posh lav" as Jonny had called it.
Not that there was anything posh about that particular piece of
sanitary-ware after twelve men had been using it for thirty-six
hours. The smell of ammonia and human excrement was so thick
you could almost cut it with a knife, but at least they had a little
window that they could keep open and mercifully, at least so far,
the toilet hadn't blocked. So, despite there being practically no
furniture, there was shelter and there was plenty of open space
for recreation, both physical and cerebral.
Indeed it was the latter which most astounded Charlie and
Jonny. Almost as soon as they arrived, there were internees
setting up rudimentary classrooms with lectures being given by
"Professor This" or "Doctor That." Subjects ranged from
chemistry and physics to bird-song and butterfly identification.
Someone had even got hold of a rusty 1920's BSA "A" series
motorbike and a group of enthusiasts were doing their best with
the basic tools they had managed to get from God-knows where
to strip it down to rebuild it. Even those who knew nothing about
the mechanics of motorcycles were made welcome and
knowledge was willingly passed on to those who were interested
to learn. Everywhere the boys turned, the desire to impart
knowledge to others seemed to be being used as a strategy for
coping with the deprivations of war and internment. Somehow
the passing on of training and experience seemed to bring back
some sort of meaning to the lives of people who had literally lost

everything; materially, physically, psychologically and socially they were bankrupt.

This thirst for knowledge was to have a specific impact on Charlie and Jonny when they returned to their house a little while later. Just as they opened the front door, one of the housemates, an old, grey-bearded Jew addressed them in German. He said that he was from a little village just outside Linz in Austria. He showed them a crumpled letter which he explained he had received at his home just an hour before starting the journey that had eventually seen him arrive in England. The letter was in English, a language which he knew only very little. He had not felt inclined to trust anyone to translate it for him before now, but, feeling that they were likely to be staying here for a while, he wanted to know what the letter said. He had observed Charlie and Jonny, knew they both spoke German as well as English, and felt that he could rely on them to be discreet. At this Charlie and Jonny looked at each other. No one had ever said that sort of thing to them before. Trusting them to be discreet – whatever next.

Enormously touched by the old gentleman's faith in them, they easily and quickly translated the letter which turned out to be from someone in Devizes offering him support if he was able to get to England. Suddenly the old man's face beamed and tears came to his eyes with the realisation that there was hope for him still. He shook both their hands vigorously and then, almost coquettishly, asked if they might find some time to teach him some more English.

"Us?" the boys said together. "We're not teachers" added Charlie in German.

The old man smiled at them and explained that he didn't want formal teaching; he just wanted to be able to communicate better, to learn a few phrases. Flattery fluttered its eyelids and the boys were anybody's.

They decided to meet at around four o'clock on the following day on the corner of the field where endless games of football were played if it was dry and in their own house if it was raining.

"I'm sure we can find somewhere quiet" said Jonny, who had really warmed to the idea of himself becoming a teacher.

So it was, with the sun almost cracking the pavements, that the boys walked towards the field, having spent most of the morning discussing the how's and the what's of their task.

"Are we ready, Professor Darling? said Charlie, with a smile at his brother.

"As we ever will be Doctor Darling."

With that they turned the corner of the last building before the field and were astonished to be confronted with about a dozen men sitting in ranks on the corner of the field.

"Bloody Hell!" cried Jonny.

"Jesus!" came from his brother as his jaw dropped. Hurrying towards the men, they stopped in front of them and sought out the original old gentleman. It was easy enough to find him. He was the one with the grin from ear to ear. "Freunde" he said as he gestured around him. "My friends all want to learn better English" he said in German.

Charlie turned at his brother who looked absolutely petrified. "What do you think now then, Professor?"

"Eh…. I think I need the toilet" was the only reply he got.

"Let's give it a go" said Charlie. "It might be fun."

So the boys began their lesson. They had decided to use everyday expressions and forget about the intricacies of spelling and grammar – mostly because they realised what a waste of time it would be, not to mention somewhat embarrassing for them. Charlie began. "Today we are going to concentrate on what we can see from sitting here" he said in German. "We will use English wherever possible. The more you hear it, the better and quicker you will understand."

Nervously, Jonny pointed upwards. "This is the sky" he said with the most confident smile he could manage. Everyone dutifully looked up and in unison chanted "This is the sky."

"The sky is blue" said Jonny.

"The sky is blue" replied the audience.

"This is the sun."

"This is the sun" came the response.

"The sun is hot."

"The sun is hot."

Having covered green grass, brown houses and black trousers, Charlie and Jonny became aware that they were beginning to loose their audience. Every time they pointed to something, there were new smiles and constrained laughter. It was when Jonny said "This is a soldier", pointing to a soldier standing on the other side of the perimeter fence watching them, and all the pupils burst out laughing, that they knew something was not quite right. Then, turning round, they saw Manny doing an impression of a soldier marching with his rifle on his shoulder.

"This is my friend" said Charlie quickly.

"This is my friend" repeated the men.

"His name is Emmanuel."

"His name is Emmanuel."

"Emmanuel is a smelly git." Jonny pinched his nose.

"Emmanuel is a smelly git." Everyone pinched their nose and laughed.

"Emmanuel is going away" said Charlie, aiming a playful kick at Manny's rear.

"Emmanuel is going away" the audience chanted.

Manny feigned offence but then smiled and waved. "Goodbye everybody" he said.

Immediately, the pupils stood. "Goodbye Emmanuel." Then they all sat down. Then the old gentleman stood up again before either Charlie or Jonny had had chance to resume the lesson.

"This is Samuel" he said, patting both hands on his chest. Then he turned to the man sitting next to him. "This is Moses" and he lifted Moses to his feet. Then turning to the man sitting on his other side "This is Abraham" and he too was made to stand. One by one he introduced all his classmates and in English.

"Well done, Samuel" said Charlie. "That was very good. Thank you."

"Wonderful" added Jonny. Everyone clapped while Samuel beamed his biggest smile for a long, long time.

Charlie turned to Jonny and whispered "What shall we do now, numbers or days of the week?"

"I................"

"Why don't you teach them to say "I'm a fuckin' parasite: a filthy, fuckin' Jewish parasite.""

All eyes turned to the edge of the field, behind Samuel and his friends. Four hard-looking lads, about Charlie's age or maybe a bit older, stood with their hands on their hips. One of them said

"Well, go on then. Teach the fuckin' Yids something useful. What about something simple like "I have stolen everything from the working man and now I deserve nothing?" What about it, then, Teacher?"

Jonny looked across at Charlie who looked as white as a sheet.

"I, eh…I don't think you're wanted here" said Charlie feebly, his mouth bone-dry. "We are not doing any harm" he pleaded.

"Oh, really" said the loud-mouth. "And what do you think this scum are going to do when they learn English? Work for the good of us all? I'll tell you what they're going to do. They're fucking going to strangle the life out of everything in this country just like they've done in Germany. Blink your eyes and they'll be running the whole bloody shop. Blink your eyes again and the pound'll be worthless and everyone'll be unemployed. The only jobs we'll be left with will be the dirty ones that this lot don't want to do and while they sit on their arses and take all the fuckin' money we'll be just lucky to survive."

Charlie was scared. Confrontation was something he had always feared and avoided, always left to his brother, Pete. He felt Jonny willing him to say something to the thug, to stand up to him but nothing came. Samuel and his friends, sensing that they were on their own, yet again, rose to their feet and began to move disconsolately away.

"Wait" shouted Charlie. "Wait." They all stopped and turned towards him. Then in German he said nervously "I am not a fighter. These people scare me. But if we let them walk over us now, they will always do it. We will be treated like cowards – and we will deserve to be. Thousands of men are fighting and suffering in an attempt to stand up to the likes of these ignorant thugs. We must not let their sacrifice be wasted. These men who talk anti-Semitism, what do you think is really their problem? I'll tell you. It is their own inadequacies, their own idleness, their own guilt. That's what keeps them poor and ignorant. They have no goals to reach, no ambition to make a better life for themselves, only an arrogant and selfish view of life and those around them. We must stand up against them, shoulder to shoulder."

The thugs, each a paid-up member of Oswald Moseley's black-shirted British Union of Fascists and veteran of the Battle of Cable Street in October 1936, could speak little German, but they weren't stupid. They each recognised a change in the body-language of the men before them. Instead of heads bowed and cowering, every one of the Jewish men now turned to face his aggressors: heads up, shoulders back and fists clenched.

The loud-mouth sneered as he looked from face to face. Recognising that this wasn't going to be the pushover he had expected, he said "There'll be other times, Teacher. Just keep lookin' over your shoulder." Then he turned and, with an exaggerated swagger, walked up the road laughing with his mates.

"Christ, Charlie. Where did all that come from?" said Jonny, patting his brother on the back. "Never thought you had it in you."

"I think I'm going to be sick" replied Charlie, who was then surrounded by Samuel and his friends, each of whom insisted on shaking his hand or patting him on the back. However, despite the euphoria, Charlie realised they were all marked men now and him in particular. He'd made a dreadful mistake.

That evening, Charlie relived the events of the day – over and over again. The more he thought about it the more scared of reprisals he became. He had quickly come to the conclusion that he should have kept his mouth shut and let the class disperse – at least everyone would be safe. "Who are we kidding? What good would those rubbish lessons do anyway?" he said to himself. "They'll manage without me. I'm not even Jewish so why should I put my neck on the block."

After a very restless and sleepless night, Charlie started the following day with one thought in his mind. There was no way that he was going to continue with the lessons. If he did, he would be beaten up or worse. "I'm not going out today" he told his brother.

Jonny looked at him quizzically. "After everything you said yesterday, you're not going to let those bastards get to you, surely?"

"No, it's not that. I, eh, don't feel too good. Must be something I ate."

"Yeah, right" said his brother. "You're a coward after all" and stormed out in disgust.

Charlie sat on the floor in the corner of the room he shared with the others, embarrassed at his own cowardice but unable to shake off the fear that ate away at him. He tried to convince himself that while everyone might think him weak, it was for the best. No point in creating trouble unnecessarily.

Jonny walked down the road towards the playing field wondering how he was going to explain his brother's pathetic weakness. Manny was standing on the corner, waiting for him. "Where's Charlie?" he said.

"He's nursing a great big yellow streak that he's got down his back."

"Eh?" said Manny, totally bewildered.

Jonny went over his brief conversation with his brother.

"You're joking!" exclaimed Manny. "After that speech he made yesterday. I don't believe it."

"That's exactly what I said to him" said Jonny and walked off sullenly towards the playing fields without another word.

"Hang on" shouted Manny and ran to catch up with him. "What're you gonna say to Samuel and his mates?"

"How the hell do I know?" said Jonny angrily and again stormed off.

Samuel and his friends were all there. Despite the threats of the previous day, not one of them had cried off: in fact they all looked eager and confident. They all looked at Jonny – first with expectation and then with unspoken questions in their minds. Jonny stood in front of them, trying to think of what to say. Seeming to sense his predicament, Samuel got slowly to his feet. "No brother? No Charlie?"

Jonny looked at him then said "Eh, no. My brother is not feeling very well this morning." Although he hadn't thought to speak German the sense was plain to all – not only the superficial meaning but also the covert one as well. There was much shaking of heads and mumbling. Jonny took a deep breath and then said, in German this time "Do you want me to continue with the lesson?"

Immediately the shaking of heads turned to nodding of heads and the smiles returned and so the class spent the next hour doing numbers linked into the previous day's lesson.

"There is one sky."

"There is one sky" they repeated.

"There are two legs" he said, pointing to each of his own.

"There are two legs." And so on until everyone seemed to have learnt numbers up to ten as well as revised what they learnt the day before. And there were no interruptions – no sign of the thugs.

At the end of the lesson Jonny was walking back towards the house when he heard footsteps coming up behind him. Thinking it was the yobs from the previous day, he tensed and clenched his fists and was just about to turn and face his aggressors, when Samuel shouted to him, "Herr Jonny." Jonny turned and waited while Samuel hurried up to him.

In German he panted "I must talk to you."

Jonny waited while the old man got his breath back. "I am sorry about your brother. I know he is a good man, but even good men know fear. And it is fear which makes us behave in ways we would not wish to behave. I know this to be true. I have seen so many things in my lifetime that have made me scared and caused me to do things I am ashamed of now. I must speak with your brother, if he will let me talk with him."

"Please yourself" said Jonny. "I think you'll be wasting your time."

"So I am so busy at the moment?" replied Samuel with a grin.

Jonny smiled at him. "Come on then. I'll show you where he is, or at least where I left him." And indeed, Charlie hadn't moved.

"Brought someone to see you" said Jonny.

"I don't want to see anyone" said Charlie. "Just all of you leave me alone. Sod off" and with that he lay on his mattress with his face turned towards the wall.

Jonny gestured to Samuel as much to say "He's all yours" and turned on his heels and left the building to find Manny. Samuel coughed.

"Go away. I don't want to see anyone."

In German, Samuel said "Herr Charlie, I am thinking that you are frightened. You are scared that you will be hurt. This is nothing that you should feel ashamed of. A perfectly normal human response to a threat, I think. In fact, if you do think of it, the human race would not have survived very long if it hadn't recognised the signs of aggression and acted accordingly. Fear is a good thing. It makes us careful, wary. Our subsequent actions are more controlled, more measured because of it. But we must take these actions. We cannot just do nothing. We cannot allow fear to paralyse us because then it becomes the fear of fear itself. Do you understand what I am saying?"

There was no reaction from Charlie so Samuel continued "If you think back in your life to all the occasions when you were scared and frightened, the fear was concerning things that hadn't yet happened. Indeed, I am sure that often the things you were scared of didn't happen anyway. And if the things that you were scared of did happen, then you dealt with them as best you could. But I think you will find, if you search your recollections, that you no longer felt fearful. You may have felt other things, but you weren't scared. There was no time to be scared. This is how the human body works. It analyses the threat and decides whether to run away or fight. If it thinks you can win, it doesn't say to run away.

"And I will tell you this from my heart. Yesterday I was going to run away. Yes I was. Then someone touched my heart with words which made me realise that we could win this fight. We do not need to run away if we stand together and help each other overcome our fears. Shoulder to shoulder, we will be strong."

He paused but still there was no reaction from Charlie.

"So, I will leave you to your thoughts, Herr Charlie. Thank you for giving me the courage to try to help my friends." He touched Charlie's shoulder and then turned and left the room. He walked slowly down the road, wondering if he had said the wrong things. Maybe he could have said it better. Then, something made him stop and turn round. Back at the house he had just left, Charlie was standing, leaning against the door, and then he smiled at Samuel and gave him the thumbs-up. Samuel smiled elatedly in return, knowing that he had said the right things after all.

Chapter 8

June 1940

Mercifully, the train journey from Douglas Station to Port Erin on the south-west corner of the island had been a short one, but, even so, the women were absolutely worn out. By now, most of them couldn't have cared less what the immediate future held for them; they just needed to stop travelling and sleep. But of all the women, it was Tilly who had been the most in shock. Since leaving Liverpool she had been buoyed up by the memories of her childhood holiday on the Isle of Man. However, the idyll had been blown apart as she had come up on deck of the Princess Josephine Charlotte as it was being tied up to Victoria Pier in Douglas. She wasn't prepared for the sight of the high, barbed-wire fencing running as far as she could see between the sand and the coast road. As she looked along the promenade, which she remembered walking along with her friend and her friend's parents holding sticks of candy-floss, she could see that every hundred yards or so there was a lower fence running at ninety degrees from the seafront to the old hotels and boarding houses which still lined the front. These lower fences, each of which had a gate in the middle, effectively sectioned off the whole of the seafront. "They must be to keep the different nationalities and threat levels apart" she had said to Ruby and Amalia.

Slowly, the internees were formed into columns and then ushered through booths where they were photographed as they held their number up on their chests.

"I feel like I'm a cow at a cattle market" said Tilly.

"I feel like I'm a criminal" said Ruby.

As the women were slowly marched up the hill along Lord Street, they were surrounded by fences and barriers. What had been, in Tilly's mind, beautiful white buildings with strange and exotic palm trees growing in the gardens offering welcome shade from the incessant sun beating down, were now cold, grey and forbidding prisons. From almost every window, men shouted and

waved; some with delight and support but most with a sadness
written across their grey faces as they examined every woman's
face in the hope that they might see someone precious: someone
who had survived.

Now, two weeks later, she sat on the end of Ruby's bed,
waiting while her friend was enjoying a soak in the bath. Tilly
stood up and walked to the window which looked out across the
Spaldrick with Bradda Head and the full expanse of Port Erin
Bay beyond. No matter how many times she stood here, taking
in the view, she didn't think she would ever stop feeling that it
was somehow unreal, a dream from which she would awaken at
some point.

Having taking every opportunity to explore the immediate
area, she now felt like she was almost one of the locals. She
watched a couple of girls walking, arm-in-arm, down the road in
the direction of the station and the centre of Port Erin. She
remembered walking the opposite way with Ruby and Amalia on
their first day here.

They had arrived at Port Erin Station in the early evening. All
three of them had had rotten headaches brought about by the lack
of refreshments on the journey from London. Fortunately, the sky
had turned cloudy but, even so, they still had to shade their eyes
against the light as they climbed down from the train. From the
station all of the women were marched out on to Station Road
and then towards the stunning turquoise sea. They were then
turned right to walk along the Promenade for some hundred or so
yards to St Catherine's Church and then into Church Road and
the Church Hall where friendly faces were keen to offer them
cups of tea, sandwiches and cakes. Tilly had never seen so much
food. "I wasn't expecting this sort of reception. Were you, Ruby?"

"No, not likely. But I'm not complaining. I could eat a horse
if only my tongue wasn't so dry."

"Would you like some more tea, dear" came the immediate
response from a short elderly lady in a maroon, smock-dress with
a flowered pinafore wrapped over it. She was carrying the most
enormous metal teapot, seemingly without any effort at all.

"Oh, you're a star" said Ruby holding out her cup for a refill.
Tilly held hers out too and was immediately followed by Amalia.

"Golly, you are all thirsty" said the lady.

"We've been travelling since six o'clock this morning and this is the first time we've been given anything to eat and drink for hours" said Ruby.

"Oh, you poor things" said the lady.

"Do you mind if I ask you a question?" said Tilly suddenly, before the lady had had chance to turn away to serve someone else.

"Not at all" came the jolly reply. "How can I help you?"

"All of you, the ladies here who have made all these refreshments for us, you seem happy to see us. I don't understand. Everywhere we've been so far we've been treated like we were spies and traitors." Then as an after thought, she added "And we're not at all."

The lady laughed. "My dear" she said. "Firstly, we are hundreds of miles from London. We don't see things quite the same over here. And secondly, before the war, this was an island that made much of its living out of tourism. Most of the ladies you see here run guest houses and small hotels. With the uncertainties of last year leading up to Mr Chamberlain's Declaration of War, people have stopped coming here for their holidays. Now the Authorities are paying us a guinea a week to look after each of you until, well, whenever. So we are happy to see you; well most of us are anyway. Anyway, I must rush. I'm sure I'll see you all again soon. Maybe some of you will be staying with me. Bye bye."

"There you go" said Ruby. "Somebody loves us. Isn't it smashing?" Then turning to Amalia she gave her the gist of the conversation in German.

It was at that point that some people began to climb onto the stage at the end of the Hall. Conversations were halted in mid-flow. In almost total silence, a man in a black jacket, pin-striped trousers and holding a black bowler hat in front of him, stepped forward together with another man in a less formal sports jacket and grey flannels.

"My name is Sheridan-Steele. I have been sent here from the Home Office to ensure that you are all suitably, but I must stress, securely looked after." The man in the sports jacket then translated what Mr Sheridan-Steele had said into German.

"You are now on the Isle of Man and this is where you will stay until such time as it is deemed appropriate for you to return to your homes. I would now like to introduce you to the Commandant of this Camp. Dame Joanna Cruickshank." As Sheridan-Steele stepped back, a rather rotund and determined-looking woman in her mid-sixties stepped purposefully forward.

"You are all in Rushen Camp." Her voice easily carried the length of the Hall.

"But I'm English, not Russian" came a shout from someone towards the back of the room.

"R.U.S.H.E.N. Not as in Russia. Rushen is the name of this area of the Island and it includes Port Erin and Port St Mary. As a result of assessments made by the Home Office's various Enemy Alien Tribunals, each of you has been classified as a threat to the British nation in this sorry time of war. As such, you have been interned here on the Isle of Man for an indefinite period. You are not allowed outside the Camp." She stopped and waited, with obvious frustration, while the translator spoke. Then she continued. "I have been asked by the Home Office to take charge of this Camp. You will all be treated properly, and providing you do as you are told and behave responsibly, you will be free to do as you wish. However, I do not expect, nor will I tolerate, any rule-breaking. Discipline will be strictly maintained."

As the translator spoke, Dame Joanna looked at her watch as if there was something more important she felt she should have been doing. When he had finished, she quickly followed on with "Although the perimeter fences have not yet been built, all roads surrounding the Camp are clearly marked and guarded. There is a curfew at nine o'clock in the evening. This will be strictly observed." The translator did his best to add gravitas to his presentation in an attempt to match the Commandant's tone.

"You will each be allocated to an address and you will live at that address. If you want to change addresses within the Camp, it is permissible but only on an exchange basis. You must advise your landlady and she will inform us.

"When your name is called out, you will come forward and collect details of where you will live. You will then make your way to that address and settle yourselves in. Your landladies will tell you what jobs you will be expected to do. These will be unpaid. There may be a small number of other jobs which need to be done and these may attract a small allowance. Your landladies will give you details of these also." With that, and while the translator was still speaking, Dame Joanna turned on her heels and, without a backward glance, left the stage with the man from the Home Office.

As it turned out, Ruby and Amalia, presumably because the allocation was done alphabetically, were given the same address while Tilly's piece of paper showed something completely different.

"Let's find your place first," said Ruby to Tilly "and then we can find where we're staying."

"Sounds good to me" said Tilly, who was surprised how disappointed she was that she was not sharing with Ruby. "This time last week I didn't even know you existed" she said "and here I am all upset that we've been split up."

Tilly's note gave an address of "Cheer ny Yindyssyn, Shore Road." So, surmising that Shore Road would be running along the shoreline, they walked back onto the Promenade, turned left and then right and down onto the little road running part-way round the bay. Choosing to turn left along it, they were surprised and delighted to find that "Cheer ny Yindyssyn" was the first house they came to as evidenced by the little wooden plaque that hung from a nail on the wall by the front door. It was the end one of three grey, stone cottages which faced out onto the harbour.

"Oh you lucky thing!" exclaimed Ruby. "This is lovely."

At the front door, Tilly rang the bell and turned to enjoy the wonderful view across the bay. In the early evening light, it was idyllic.

"Yes" came a stern voice from behind her.

"Oh" Tilly said, startled, and turned to see her new landlady. She was shorter than Tilly, about five feet two or three with very short, almost cropped, dark hair. She was wearing a blue jumper and baggy black trousers. Both had what looked like paint all over them.

"My name is Nussbaum, Matilde Nussbaum" said Tilly. "Err, I have been told I am to stay here."

"Yes, I was expecting you. But only you. I have no room for anyone else" said the lady, her broad Irish accent easily discernable.

"Oh no" said Tilly, quickly. "These are my friends. They are staying somewhere else but we decided to stick together until we found both places. I'm sorry if we startled you."

The woman relaxed her somewhat stern expression. "You'd better all come in then." Gesturing to Amalia and Ruby she added, "You can leave your things out here. They will be perfectly safe."

Ruby translated to Amalia and they both stacked their cases and gas mask boxes by the front door. Then they all followed the woman inside.

"My name is Georgina Spiers, but everyone calls me George. Would you all like a cup of tea?"

"That's very nice of you" said Tilly, "but we've just had some in the Church Hall so would you mind if we went and found where Ruby and Amalia are staying before the curfew starts?"

"Of course not" said George. "Let me just show you your bedroom first so you can get rid of your things and then I'll see if I can give you directions."

Tilly's bedroom turned out to be little more than a large cupboard, about eight feet square with a small bed, a wardrobe and a straight-backed dining chair crammed into it. The window, disappointingly, looked onto a high bank at the back of the bungalow. "This is lovely" she lied. "Thank you."

"We all have to do our bit" said George, putting her hand on Tilly's back. "Now, let's go and find out where your friends have to go."

Ruby gave her the slip of paper she had been given.

"Oh, the Golf Links Hotel. That's not difficult. If you go back the way you came, get back onto The Promenade and continue walking up the hill with the sea on your left, you will come to it on the right. In fact, I can show you from the front door." She took them back to the front of the cottage, opened the door and pointed to a large building across the bay."

"That's great" said Ruby. "Thank you."

"You're welcome" said George. Then to Tilly she said "It should only take you about half an hour or so. I'll run you a bath in time for when you get back. I'm sure you could do with freshening up. Then we can have a nice chat over dinner."

"Oh" said Tilly, feeling more than a trifle apprehensive about just how her relationship with her new landlady was going to develop. "That would be absolutely marvellous. Thank you."

It did indeed only take the girls a short while to walk up to the Golf Links Hotel, which was a large Edwardian establishment overlooking the harbour. Ruby and Amalia introduced themselves and Tilly to Mrs Mylechreest, the owner, who was a stern-faced, middle-aged woman with her hair in a bun and wearing a spotless white pinafore over a voluminous black dress which came down to her shoes.

Amalia was to share a room on the first floor. Her room-mate was sitting on her bed as she and Mrs Mylechreest walked in. She was looking at a photograph of two children and had tears running down her cheeks. Mrs Mylechreest chose to ignore her and just said "This is your bed" to Amalia "and you can put your clothes in there with her's" and she pointed to a small wardrobe between the two single beds. Amalia didn't understand the words but she got the gist. She looked concernedly at her room-mate but the latter still didn't acknowledge anyone in the room. Amalia and Ruby exchanged glances and then Mrs Mylechreest said to Ruby "Your room is on the next floor up."

Without knocking Mrs Mylechreest opened Ruby's door and went into the room, followed by Ruby.

"Oh my God!" exclaimed Ruby, for standing against one of the beds, unpacking her suitcase, was Tuppence.

Tuppence turned and then, seeing it was Ruby, sneered. "Ja, eet is gut that we haf dis room. Friends we will be. Ja?" she said menacingly.

"Is this the only room you have, Mrs Mylechreest?" asked Ruby.

"Yes it is" said Mrs Mylechreest tartly, sensing the friction between the two girls. "And I don't want any trouble. Do you hear? Both of you will have to make the best of it. Like we all have to do while your Herr Hitler is causing trouble all over the place."

At the mention of his name, Tuppence's immediate reaction was to raise her arm in a Nazi salute saying "Heil Hitler."

"Don't you ever do that again" said Mrs Mylechreest, rounding on her so ferociously that Ruby thought she might even slap her. "I am being paid to provide you with board and lodgings but I don't have to tolerate that kind of behaviour. Do you understand?"

Tuppence's bravado deflated in the face of the formidable Mrs Mylechreest's onslaught.

"Yes!" thought Tilly, who was standing in the corridor listening. "Mrs Mylechreest for Queen!"

"Right" said the red-faced hotelier, turning to Ruby. "The bathroom is next door. You are allowed one bath a week and the rota is on the door. You will leave it cleaner than you found it. There will be another rota which will show your duties on this floor. If you all do your share, everyone will benefit. You will find that the tasks are not that time-consuming. Anything else you want to know, just ask. I will leave you two to come to some amicable truce and you Miss," gesturing to Tilly "I think you should be getting back to your place now." With that she went off towards the stairs.

Tilly said to Ruby "Are you sure you're alright sharing with her?"

"I'll be fine, thanks" said Ruby. "It was just a bit of a shock, that's all. And anyway, nobody's going to get on the wrong side of Mrs Mylechreest are they?"

Tilly looked across to Tuppence and pointed at her. In German she said "We are all on this island together, so we must all make an effort to tolerate each other. But if you so much as look at my friends in the wrong way or say one word out of turn, there won't be much left of you for Mrs Mylechreest to have a go at. Do you understand me?"

Tuppence just stared, sullenly at her.

Tilly's face seemed to register a thought and she said "And just to start the ball rolling, I will no longer call you Tuppence. Your name is Hannah?"

Tuppence nodded.

"So Hannah, I will wish you a good night, and remember what I've said." Turning to Ruby, Tilly said "See you in the morning. Bright and early – we have a lot of exploring to do."

"Are you sure you're alright walking back on your own?" asked Ruby.

"Yes. I'll be fine and it's not far. To be honest, it's not the walk back that's worrying me."

Indeed, the walk back to "Cheer ny Yindyssyn" was absolutely wonderful with an apricot-pink sky and the turquoise sea lazily lapping the golden sand. It was to Tilly everything that she remembered from her previous time here and more. Arriving at the cottage, she knocked on the door. No answer. She knocked again but there was still no sign of George. She lifted the latch and pushed. The door opened with a squeak. There was loud classical music coming from the kitchen and it was there that she found George chopping vegetables.

"Oh there you are Matilde!" exclaimed George with a smile. "Found you way back without any problem, then?"

"Yes" replied Tilly. "Ruby's place was easy to find, and please call me Tilly."

"Oh, I'm glad. I don't think Matilde is quite you, somehow. Now, I've just run you a bath, so you go and enjoy it and I'll bring you that cup of tea in a little while. And it's Fisherman's Pie tonight."

The bath was just the right length for Tilly to stretch out in and there was so much lovely hot water and perfumed bubbles in it that she just couldn't help but lay back and let her thoughts drift away. Such luxury.

It must have been some sixth sense that caused her to open her eyes some time later. Sitting on the side of the bath, watching her, was George, now dressed in an orange satin dressing gown which had gaped open revealing the whole of her left breast. Tilly forced her glance away, but George smiled and said "Do you like what you see?"

Tilly was dumbstruck.

"I've brought you a cup of tea" said George with a new edge, almost a purr to her voice, "but I didn't like to wake you. You looked so beautiful just lying there, I nearly…"

"Couldn't you have knocked" said Tilly, angrily reaching for a towel to cover herself.

"I'm sorry, my dear" said George, standing and tying her dressing gown tighter. "I didn't think you'd be so shy. You

London girls are supposed to be so sophisticated and open-minded. I thought we might…become very good friends.”

“Well you thought wrong………..and I’m from Watford.”

If Tilly hadn’t been starving, she would have stayed in her room, but she was so she didn’t. Instead, she put on the most plain skirt and blouse she had with her and went into the kitchen where George was sitting at the table nursing a glass of what looked to Tilly like whisky.

George looked up as Tilly entered . She had obviously been crying. “I’m sorry” she said. “I’ve been so looking forward to you coming. I just thought you might…..well….I was wrong and I apologise. Can you forgive me?”

“Forget it” said Tilly, “But don’t you ever try anything like that again. Deal?”

“Deal” said George with a weak smile.

“Right, what about that Fisherman’s Pie you promised me? I’m starving.”

During a very tasty dinner, Tilly found out that George was a painter, seascapes mostly, but when she found the right model she had promised herself that she would try “something different, if you know what I mean.”

“Well don’t look at me” said Tilly, but this time it was with a smile.

It turned out that George had had a long relationship with someone but her partner had died of lung cancer a few years before and so George had come to Port Erin to make a new start. She had only been on the Island for just over two years. As dinner progressed, Tilly found that, despite trying hard to remain angry, she was warming to her landlady; not in any physical sense, but she found her interesting and easy company. “What does “Cheer ny Yindyssyn mean?” Tilly had asked at one point.

George had laughed. “It was just a little joke to cheer myself up. It’s Manx for “Wonderland” as best as I can tell.”

It was after dinner, as they were washing up the dirty plates that Tilly had an idea: if it worked then she would be able to kill two birds with one stone. As she was going off to bed she said “George?”

"Yes, my dear" said George, wondering for an instant if Tilly had changed her mind.

"What do you think about German girls?"

When Ruby opened the door, Tilly was still looking out the window.

"Oh that was simply wonderful" said Ruby. "You have no idea how much I look forward to my weekly appointment with the bath tub. A whole hour all to myself. Absolute bliss. What were you doing while I was away with the fairies?"

"Oh," said Tilly wistfully, "I was just thinking about when we first arrived here. Before Hannah and I swapped houses. I just love this Island, even in the current circumstances."

"Mmm, I know what you mean" replied Ruby. "But I do worry about my mum a lot. I thought I might have got a letter before now."

"I'm sure she'll be fine and I don't suppose she gets much time for letter writing. She might not even know where you are yet. Come on, get yourself sorted and we'll go and see if there are any more paid jobs going."

"Mmm, I suppose you're right. The money I earn from Mrs Mylechreest shovelling coal and stoking the boiler doesn't seem to go that far, that's a cert."

"Well, you didn't have to buy those sunglasses" laughed Tilly. "And if you could cook, you could have worked with me in the kitchen."

"Yes, but I haven't seen sunglasses in the shops at home for ages" replied Ruby with a laugh.

"Oh! By the way," said Tilly, "I just saw George and Hannah walking arm in arm up the road. Talk about cats and cream. Hannah really does look totally different with that new hairstyle. I wonder if George has painted her yet?"

"Funny how that worked out so well" said Ruby. "I'm still amazed that you knew that Hannah was… you know...like that."

"Me too. Just came in a flash. Oh well, takes all sorts" said Tilly, moving towards the door. "I'll just go and see if Amalia wants to come with us. See you outside in a minute."

Two minutes later she was back. "Ruby, you'll never guess what's just happened."

Ruby looked up from brushing her hair. "What?" she said, alarmed.

"Amalia's room-mate, Edith. She's just been taken off to Braddon Mental Hospital, poor thing."

"Oh. That's so awful, but I can't say I'm surprised. She's been getting worse every day. We both know what a nightmare it's been for Amalia, having to share with her. Fancy having to leave your children behind with people you don't even know, just because you're married to a German."

"Mm, and they're still only babies. No wonder she's had a breakdown. I'll bet Amalia's in a right state. Come on. We need to make sure she's alright."

Amalia was lying on her bed, crying her eyes out. The strain of coping with Edith whilst still trying to come to terms with the trauma of leaving her mother and sister in Holloway Prison was bringing her very close to her own nervous breakdown as well.

Eventually, after much comforting from Ruby and Tilly, Amalia agreed to go for a walk to the Church Hall to see if they could find something to do that would pay even just a few coppers. The three of them walked down The Promenade and turned left into Church Road. Suddenly Amalia screamed and started running towards the Church Hall. Ruby and Tilly quickly glanced at each other and then ran after their friend, fearing she was going to do something awful; but they needn't have worried, for Amalia threw herself into the arms of her mother and sister who were trudging along the road towards them, clutching a piece of paper with their new address on it. After much excited hugging and kissing, and having worked out where their new address was, Ruby and Tilly left the family to themselves.

"I don't think we'll have to worry about Amalia any more" said Ruby.

"Me neither" said Tilly. "Come on, let's leave them to it. We've only got a couple of hours before we have to get back."

"What do you know about farming?" asked the lady from the Camp Office.

"Nothing at all" said Ruby.

"I went on one once" said Tilly. "It was a school-friend's birthday party and a horse bit me."

"Not what you would call "skilled agricultural workers", then. Are you?"

"Well, we're both pretty adaptable and we could do with some more money" said Ruby.

"And although we've both got jobs at the Hotel, there still seems to be so much time just doing nothing" added Tilly. "What do they need doing?"

"Well, Mr Roberts down at Ballamaddrell Farm has just this minute been in to say that his wife's about to produce their fourth child so he needs some help with castrating some of their lambs. I don't suppose you'd……….."

"No thanks" said Ruby immediately.

"Kind of you to offer" said Tilly. "Maybe next time."

"Well that only leaves archaeology, I'm afraid."

Chapter 9

The stench was awful. It reminded him of the time he had found a dead cat in the hedgerow when they went with their Mum to visit his grandad in St Albans. That was years ago – this was now. The trouble was that what he could smell was himself.

He'd tried to keep himself clean and had even got used to washing in freezing cold water when he got the opportunity to get under one of the dozen or so taps. No soap, though. But it was his clothes that stank and there was no provision for washing them. There was a rumour that laundry equipment was being brought in, but it was generally thought that the War would be over before it arrived. So, in the mean time, what would easily dry, like underwear, was rinsed under the tap and carried around until it dried. What wouldn't dry easily, like the one pullover he had, stayed filthy and increasingly smelly.

Everyone seemed to have established a semblance of ownership of a small space somewhere in the Mill: just enough room for each of them to lay his mouldy straw-filled sack on which to dream his dreams. Pete's space was in what looked like it used to be the Main Hall. The trouble was that he shared it with four hundred and eighty-two other men who smelled equally rank. He knew there was that many because he had stood and counted them a few times. Why had he counted them? "So there's something else to do?" his friend Manny would have said.

Because all the electricity to the Hall had been cut off, there was no light beyond what came through the windows and skylights: the broken ones affording more than the few dirty ones that remained intact. It was during the hours of darkness that this lack of light added to the confusion suffered by many of the men, particularly the elderly. With only enough room for one person to pass between the palliasses, it was easy to become disorientated, even for the most aware. It was therefore not uncommon for there to be a mishap on the way to the urinals which were in fact five gallon oil-drums situated in an adjacent room. On two occasions Pete had awoken to find someone pissing over him. No wonder his clothes stank.

In the fortnight that he had been in this dreadful place, Pete had got used to eating his meagre meals standing up because there was nowhere else to go, no tables, no chairs. At one surreal point he felt like he was watching a scene from Dickens' Oliver Twist: convinced that someone was about to walk to the front and say "Please Sir. I want some more." Except that you really didn't want more of the slop that was dolloped onto their battered metal plates.

The arrival of the Italians only made things worse. It meant longer queues for the food, for the toilets, for the taps and it lead to numerous fights in which the weak, sick and elderly never won. Sleeping arrangements became even more cramped, space to put their mattresses even more precious. And there was more friction between the inmates themselves and between the inmates and the soldiers who called everyone "Jerry" and took wallets, suitcases, watches and even treasured wedding rings with impunity.

In the main, Pete's days and nights were spent in much the same way as the rest of Warth Mill's "guests". He was constantly avoiding the threats and intimidation of the bully-boys of whatever persuasion and at the same time managing with the halfway edible food, the shelter that was wet when it rained and damp when it didn't, the fighting off of the rats which were constantly trying to share his already crawling bedding as well as his food and, on one occasion, his toes and surviving the sickening stench of hundreds of unwashed men. On top of all this, there was the constant coping with the numbing boredom of having absolutely nothing to do.

There were the usual, and endless, games of football of course but after playing three games a day for the first four days, Pete had given up on them. He no longer had the inclination nor the energy. If football ever became a banned sport, he didn't think he'd loose any sleep over it. Not that sleep was too much of a problem for him. Never had been.

He had managed to retain his relationship with Captain Burfeind and his crew although they were billeted in another part of the Mill and had even got to know some of them quite well. As the rest of the SS Adolf Woermann's crew had been brought up to the Mill, Pete had also made contact with his namesake, Oberbootsmann Felix Darling, although as far as they could tell they weren't related. This suited Pete fine because he found the seaman's unswerving support of the Third Reich difficult to stomach. But in a way, not liking the man made what he had to do that much easier. However, he found that he did still enjoy the company of Captain Burfeind, even though the officer's opinions were closer to those of his colleague than to his own. Pete had tried very hard to remain detached from the Burfeind's views, but he always found a sort of comfort in their conversations. Maybe it was because he was so much like his dead father, he thought.

Pete tended to stay outside as much as possible, sitting in on some of the informal lectures from time to time. He had particularly enjoyed a talk given by a former Professor from one of the Austrian Universities in which he suggested that thousands of years ago the Earth had been visited by an alien race from one of the distant stars. In time, these aliens had bred with the early humans and this was why there was such a gap between man and the apes. They were "The Missing Link." Seemed plausible.

It was after attending one such session that he literally bumped into a short, middle-aged man who was coming out of one of the buildings.

"Sorry, mate!" said Pete.

"Nae matter" replied the man in a Scottish accent. He then looked about him as of trying to get his bearings. "D'yer ken where is medical hut?"

Pete pointed it out.

"Just a wee dose of trots" said the man. "They have something, maybe?"

"You'll be lucky" said Pete. "And you'll have to pay for anything they do give yeh."

"Oh. That not good."

Pete was puzzled by the accent: Scottish and something else. Italian? "How come you're in here?"

The man shook his head, sadly. "It is my fault. I born in Sicily. I come to Edinburgh after last war to find my brother. I stay. I marry my wife, my bella Edith. She from Edinburgh. We have two boys. They now in British Army. I have best transport cafe in Selkirk. Now bloody stupid I'ties join Krauts everything upset."

"I don't understand" said Pete.

"I forget to get British citizenship" said the man, disconsolately. "Now I go try get something to plug my arse." He walked off in the direction of the medical hut, still shaking his head gently as he continued to admonish himself.

"Don't turn around" said an unfamiliar voice behind him. "I always like looking at the oak trees in May."

"Especially when the sun shines on them in the late afternoon" replied Pete automatically, as the hairs on the back of his neck stood to attention. Then, while he tried to look innocently over the Camp, he proceeded to pass on what he had learned from Burfeind and his crew; his part of the bargain.

With newspapers and radios banned in all Prisoner of War camps in Britain, it was no wonder that rumours abounded. Indeed, it provided the only interesting pastime that many of the men had. They would sit in their little groups exchanging gossip, embellishing where they felt it necessary to achieve the right effect:

"All prisoners were to be put into uniform."

"Red Cross food parcels, intended for the inmates, had been purloined by the guards."

"All the bread was laced with bromide to make sure the Nazi-boys didn't turn into Nancy-boys."

"Two coach loads of prostitutes were going to be brought in from Manchester."

"All prisoners were about to be loaded onto a ship and deported to Australia."

But the rumour that had the most far-reaching impact was that the Axis forces had landed near Brighton. "With overwhelming air support, hundreds of German tanks had taken up positions on the South Downs and thousands of infantry soldiers were currently marching on the London. In the face of certain defeat, the Royal family had been flown out to Iceland en-route to Canada, taking some senior members of the Government with them. Apparently Winston Churchill had refused to go with them. Accordingly, Sir Oswald Mosley had been released from his prison cell, and, together with the Duke of Wellington who was well known to be pro-Nazi, was about to sue for peace with Herr

Hitler, who was coming to London personally to take charge of negotiations. It was further understood that one of the chief demands of the Third Reich would be that all British Prisoner of War camps would be handed over to the Germans."

The effect that this rumour had on Warth Mill was astonishing and immediate. The place dissolved into total panic. Prisoners, especially the Jewish ones rushed in all directions seeking advice, clarification and support. Some tried to storm the gate, only to be repelled by a squad of soldiers firing over their heads. Tunnels were begun but, with the proximity of the river, these soon became waterlogged. Other prisoners tried more drastic and permanent solutions to escape. An elderly father was seen trying to revive his son who had tried to drown himself in the piss-drums. Two others managed to find their way onto the roof of the Mill and jumped. One had died instantly, impaled on an iron post, while the other survived, albeit with injuries which would certainly mean he would never walk again.

In the ensuing chaos, one wretch managed to get through the mound of barbed-wire that engulfed the metal ladder running up the side of the seventy foot chimney but, when he was no more than halfway up, he had panicked and froze. Despite the shouts and threats of shooting by several soldiers who were lined up at the bottom of the chimney, the man could not move up or down. It was only when someone persuaded the soldiers to let him try to talk to the man that they lowered their rifles. It wasn't as if the man could escape, after all. Slowly, the would-be rescuer inched his way up the ladder until he was able to talk to him without shouting and to touch him without invoking panic.

Pete was too far away to hear anything that was being said but after about ten minutes of gentle persuasion, both men returned to earth. The original climber, who was sobbing his heart out by now, was immediately grabbed by the hair by one of the soldiers and punched several times. As he fell to the ground holding his face, he was kicked in the head, back and stomach by the other soldiers. One of them then stamped on his legs. But just as he was aiming to repeat the treatment, he was grabbed by one of the prisoners and spun around. It was the man who owned the transport café in Selkirk.

"Do ye ken what is Glasgow kiss, son?"

The soldier, for an instant, looked bewildered and then his much-smaller opponent jumped and smashed his forehead into his face, smashing his nose flat. With cheers from the crowd, the soldier reeled away in a plume of blood and fell unconscious. By the time he hit the ground, the onlookers had swallowed up the café owner and smuggled him away. Amid the ensuing shouting came the sound of several whistles as more soldiers, including at least one officer, ran to the mêlée and pulled their colleagues off the now-unconscious climber. The officer was shouting orders and the surrounding, and now threatening, prisoners were shouting back, fired up by this and a thousand other injustices.

Pete was quite disappointed when the air-raid sirens suddenly sounded and the whole episode was concluded as every man rushed to his own place of relative safety and the two casualties were dragged away. As the anti-aircraft guns on the edge of the nearby lake opened up, Pete was probably not the only prisoner who was wondering if this was the final episode in the take-over of Britain.

The air-raid continued all night.

In the morning light, the bleary-eyed and traumatised prisoners were assembled for the usual roll call. As usual, it was a farce. The numbers never tallied. It was generally considered by the inmates that the British authorities had no accurate idea just how many men were actually detained in Warth Mill anyway. But this was no ordinary roll-call, as evidenced by the senior officer marching into the compound escorted by seven or eight rifle-carrying soldiers. Pete guessed that if you were to put a spirit level against the officer's back, the bubble would be dead centre. He climbed up onto an orange-box and raised a loud-hailer to his lips.

"There will be no repeat of yesterday's attack on my men" he said as if he had a nasty smell under his nose. In a way he had: several hundreds of nasty smells.

"I don't believe this" said Pete out loud as he stood towards the back of the assembled fragrant mass. "Pompous git."

"The culprit will be found and severely punished" the officer continued. "There will be no tolerance of unruly or threatening behaviour. My men have orders to shoot any offenders.

"Secondly, I understand that there has been some disquiet concerning rumours that the Axis forces have landed on the South coast. I can tell you that this is not true. No such landing has taken place. There is no invasion." This was obviously a bitter disappointment for many of the "A" category prisoners, who booed and jeered at the news.

"Thirdly" shouted the officer trying to be heard, "many of you are to be moved to a new Camp tomorrow." Hundreds started to cheer but most looked around, totally bewildered. The officer continued, uncomfortably. "The lists of the names of those who are being moved are being pinned to that board." He pointed to a large wooden notice-board being hammered by two soldiers to the side of a derelict outhouse. "If your name is on the list, you will get your things and return here at 07.30 ready for loading onto the transport.

"Finally, I repeat. No further indiscipline will be tolerated."

"Does the same apply to your men?" Pete shouted from the rear. Those who understood cheered. Those who didn't cheered anyway. The officer looked around again as if he was about to answer but, instead, he decided that a dignified and immediate retreat was called for. He climbed down off the orange-box and marched swiftly out of the compound, closely followed by his entourage.

Pete shook his head and smiled ironically as he realised that at no point had the officer acknowledged that most of his audience did not speak English. No wonder there was utter confusion; most of the poor bastards in the Camp were left totally unaware of what they had just been told. Pete stood and watched as the men crowded, pushed and jostled around the notice-board. Identity papers were openly being exchanged as father tried to stay with son, brother with brother, friend with friend.

"Bastard War" said Pete.

Pete's name was on one of the lists. Thank God! he thought and breathed a sigh of utter relief that he had only one more night to spend in this awful place. Burfeind's and his crew's names were also there, although on a different list. "Thought they might be, somehow" said Pete, smiling to himself.

Chapter 10

"Jesus Christ" Corporal Taf Allcott said, more to himself than to those who stood with him watching the spectacle develop as the rain continued to hammer down. "Where the bloody hell have they been?" The first of the vehicles had just turned through the gates and the occupants unloaded and lined up beside them. Allcott had seen better dressed and fatter tramps.

Over the next half hour, all manner of bus, truck and coach came into the Camp, spraying plumes of muddy water over those unfortunate to get too close. By the time the last one had arrived, the whole area around the gates was a quagmire.

"Looks like the bleedin' Somme. Don't it Corp?"

"Fuckin' Hell Higgins!" shouted Allcott over the noise. "Is that you? There's so much mud over your face I thought it was bleedin' Al Jolson".

He stepped out of the Army lorry and looked around at the half-finished houses and the hundreds of tents in the surrounding fields. Compared with Warth Mill, this was paradise, even though it was chucking it down and he was ankle-deep in mud. He walked with the others out of the mud and stood in line, amid masses of builders' rubble, waiting for the strip search and identity check. He was sopping wet, through to his skin. His head was throbbing and he felt lousy but he didn't care. It was as if they were being cleansed by the rain: the past was being wiped away and their future, wherever it lay, was being put back on track.

The queue was only about twenty yards long when Pete joined it, having had the good fortune to be on the first coach to arrive. He could see that it led straight into one of the houses on the edge of the housing estate. Around him, the Warth Mill exiles were in a sorry state – half-starved, dirty and, the vast majority, ill. Already two had collapsed and been taken away by Red Cross workers. In fact, while he had been standing in line, a man wearing a Red Cross armband had walked passed him with an army officer. Pete heard him say "Major, this is absolutely disgraceful. Get these men under cover at once and then give them everything you can in terms of special care and attention. They're all in an appalling state. God knows what's been going on. It's simply unacceptable."

The Major was obviously just as shocked because Pete heard him say "I just don't understand how they could have been allowed to get into this condition" before the two men continued their inspection further down the line.

As Pete got to the front of the queue and stepped inside the building, he knew that he wasn't well at all. Vile-smelling steam was rising out of his jacket as he put his hand to his still-throbbing head and felt himself burning.

"Papers?" said a soldier. Pete gave them to him and the soldier passed them to another who was seated behind him. The first soldier carried out a quick search of Pete's suitcase and handed it back to him.

"Through there" said the seated soldier, pointing to a closed door with a "KNOCK AND WAIT" sign hanging from a nail. As Pete walked the three yards to the door, it felt as if his legs belonged to someone else. He knocked on the door.

"Enter."

Pete tottered into the room which contained a desk, two chairs, a single bar electric fire and a three-panelled mobile screen on casters. Nothing else. Even the light bulb hung shadeless. Behind the desk sat a painfully thin, bespectacled man in a white coat. On his lapel he wore a name badge which just said "WHITE". Was this his name or was it just an endorsement of the colour of the coat? Pete felt himself wanting to giggle hysterically but with considerable effort simply allowed himself a smile.

"Something the matter?" asked the man, his face having hardly any more colour than his coat. His glasses sat precariously on the end of his nose.

"Eh…no…sorry" said Pete, straightening his face. "Just good to be in the warm."

"Papers?" continued the man, peering over the lenses. Pete gave them to him.

"Darling Peter" said the man quietly to himself as he ran his finger down a list of names. Pete nearly lost it.

"Ah, there!" said White and he placed a tick at the place and handed the papers back to Pete. "Take your clothes off" he said abruptly.

Pete removed his foul-smelling clothes, shivering uncontrollably as he did so.

"Stand closer to the fire if you want to."

"Cheers" said Pete and shuffled across until he was almost touching the fire. This was the first man-made heat he had felt since he had left home weeks ago.

"Stand back a bit. You're going to burn yourself otherwise" said the man, who was appraising Pete's condition with obvious concern.

Pete moved away a few inches.

"Right, put your clothes back on now, please." Pete bent down to pick his clothes off the floor where he'd put them but, as he straightened, the room began to close in around him.

"Oh Christ!" said the man, grabbing Pete's arm just in time to stop him collapsing to the floor. "Sit on this chair and put your head down as far as you can."

Pete did so and felt the room return.

"Right. You stay there for a minute. Don't move" and the man hurried out of the room.

No more than twenty seconds later another man, much younger and wearing a tweed sports jacket, came through the door. "You feeling a bit better?"

"Yes, thanks" said Pete, although he was still naked and shivering and his head was pounding.

"Come on. Let me help you get dressed, although you could really do with some dry clothes."

"It's fine" said Pete sharply, embarrassed at the stench that was coming from the steaming pile of rags next to him. "I can do it."

"Please yourself" said the man.

Pete pulled on his underpants and trousers and was buttoning-up his shirt when the man said "I always like looking at the oak trees in May."

Pete raised his head and looked at the man, who was not that much older than he was himself. He was so stunned, he couldn't remember what to say. This would have been the last place he would have anticipated a contact. The man just stared at him.

"I…eh…" said Pete. Then it came. "Especially when the sun shines on them in the late afternoon."

"Thank God for that. I thought I'd got the wrong chap for a minute. Continue getting your clothes on. We don't have much time and I want to get you squared away sharpish."

For a few more seconds, Pete continued to look at the man and then he went back to buttoning up his shirt. This was the first time since the beginning that he had actually come face to face with these people. He was pretty certain he hadn't heard this one's voice before though.

"Right. Now, just listen. I'm assuming you haven't been told why you were asked to keep an eye on our little German sailor."

Pete shook his head.

"I should hope not. Need to know and all that stuff." Suddenly the man reached into his trouser pocket and pulled out a perfectly folded handkerchief and sneezed into it. "Sorry about that. Things have changed somewhat and so you need to know more so you can push a bit harder.

"For some time now, we have been getting reports that there is a highly secret organisation within the German High Command which is developing new weapons."

"What sort of weapons?"

"I'm afraid I can't tell you that because frankly I don't know myself. What I can tell you is that this is serious stuff. We do know that a lot of resources are being ploughed into this project and all the boffins that Adolf can lay his hands on are being channelled onto it. Not just the committed supporters but anyone else they can get.

"We're pretty sure, for instance, that a group of Jewish scientists and engineers was assembled recently near Hamburg and taken abroad to a secret location. And this is where you come in.

"Our little German sailor chappy and his merry men have been regularly making trips to somewhere in Africa and we think he's been carrying the personnel and equipment for this new project."

"Why Africa?" asked Pete, his eyes just slits as his head was feeling as if it was about to split open any minute.

"We're not a hundred percent sure but think about it. What better place to develop something that you don't want the rest of the world to see."

"Umm" said Pete vacantly, now really struggling to concentrate.

"Trouble is we haven't a clue where it might be and that's your job."

"Thanks a lot."

"Right, so no pressure but we do need to get this information pronto. And I understand that it is essential if we are going to be able to keep to our side of the bargain, whatever that means."

Pete looked into his eyes. Cold as ice despite the friendly approach. Bastard. He knows perfectly well what it means.

"Right. Unless there are any questions, we're finished." Pete's brain couldn't have formulated a question if his life had depended on it.

"No? Just sit still, then, for a minute while I get the MO to come back. Best of luck."

Pete's head really was about to split open. He couldn't open his eyes because the light bored straight into his brain. He was sweating and thought he might be sick any minute. He could no longer hear a thing. He bent down and put his head between his legs but as he did so the floor came up to meet him and everything went black as he felt himself pitching forward.

By six o'clock the following morning, the weather had changed. The rain, having sped eastwards towards the Pennines during the night, had left enormous muddy puddles in the unfinished roads and across the fields. Those unfortunate to have been allocated to the tents were now trying to dry off their clothes and blankets by draping them on the guy-ropes. Steam was rising out of them as the hot morning sun got to work. The field in which the tents were pitched now resembled a lake – an expanse of about three hundred yards across was just water.

As Charlie opened the front door to his house, the road outside was a sea of mud and water with squads of young soldiers pushing and pulling at vehicles, trying to keep them moving. They looked like they had each been dipped in chocolate.

"Brilliant, eh?" Manny was at his shoulder. "C'mon, get your backs into it!" he shouted at the squaddies. One of the soldiers raised two fingers at him. Another raised only one. Yet another suggested he might like to procreate somewhere else.

"Charming" said Manny, with a grin. "Seen Jonny? He's not in his bed."

"No idea. Perhaps he's gone down the shop for a paper."

"Wouldn't that be nice" said Manny. "Some real news for a change. Fancy some breakfast?"

"You payin'?" asked Charlie.

"You twisted my arm. Come on. Let's go. We'll probably see Jonny there."

As they walked in the direction of the Mess Hut, holding their aluminium plates and mugs, Charlie said "In a way I hope Jonny's not there."

"Why?" asked his surprised friend.

"He's been goin' on and on about this Mind Over Matter stuff that he heard at somebody's lecture yesterday. As far as I can understand, you just have to concentrate your mind on what you're doin' or eatin' and you can make your brain think it's somethin' else."

"So if I concentrated hard enough you'd turn into Jane Russell?" and Manny put his hand on Charlie's bum.

"Piss off!" laughed Charlie, shrugging him off.

"Thought we might find you here Jonny" said Manny as they came up to him in the Mess Hut. "What have we got on the menu today?"

"Oh…right…Charlie told you. Well it works….well almost. I'm workin' my way through a full English. Two eggs, two sausages, black pudding, tomatoes, mushrooms and the best fried bread you ever tasted. And the tea's terrific as well" he added with a grin.

"Christ" said Manny, "No wonder you've been puttin' on weight. I'm just goin' to stick to toast and marmalade, as usual. What about you, Charlie?"

"I dunno" said Charlie, scratching his head. "I'm torn between the full English and the Arbroath Smokies."

After they had finished their breakfasts; bread, cheese and tea as usual, they went outside where they scoured their plates and mugs clean with the builders' sand that was lying in small heaps all over the place.

"Have you seen that notice on the board?" asked Jonny.

"Which one?" asked his brother.

"The one about wantin' volunteers with medical experience to help with that lot that came in yesterday."

"Yeah. Some of 'em looked in a right state" said Manny. "Like bloomin' skeletons some of 'em. God knows where they've been."

"I heard someone say this mornin' that they'd come from another camp and conditions there were diabolical" said Jonny, quite proud that he had got hold of some news before Manny.

"Well, we should join up and help the poor bastards, then. And besides, it'll be something to do" said Charlie.

"We don't have any medical experience, though" said Jonny.

"You've bin in 'ospital, ain't yer?" said Manny.

"Exactly" said Charlie. "Almost over qualified we are."

They were given the job of washing those who couldn't do it themselves - one bowl of lovely hot water to every three men and then throw it away and get fresh, "whether it needs to be or not" they were told. And soap….albeit the red carbolic variety.

"Oh, this is goin' to play havoc with my 'ands" laughed Manny, effeminately waving his hands about.

"If there is an open wound of any sort" the Medical Officer had told them "get fresh water and throw it away afterwards. We don't want to make matters worse, do we?"

So, each armed with a bowl of hot water, a towel and a block of soap, they got to work.

"Watcha mate!" said Jonny to his first customer, a young man in his twenties who was sporting a filthy jumper with the words "GREAT BRITAIN" across the chest. He was lying on a fold-away canvass bed with his eyes closed and his arms down by his side. The man opened his eyes and turned his head to look at him, but said nothing.

"Do you speak English?" asked Jonny.

The man said nothing but continued to stare at Jonny.

"Sprechen Sie Deutch?" Jonny felt that the stare was now directed through him not at him. "Eh... well…I'm just goin' to give you a bit of a wash and brush up" said Jonny showing the man the soap in his hand.

No reaction except the faintest of shrugs. Jonny thought the easiest way was to start without removing any of the man's clothes so he pushed up one of the sleeves of the jumper and went to work with soapy hands and the towel. Jonny had never seen such a thin, scabby arm in his life. It was like washing an old man, not a young one. When one arm was clean and dry, Jonny move round the bed and started on the other one. The scabs on this arm were, if anything, even worse – red and raw- so he tried to be as gentle as he could.

"Christ, that stings" said the man suddenly through gritted teeth.

"Sorry, Mate!" said Jonny. "I'll rinse it off straight-away." That done, the man relaxed and Jonny went to work on his feet, not something he relished as he knew from the smell that it wasn't going to be pleasant.

"So you're English" he said as he removed the man's socks and saw more sores, some of which were oozing puss. Jesus, the smell was horrendous. Jonny thought he might be sick. "Mustn't shoot the cat. Mustn't shoot the cat" he mumbled to himself as if in a trance. "This is goin' to hurt, mate. But I'll be as quick and as gentle as I can."

"Half - Italian" said the man, weakly. "Born in Romford. Christ, that stings."

Jonny continued as best he could. "What's your name?"

"Romund. But everyone calls me "Fish.""

"I'm Jonny….. Johann really. Why do they call you "Fish"?"

"Cos I'm a bit of a swimmer – competitions and stuff."

"Any good?"

"Not bad" said Fish between winches. "I swam in the last Olympics, in Berlin."

"Never!" said Jonny, impressed. "I've never met a star before" he laughed and looked up to the man's face. Fish was sweating with pain and looked as white as a sheet, but he smiled at Jonny. "Who did you swim for, us or Italy?"

Fish just pointed to his jumper.

"Ah, so that was the official team jumper, was it?"

Fish just nodded.

"Right, well let's try 'avin' it off yer, shall we? Now that I've done yer feet."

As Jonny gently washed Fish's back, which was also covered with bites and sores, he tried to keep the conversation going to distract his attention. "Daft, ain't it. Swimming for your country in the Olympic Games one minute and the next they've locked you up. Bloody madness, if you ask me." Fish smiled again, but this was obviously taking its toll - any colour he had had in his face had gone. And by the time Jonny had finished, Fish was unconscious.

By now both Charlie and Manny were well into their second patients, both of whom seemed to be elderly Jews with long, matted and tangled beards. Jonny emptied his bowl down the drain where he had been shown and returned to refill it with some more hot water. His next customer was also lying on his bed, eyes closed, but as Jonny approached he opened them. "Hello, mate. Speak English?"

"Hello, Jonny" Pete croaked, hoarsely. "Don't you even know your own brother?"

"Bloody Hell. It's you. I wouldn't have recognised you in a month of Sundays. How are yer? You look awful. Where've you been? Jesus, I don't believe it. CHARLIE. IT'S PETE!" he shouted to his other brother.

As the days went by, Pete became stronger but, much to Charlie's puzzlement, there was something different about him. "Do you think Pete's a bit strange?" he'd asked Jonny one evening.

"A bit quiet, maybe. But he's been through hell. Stands to reason he's not going to be leapin' about much. He'll be alright in a few days, you see."

"Mmm, maybe." But although Pete always seemed pleased to see his brothers, Charlie got the impression that he was trying to be distant, like he wanted to be somewhere else. This was confirmed a few days later when, as Charlie was helping Pete wash himself, Captain Burfeind came into the Hut and immediately made his way to Pete's bed.

"I wondered where you had got to, my friend."

As Pete introduced them, Charlie felt that Pete was embarrassed somehow. "Captain, this is my brother, Charlie. He's been here all the time we were at the Mill." As he said this, Charlie got the distinct feeling that Pete did not want him coming between him and his friendship with this German Officer.

"I am please to meet you. Your brother has become almost like one of my crew" said Burfeind, offering his hand to Charlie. Then to Pete he said "I didn't know you were here until one of the men mentioned it. Are you feeling better?"

Pete glanced quickly at Charlie and then turned to Burfeind. "Yes, much. The food's better here. Not like that crap we've had to put up with for the last few weeks. Like paradise, this place is in comparison. How are you and the rest of the crew?"

Charlie felt like an outsider. He had taken an instant dislike to the seaman and couldn't understand why Pete obviously hadn't. "I'm going to find Jonny and Manny" he said getting to his feet. "See you tomorrow."

"Don't worry - you've got other stuff to do" said Pete tersely. Charlie just looked at his brother, but said nothing.

It was Burfeind that broke the silence. "I am glad to have met with you, Herr Darling."

"Yeah" said Charlie and walked out of the Hut.

"I think he's gone over to the other side."

"What do you mean?" said Manny.

"I think all that time in the company of those Nazi seamen has turned him into one of them. They've brainwashed him" answered Charlie.

"He wouldn't do that" said Jonny. "Would he?"

"Well something's happened to him, that's for sure. And you should have seen how pally they were together."

"He'll be as right as ninepence when he's fully recovered" said Jonny. "Just needs time, that's all.

"Jonny's right, Charlie" said Manny. "Just give him time. And speaking of time, they're holding a snail race this afternoon down the street. Fancy giving it a go?"

"Yeah" said Jonny. "Come on, Charlie. Stop fretting. Pete'll be back to normal in no time. Let's go and have a bet on the snails."

"Sounds terrific" said Charlie sarcastically, his mind still churning away at his other brother's attitude.

Pete lay in he bed. Burfeind had gone soon after Charlie had left in a huff. Pete didn't blame him. Probably would have done the same if the roles were reversed. But they weren't. It wasn't down to Charlie or Jonny to get the information from Burfeind. It was him, only him. And there was no way he could say anything to them. They would say something to Manny, who would say something to someone else and pretty soon the whole Camp would know, including Burfeind. Best keep schtum.

Two days later, Pete was strong enough to leave the Medical Hut. Charlie came armed with some new clothes that he had managed to scrounge from one of the Red Cross people. "Cheers mate" Pete had said, genuinely.

"I've got you a bed in our billet" said Charlie. "One of the other chaps didn't mind moving out."

"Look, Charlie" said Pete, trying desperately to look his brother in the eye but not quite making it. "The thing is.... I've already arranged with the Captain to move in to one of the houses they've got."

Charlie felt someone had kicked him in the stomach but strangely he wasn't surprised. "I see" was all he said.

"Look, don't take it like that" said Pete. "I do appreciate what you've done, but I've been with these blokes for weeks now. They're mates."

"And what about us? Jonny and me are your brothers. Don't we count?"

"Course you do. It's just....it's just that I need to be with them at the moment."

"Why? What hold have they got over you, Pete? For Christ's sake, look at yourself. You're not the same. The old Pete wouldn't have given these people the spit off the end of his tongue. They're Nazis for fuck sake. Don't you see that?"

"Look, Charlie, I gotta do this, so let me go."

"Is that it? You've sided with them. Believe that Adolf's got it right, do you? You always were a bloody idiot, Pete. Now you've proved it. Can't you see that bloke, that Captain, is using you? I don't know why, but he's using you for something. For Christ's sake Pete!"

"You couldn't be more wrong" said Pete. "Now just leave me alone, will yer?"

"Oh I'll leave you alone, alright. You can do what you bloody well like, but I'll tell you what…"

"What?"

"This" and Charlie poked Pete hard in the chest. "If Mutti knew you'd sided with that lot, it'd kill her. You know that. Is that what you want? God you're a selfish bastard." And he walked away without a backward glance.

Pete stood and watched his brother walk away from him. After a time, some minutes after Charlie had gone from sight, he wiped a tear from his eye and walked in the other direction.

The following day saw Charlie and Jonny out on the field early, before Samuel and his friends had arrived. Charlie had not slept at all and was in the foulest of moods. "For fuck sake, Jonny, stop going on about it. I saw Pete and he doesn't want to stay with us. End of story."

"But I don't understand why" said his brother. "Why does he want to hang around with them? He hates Nazis."

"Not any more he doesn't. Now just give it a rest. We've got a class to teach, and they're coming now." Samuel and his friends were laughing and joking as they came round the corner.

"Good morning gentlemen" said Jonny. Charlie did his best to smile and gave a nod to Samuel and the rest.

"Today we are going to get you speaking to each other. It is called holding a conversation" said Charlie while Jonny arranged the men into pairs.

"So, using just English, you will ask how your partner is, his name, his profession, his place of birth and his age. If you have a problem, just raise your hand."

Samuel immediately raised his hand.

"Yes Samuel?"

"My age is my secret."

Everyone laughed and those closest to Samuel playfully pushed him or patted him on the back.

"Very well" said Charlie. "Use the age you would like to be." Samuel and everyone else were happy with that. Within minutes, their corner of the field was full of laughing and chattering black-coated men, occasionally putting their hands in the air. It became quite a spectacle and soon attracted a sizeable audience which watched, captivated. It was the best entertainment most of the men had seen in weeks, even months. Everyone was enjoying themselves, participants and spectators alike until, suddenly, there were cries and shouts from the back of the crowd. A chant of "KRISTALLNACHT – JUDENFREI" was started and gained both momentum and volume. As all eyes went to the direction of the rumpus, the crowd gave way and about twenty of the SS Adolf Woermann's crew spewed onto the field. The Jewish men immediately jumped to their feet and bunched together as the seamen menacingly formed a line between the crowd and the Jews – some watching the crowd to ensure that no one was foolish enough to intervene, while the rest continued chanting at the frightened men in black coats.

"Glass night – Jew free?" shouted Jonny at Charlie's side. "I don't understand what they mean."

Charlie didn't reply. He just stared ahead. He knew that Kristallnacht was the night about eighteen months previously when the Nazis had moved against the Jews. In the space of a few hours, thousands of synagogues, Jewish businesses and homes were destroyed. This became known as "Kristallnacht" or "Night of the broken glass" because of all the shattered windows which littered the streets. The newspapers had estimated that thirty thousand Jews had been rounded up on this one evening alone and sent to concentration camps in Buchenwald, Dachau and Sachsenhausen. Once the Jews had been taken from a building, the word "Judenfrei" was painted on the brickwork outside to show that it was free of Jews. Hundreds of Jews had died within weeks of their arrival at the camps and they were only released once they had signed over all of their property and arranged to leave the country for good.

Samuel and many of his friends remembered it only too well.

"I don't understand" said Jonny again, but again he received no reply as Charlie continued to stare sternly ahead. He was looking at one of the German seamen: the one who was shouting and chanting loudest, the one who was the most menacing, the most serious. It was Pete.

Pain and utter contempt for his brother racked through him as he continued to watch. He knew Pete knew he had been noticed but had refused to engage in any form of eye contact, so Charlie just stared until he was dragged away by Jonny.

There were no physical injuries, but the pain Charlie suffered was worse than any physical pain. How could his brother have changed so much?

The class broke up as the students ran in all directions. There were to be no more English lessons.

"Quiet, ain't it, Corp" said Private Jonathan "Jonah" Higgins.

"Bloody lovely" replied Corporal Taf Allcott as he surveyed the sight in front of him: foot deep furrows in the mud from the motley selection of vehicles that had come in at dawn; discarded metal plates and mugs all over the place; a forlorn-looking motor bike laying on its side in the front garden of one of the houses; and silence – absolute blissful bloody silence. Except for those too sick to move, the camp was empty.

At four o'clock on the morning of July 2nd 1940, the Arandora Star, having unloaded about 1700 troops and refugees from the Dunkirk evacuation, left her berth in Liverpool docks and made her way north, bound for St John's, Newfoundland and Labrador. On board were 174 officers and crew, 200 military guards, 479 German internees, 86 German Prisoners of War (including most of the crew of the SS Adolf Woermann) and 734 Italian internees.

In a cabin on "A" Deck, which in better times accommodated just two passengers in some splendour, Charlie and Jonny shared with a German garage owner from Woking and an Austrian violinist who had married a Jewish girl in Munich and had fled with her to England six months ago.

In a similar sized, but no less utilitarian, cabin above them on "C" Deck, Pete found himself sharing with three members of Burfeind's crew, one of which was Oberbootsmann Felix Darling.

The bewildered passengers were herded in like cattle; prodded with rifles, shouted at by abusive guards. This was definitely not going to be a luxury cruise. Packed into every available space, they knew they were destined for Canada: word had spread so fast it might just as well have been announced over the tannoy system, but most of them were so cold, hungry and both mentally and physically exhausted that they really couldn't have cared less. Life for them now was just a matter of survival.

Chapter 11

"My back's killing me already, and we've only been at it half an hour. What time's lunch? I'm starving." Tilly used the back of her hand to wipe the sweat from her forehead.

"Just not used to physical work, that's your trouble, my girl" chided Ruby. "Now in my day…………" she added.

"Bloody cheek! I'll have you know I work just as hard as you do. It's hot and tiring work in that kitchen."

Ruby laughed. "Such a shame. Poor thing."

"Oh shut up" said Tilly, but she was laughing too. "When was the Iron Age anyway?"

"God knows."

"In Europe it is considered to have started around 1200BC and finished about 400AD, when the Romans left." The voice, in German, was that of Professor Gerhard Bersu, their new, occasional boss, who was standing behind the girls. They turned and saw that he was with another much younger man. The Professor continued to speak in German. "This is Enrico. He is Italian and will help you today. It is also his first day so can you show him what you are doing. Thank you." He gave a slight bow in the girls' direction, turned and walked away to one of the other digs that he was organising.

"Hello, Enrico" said Ruby but he just stood staring at Tilly. Ruby turned to Tilly but she seemed equally dumbstruck. "TILLY!" cried Ruby.

Tilly jumped but her eyes never left Enrico. "Oh! Sorry…er…sorry…."

"Oh for God's sake! Tilly!" Ruby tried again. "Enrico. ENRICO! That's better." He had turned to look at her. "I'm Ruby and this is my friend, Tilly. Can you speak English or German?"

"I can speak English. My name is Enrico Salvatori but you must call me Rico, please" and he held out his hand to Ruby, who, despite having muddy hands, took it and shook it slightly. He then offered his hand to Tilly but she just stood there staring at him.

"Oy! Little Miss Cow Eyes!" cried Ruby and then took Tilly's hand and gave it to Rico to shake. As soon as Tilly felt Rico's hand she sighed. Neither seemed prepared to let go of the other's hand.

"Oh, I give up" said Ruby and went back to digging the trench as Dr Bersu had instructed. After a couple of minutes the other two, armed with spades, joined her in slicing the turf away from the area of the field which had been marked with stakes. Continually watched by the armed soldiers that patrolled the field, they worked their way across the trench. Periodically, Doctor Bersu came over to them to say "Ja, das ist gut" or "Nein, ein wenig tiefer" – a little deeper. But he never stayed for long and his absences gave the girls, and particularly Tilly, chance to find out about Rico and also about what was happening with the War. Rico's father, he explained, had come over to England after the First World War when Rico was just a baby and had set up an ice-cream business in Brighton. "The best ice-cream on the South Coast" he exclaimed, proudly puffing up his chest. When his father had died suddenly, Rico and his mother continued running the business. She had remarried after a few years and now, with Rico away, ran the company with her new husband who was English. "He is a good man" said Rico. "Good to my Mama and good to me. But I miss my Dad very much."

Tilly's feeling that a fairground balloon was lodged somewhere in her stomach gradually disappeared and soon she was telling Rico all about herself and Ruby and what they had been doing since they had been on the Island.

"What is Professor Bersu like?" Rico asked when they took a bit of a breather.

"He's actually very nice" replied Ruby. "Apparently he was running some important archaeological centre in Germany but Hitler sacked him because he's a Jew. He came to England with his wife, Maria..."

"That is my Mama's name, Maria" interrupted Rico.

"That's a nice name" said Tilly, looking into his oak-brown eyes and still getting an amazing tingle through her body every time Rico said something.

"Yes, well" said Ruby, exasperatedly, "Anyway, they were both interned here but someone high up thought it was a waste of his talents if he was just festering in one of the camps somewhere so he and his wife were asked to investigate these mounds that you see in the field."

"Mrs Bersu's ever such a strange old stick" contributed Tilly. "We've seen her once or twice today in her wellies, just wandering around with a huge tape-measure and scribbling stuff in a little notebook. She doesn't seem to get involved at all in the digging. Just tells her husband where to dig and leaves him to it."

By the time four o'clock came and they were instructed to finish for the day, Tilly, Rico and Ruby had explored each others pasts in considerable detail, although Ruby had been somewhat economical with the truth when it came to discussing her background.

"Are you here every day?" asked Rico as they walked to where the trucks had been lined up to take them back to their respective camps.

"No, just Tuesdays" said Tilly. "What about you?"

"I am here Tuesdays and Thursdays" said Rico.

"Oh" said Tilly, noticeably disappointed. "Well perhaps we can get onto the Thursday rota as well" and she looked at Ruby, almost pleading.

"I don't think that's likely" said Ruby. "You know half of Rushen Camp applied to come on this. That's why we're being rationed to just one day each a week."

"Well I'm going to try my damnedest to get Thursdays as well" said Tilly, looking at Rico.

"Well I wish you luck" said Ruby.

"So do I" said Rico meaningfully.

"Oh I think I've died and gone to heaven" swooned Tilly as they rocked about in the back of the army lorry on the journey back to Port Erin.

Ruby smiled, indulgently. "Well my back doesn't feel like it's in heaven…Oh Christ. I've just remembered I've got to move half a ton of coal before I've finished for the day."

"Mmm and I've got to cook for 120 people" said Tilly, still with a Cheshire-cat grin "but I don't care. Don't you think he's wonderful? So handsome."

"Yes, but don't forget he's married."

"WHAT!"

"He's married."

"He's not married!"

"Course he is. You've seen his wife."

Tilly looked puzzled for an instant, then, as Ruby started collapsing with laughter, she understood.

"Not Bersu, you sod. Rico!"

The following day, after the daily chores had been completed, Ruby and Tilly walked down to Collinson's Café on the Promenade. It had become the centre of life in Port Erin, the place where everyone met up. It was here that the internees could obtain material for their craft work such as dressmaking, knitting and the like as well as a place to hand in their finished work which would then be sold in the makeshift shop that had been set up: albeit that no one had much in the way of money with which to buy the goods on offer. There was also a collection of books and old magazines to read, and someone was asking for names of those who might be interested in a Keep-Fit class. It was also the place where the children who had been interned with their mothers seemed to run riot.

"What we need is a school for them" said one of the mothers who happened to be sitting on the same table as Ruby and Tilly and had seen the look of frustration on their faces as the children shrieked and shouted.

Whether it was the fatigue from all the digging and shovelling that she had been doing lately or the result of the tedium of doing the same things day after day or even some deep-seated twinge of jealousy over Tilly's relationship with Rico, Ruby wasn't sure. She didn't even think about it, just found herself suddenly saying "We'll do it."

"What!" exclaimed Tilly, looking at her friend as if she'd gone mad. "You're not serious. How could we possibly do it? We don't know the foggiest thing about teaching."

"Of course we do" said Ruby, realising she was as surprised as Tilly at her own volunteering. "We couldn't do it every day, but we should be able to manage three days a week. Say three or four hours at a time. No problem."

"You have gone mad!"

"Look, when you think about it we both speak English and German, right?" said Ruby, picking up her mug of "Camp" coffee mixed with hot, *real* milk.

"Right" said Tilly, quizzically

"And most of the kids only speak German. Right?"

"I suppose."

"So if nothing else we could teach them some English. And that would help the mothers who only speak German and there's plenty of them. Oh come on Tilly" pleaded Ruby "it'll be fun."

"I'm not at all sure fun is an apt description. How many kids are there?" she asked turning towards the mother.

"I don't know" she said, trying to count on her fingers. "About twenty, maybe."

"Well there you are, then" said Ruby, emphatically. "We could cope with twenty. Get the big ones helping the little ones. And the Mums could help as well, if they wanted to. Easy. The only problem would be where would we do it. We need a room somewhere."

"What about St Catherine's Church?" said the mother. "There's a room in the back. I'll show you if you like."

Despite Tilly's lack of enthusiasm, she accompanied Ruby on the short walk to the Church Hall, and after a brief discussion with the Caretaker, it was soon arranged.

Back in the Café, Ruby said "Look, why don't we take this lot down to the beach for an hour or two? It would give us chance to get to know them and give us some idea what we've got ourselves into."

"What *you've* got us into, you mean" said Tilly, reproachfully. She wasn't happy with the idea of anything taking up time that could possibly be spent with Rico. "And I'm not giving up the Dig. Understood?"

"Alright. Keep your hair on. Come on, let's round these kids up and go and look in some rock pools or something."

Fifteen minutes later there were seven children and two young women walking down the promenade towards the beach. Tilly led the way with four year old twins, a girl (Rilla) and a boy (Marko), holding on to each hand. Next came Gabriele, who was thirteen, holding Brigitte's hand. Brigitte was seven. Following behind them, and pretending they were marching soldiers, were Dominik aged eleven and Ulrich who was nine. At the rear, Ruby held the hand of Heike, who was also four. Once on the beach, they ran around playing chase and then, having burnt off their initial excitement, Tilly got them all drawing pictures in the wet sand. This naturally evolved into teaching the little ones how to write their names in the sand. While this was going on, Ruby took Gabriele, Brigitte and the two boys to the rock pools to see what they could find. But, after ten minutes or so, the boys decided that splashing the girls was much more fun and it didn't take long before both girls were in tears.

As Ruby was trying to dry their faces with her handkerchief, she heard shouts from the boys who had wandered round the other side of what remained of a large derelict boat, abandoned at the sea's edge. "Fräulein Ruby! Kommen Sie schnell!" Ruby raced round the boat and immediately saw the source of the boys' alarm. There, with the sea water lapping round its base, was a large black metal sphere with white writing painted crudely around it. She could make out the words "Churchill" and "Grosse" but if there was anything else written, it was covered by the mass of seaweed draped over it. "I think it is time for us to be getting back, now" she said to the boys, as calmly as she could.

"Ohhh!" both boys whined.

"Whatever this is, we will have to tell the policemen." She knew quite well what it was.

"There's a mine on the other side of that old wreck" she said to Tilly. "We've got to get everyone away, now."

"Are you sure?" said Tilly.

"Absolutely. Now let's move….quickly."

"Where's Ulrich?" Tilly said.

"He's …..Oh God." Ruby looked frantically around the beach but there was no sign of the boy. "Tilly, take all of the children back to Collinson's and get them to get the police down here straight-away. I'm going to find Ulrich" and she ran in the direction of the boat. "Stupid little bugger" she said to herself as she sprinted across the soft sand in the direction of the mine. "ULRICH. Wo bist du?"

She rounded the boat. "ULRICH" she screamed as the young lad prodded the mine with a stick. "NEIN. NEIN" she shouted "Komm dort weg!" Come away! She hurtled towards him and scooped him into her arms. Holding him as tight as she dared, she turned and sprinted away as fast as she could. It was only when they were almost back to Shore Road that she allowed him to stand while she caught her breath. "Geht es Dir gut?" she panted. The boy just looked at her in utter amazement. At that point, Ruby saw two policemen running towards them.

"You alright, Miss" said the younger of two, while his colleague bent at the waist in an attempt to regain his breath.

"We're fine, thanks" said Ruby, "but there's a mine just round the other side of that wreck."

"Right" said the policeman, "Superman here and I had better go and have a little look-see. Would you get this lad off the beach, please Miss? And could you make sure no one else comes down."

So as Ruby and Ulrich hurried off the beach, the two policemen cautiously moved forward to investigate the mine. As they hurried to safety, Ruby kept looking over her shoulder, almost expecting the explosion, but nothing came and the policemen by now were out of sight. Just as they reached the bottom of the track that connected the beach with Shore Road, Tilly came flying down it and threw herself into Ruby's arms.

"Oh" she panted "I thought you were going to blow yourself up. Are you alright?"

"Yeah, I'm fine… and so is he, thank God" and she ruffled Ulrich's hair. He looked up at her as if to say "What's all the fuss about?" but then just sat down on a rock and looked in the direction of the boat.

"Let's get back to Collinson's" said Ruby. "We need to find his Mum. Komm, Ulrich."

The three turned to walk up the track just as a policewoman and a woman the girls had met before in the Camp Office were hurrying down the slope towards them.

"Your colleagues are on the other side of the wreck, by the water line" said Ruby, pointing in the direction.

"Thank you, but I'm not here because of that" said the rather large policewoman. "Are you Fräulein Nussbaum?"

"No, I am" said Tilly. "What's the matter? What have I done?"

"Nothing, Miss. I'm Sergeant Pike and I'm afraid I've got some bad news for you. I'm sorry to have to tell you that both your grandparents have been killed in an air-raid." She gave Tilly a telegram.

Chapter 12

July 1st 1940

Having just slammed the telephone back onto its cradle, Captain Edgar Moulton sat in the glorified broom-cupboard which currently served as his office, and fumed. Not because his beautiful ship, once nicknamed "The Wedding Cake" because of its white-painted hull with a scarlet ribbon-like line at the top near the upper deck, was now a uniform and anonymous grey – there was a war on and she could of course be repainted when peace returned. Nor was his mood because all the wood panelling and fine furnishings in the state-rooms, ballrooms and restaurants had been ripped out to provide room for the additional metal bunks and mess tables– that had happened over a year ago and he'd had the time to come to terms with that. And it certainly was not because the Cinema had been dismantled and turned into a mess hall and all the expensive equipment had been ruined – it had never worked properly anyway. It wasn't because the Arandora Star, with nearly 1700 men on board, was grossly overloaded and there weren't enough lifeboats to cope with them all – he'd spoken to everyone he could think of proposing a cut to half this number of passengers only to be told he had to do as he was ordered and get on with it. And it wasn't because the life-rafts had been secured by wire with release requiring the use of special tools which Moulton had been assured would be made available to every senior officer on board once they were out to sea. It wasn't even because the ship had been virtually cocooned with impenetrable barbed-wire, although that was certainly his primary concern.

The source of Edgar Moulton's frustration was that, after dozens of telephone calls, first to Frederick Leyland & Co. Ltd who were the owners of the Arandora Star, then to its managers, The Blue Star Line, and subsequently to various boffins and paper-pushers in Ministries he didn't even know had existed, no one was even answering his calls.

"You are signing hundreds of men's death warrants" he had told each of them in increasingly violent and sometimes profane language days before. "Not only my crew, many of whom have been with me for years, but the guards and the poor wretches that we are transporting. If anything happens to this vessel, that wire will seriously obstruct access to the lifeboats and the rafts."

In the most recent conversations he had even resorted to saying "The Arandora Star is now just a floating death-trap and if anything happens, it will be on your conscience for ever." But no one would accept responsibility for having the wire removed. It was there to prevent dangerous men escaping, he had been told, although quite where in the middle of the Atlantic Ocean they would go to was beyond Moulton's imagination. "I pray to God" he had told the Chairman of The Blue Star Line "that there isn't a U-boot sitting out there with our name on it."

So despite Moulton's efforts, at around four o'clock in the afternoon, the Arandora Star weighed anchor and headed, unescorted, out of the River Mersey into the Irish Sea. She headed northward and made good progress in the calm sea. "Perhaps she will be lucky" Moulton allowed himself to think as night fell and they rounded Rathlin Island, off the north-east coast of Ireland. "Fingers crossed."

Korvettenkapitan Gunther Prien, the first sailor in the U-boat service to receive the Knight's Cross of the Iron Cross for his sinking of HMS Royal Oak some eight months previously by managing to penetrate the Royal Navy's primary base at Scapa Flow, had been woken at three o'clock on the morning of July 2nd. The engine noise of a surface vessel had been picked up. He had immediately ordered the submarine to periscope depth but the moon had provided insufficient light to make an identification. He therefore decided to track her until daybreak but by then there was a thick sea-mist and he decided to wait and watch. By six o'clock, and despite the fact that the vessel carried no Red Cross pennant nor other means of identification, Prien was satisfied that she was an Allied troop ship sailing westward at fifteen knots, and alone. In normal circumstances, his mind would be clear and he would have ordered torpedoes to be launched immediately. However, he had a dilemma – he only had one torpedo left in the rack. Continuing to track the vessel, he debated whether to engage and leave U-47 without any means of defence if she needed it or to continue his voyage home and get some long overdue rest for himself and his crew while fresh supplies were loaded. After forty-five minutes he had made up his mind and ordered his crew to go to their attack stations.

As the mist cleared, Chief Officer Hubert Henry Grace of the Arandora Star had given the order for four extra lookouts to be posted. The twinge in his left knee told him there was a U-boat around and his twinge had never let him down yet – although there was no way he was ever going to let anyone in on his secret. Standing on the bridge, with the sound of six bells, he knew it was seven o'clock. "Please God I'm wrong this time" he thought.

Pete leaned on one elbow and, with his other hand, traced a finger down Myrna Loy's cheek. She smiled in her sleep and then sighed. He was absolutely captivated by her beauty and her warm, addictive smell. She was definitely Pete's Miss Right. He rolled over onto her and, although she mumbled "Oh, not again, Pete", her legs opened to accommodate him for the fifth time that night. "What does a girl have to do to get some sleep around here?" she mumbled huskily at the same time as thrusting her hips up to him. As she urged him on, Pete could feel his very soul work its way from every part of his body, to concentrate in his loins. He tried to think of his mother's cabbage soup so that he could prolong the ecstasy, but Myrna was having none of that. "Now, Pete, now" she cried. All was lost and the pair of them climaxed together in a shuddering explosion that fired from every possible nerve ending. "Oh, Pete, the earth *did* actually move" said Myna, dreamily looking into his eyes. "Oh, Pete!"

"TORPEDO - STARBOARD MIDSHIPS" one of the lookouts had screamed, but it was too late. Almost immediately, the ship was rocked by a huge explosion as the torpedo struck home, completely wrecking the aft engine-room which was instantly flooded as the watertight bulkheads buckled and gave way under the impact.

Grace shouted to his Fourth Officer, Ralph Liddle, to get a damage report while he ordered the wireless room to issue a mayday signal giving their position. This was immediately answered by the radio station at Malin Head, some 125 nautical miles away.

"No answer from the engine-room, Sir" shouted Liddle "and all engines have stopped. The main generators have gone, too. We're on the emergency generators now but I don't think they'll last long."

With that, all the lights went out and communications between the wireless room and the bridge were lost.

"Bugger" swore Grace. "I think we're done for, Mr Liddle. See if you can get the skipper."

"No need, Number 1. I'm here" said Moulton, rushing onto the Bridge. "What's the damage?"

"Engine room's gone and we're taking water fast. All generators are down, but we did manage to get a mayday away."

"Confirmed?"

"Yes Sir!"

The ship was already listing to starboard. Moulton knew he had no choice. "Breakout the loudhailers, Mr Liddle, and give the order to abandon ship."

Jonny was thinking about home when the explosion rocked the ship. If he had but known it, he had been within ten miles of his eldest sister some hours earlier as they had passed between the coast of Ireland and the Isle of Man. He shouted to Charlie to wake up and then stood and grabbed him by the arm. "Wake up, Charlie. Something's happened!" He turned to wake the other two, but they were already on their feet and pulling their clothes on.

"What's happened?" said Charlie, now fully awake.

"I dunno" said Jonny, "But something has." With that came the sounds of shouting and screaming and people running. Then shots being fired. Someone shouted something about a torpedo as they ran passed. "They're abandoning ship" screamed another. In panic, they dressed and grabbed what they could, before heading out into the gangway. At that point everything was suddenly plunged into darkness and they could smell burning.

"Which way?"shouted Jonny over the noise.

"Let's try this way. To the left" shouted his brother, who could now definitely feel that the deck was sloping to the right. Some men ran blindly in their direction and collided with them. "Which way is out?" shouted Charlie, grabbing one of them and throwing him against the wall. The man paid no attention and carried on running.

"Come on!" cried Charlie. "We'll try up here" and he hurried forwards. As his eyes got used to the gloom, he could just make out a stairwell – stairs going up and down. From below came the noises of Hell. Looking up, he could see why the others had been running in the other direction. The steps leading up were blocked with all sorts of debris: tables, strangely contorted strips of metal and wooden panels.

"It's no good" shouted Jonny, now at his shoulder. "It'll take us ages to get through there. Let's try the other way." They went back the way they'd come, passed their own cabin, and on to where another gangway ran at right-angles to their own. An elderly man just stood like a ghost in the smoke at the crossway, unable to move; tears glistening on his face.

"Which way now?" yelled Charlie.

"This way" and Jonny moved off to the right. Charlie grabbed hold of the old man's arm and propelled him after his brother but he stopped after a few yards and sat on the floor. Charlie went to grab him again but Jonny shouted "Leave him. We don't have the time."

Charlie couldn't just walk away and leave him. He picked the old man up by his lapels and tried to get him to move again but he just slumped to the floor and the vacant stare that Charlie could just make out in his eyes told him he was wasting his time.

"COME ON!" shouted Jonny from further up the corridor. They were definitely going upwards – the ship was gradually turning on her side.

It got lighter the closer they got to the end of the corridor which then led onto a covered-in walkway. Through its windows they could see the pandemonium that was going on outside. There was a lifeboat immediately in front of them. As if it were a scene from a horror film, it was full of dead and injured men, shot seconds before the order to abandon ship had come by a terrified Private assuming he had to stop these men escaping. Bullet holes could be seen all along the side of the boat. Seamen, soldiers and civilians were rushing about in all directions: some trying to climb over the wriggling, screaming bodies of those who had come before them and become ensnared on the masses of barbed-wire.

"We've got to get out onto that deck" shouted Charlie. "Then we can see where we are and how we get to the lifeboats."

"There's a door down there" Jonny said, running along the walkway and grabbing the handle. "It's blocked!"

"Here, let me try" and Charlie applied all his strength to the handle. The door normally opened outwards, but something was on the outside, preventing it from opening. "There's no way it's going to move. Let's try further down." They ran along the tilting corridor and found another door, which this time opened freely. As they came onto the deck, there was another loud volley of gunfire not ten feet from them.

Corporal Ivor Duxberry of the Welsh Regiment was one of the guard detachment. When the explosion took place, he had had his head over the side being violently seasick and wanting to die. Wiping his mouth on his sleeve, he ran to the nearest of the lifeboats but hadn't a clue how they were launched or what the procedure was in terms of filling them, there having been no lifeboat drill. He decided to run to the next lifeboat along and see if he could find someone who knew what to do. By now, orders were being given to abandon ship and then he recognised the voice of Major Bethell, the Commanding Officer of the 109th POW unit, using a loud-hailer from the Bridge.

"Corporal, get those men out of there. Prisoners of War and Internees first into the boats."

It was then, amid the chaos, Duxberry saw that twenty or so of the soldiers who were supposed to be guarding the prisoners and internees had managed to get themselves through the wire and were desperately trying to launch the lifeboat. Duxberry ran across and shouted at the men to get out. Some ignored him. Some suggested he come in with them. None made to obey his instruction.

"CORPORAL!" came from Bethell's loud-hailer again. "I said get those men out of there. If they won't move, fire a volley over their heads. Count to ten and then start shooting them. THEY ARE DESERTERS."

Duxberry looked to the Bridge and, for a second or two, locked eyes with his CO. Then he turned and raised his Thompson submachine gun and fired a short burst into the air just above his men. They all froze.

"In ten seconds there will be another volley" he shouted, "only this time it will be six feet lower. Now get out. NOW!"

The men looked at each other as if to get confirmation that the Corporal would actually kill them. The answer to some was obvious and they began the climb back on board straight-away. As more climbed out, the diehards realised the odds of them launching the lifeboat and surviving the bullets at the same time were just about nil and they climbed back as well.

With the lifeboat vacated, the ship's personnel could take charge and two of the seamen crawled through the path in the barbed-wire created by the soldiers and prepared the lifeboat for launching. Then they called for prisoners and internees to be loaded. Duxberry and his surly and belligerent men grabbed those nearest and pushed and shoved them through the gap in the wire. Those that tried to rush the process and forge their own way were quickly caught and held fast by the wicked barbs. No one heeded their cries and screams for assistance.

"Come on" shouted Charlie holding on to his brother tightly, they pushed their way into the throng trying to get on to the lifeboat. Neither looked at any of their fellows – they had one goal and it was every man for himself.

One of the crew was counting those getting on to the lifeboat.

"58, 59, 60. Right. That's enough." Charlie was number 60. Jonny would have been number 61.

"But he's my brother" Charlie shouted at the seaman.

"Sorry mate. Any more and it'll capsize"

Realizing that they weren't going to get onto the boat, those behind started fighting amongst themselves and with the soldiers and seamen who were trying to restore order. In the mêlée, the seaman who was doing the counting was momentarily pushed aside. Charlie saw the opportunity, grabbed Jonny's hand and pulled him onto the lifeboat. Almost immediately the two crewmen on board began to winch the lifeboat down to the sea. They were safe!

In the clear early morning light, they could see the churning, oil-streaked water below as those who had survived the jump from the ship were swimming as fast as they could away from its hull. They were already having to forge their way through the pitiful bodies of those who had broken their necks in the fall or been knocked unconscious and drowned. Others just clung to any piece of floating debris they could get hold of and simply prayed.

Inch by inch the lifeboat was lowered, but as it made contact with the sea it was immediately set upon by the poor wretches who were already in the water.

"GET OFF" shouted one of the crewmen. "You'll 'ave us over!" and he brought his oar down on the head of one poor unfortunate who was trying to pull himself onboard.

"Can't we make room for some more?" shouted Charlie.

"We won't be able to stop once we've started. We'd just be swamped" shouted the same crewman without looking down at him.

But two seconds later, that's exactly what happened. With at least twenty men who were already in the sea trying to scramble onto the boat, the lifeboat rolled over depositing the sixty-three men who had had a reasonable chance of survival into the oily, salt water.

The scene now became one of absolute mayhem with the occupants of the lifeboat being pitched onto those already in the sea. Terrified screams from those who could not swim were added to those desperately shouting to maintain contact with father, brother, son or friend. Like a net full of freshly landed fish, the men thrashed around and over each other as they looked for something to hold on to. As panic overtook some, many of the frail were simply pushed under the water out of the way, their chance to survive taken from them.

Both Charlie and Jonny were good swimmers and were able to stay calm, confident that they could swim to safety and it was Charlie who managed to reach onto the side of the capsized lifeboat first. But as he tried to haul himself out of the water, he was grabbed from behind and thrown back into the sea.

Meanwhile, Jonny was using a discarded suitcase to hold onto. He looked around to find his brother and was just in time to see him thrown off the side of the lifeboat. Gradually, he manoeuvred the case in Charlie's direction and finally reached out for him. Charlie was coughing and vomiting the foul water that he had swallowed but Jonny forced him to hold on to the suitcase with both hands as he used his free arm to pull the pair of them clear. "KICK, Charlie! For fuck's sake, KICK." As he swam, he could hear the groaning and hissing of the doomed ship behind him, even above the screams and cries and the splashes of terrified jumping men and descending debris. Inch by inch they moved away from the ship, pushing the dead and unconscious away as they did so.

Even as they kicked, Jonny knew the suitcase wouldn't last much longer, it was already half submerged; they needed more floatation. As if by some miracle, there was a body ahead wearing a life-jacket; the only one they'd seen so far. Jonny grabbed the man who was lying face down in the water and turned him over. His head, streaked with oil and blood, flopped as if it were only attached by the skin of his neck. "Oh God!" he shouted. "It's Samuel. He's dead. His neck must be broken."

"Must have done it jumping" said Charlie, spitting the foul taste from his mouth. "Poor Bugger."

"We've got to get that life-jacket off him. We need it more than he does now" said Jonny, although it went against all his instincts. He'd really liked the old man. It was difficult, but finally they managed to release the straps. As they completed their task, Samuel just sank beneath the water.

"Goodbye, Samuel. Glad you enjoyed the English Lessons. It was good to have met you." Charlie's words were inadequate, he knew, but it was more of a homily than most of the dead received that day.

It was now clear that, for the moment, this was their only way of survival: they had to gather as many life-jackets and any other flotsam as they could, and as quickly as possible.

Despite Myrna wrapping her arms tightly around his neck, Pete had felt himself being dragged from her. "Mach schnell" was being shouted in his ear. It was only when he was halfway down a dark and smoky corridor that he fully awoke and realised something was dreadfully wrong. Shrugging off those that were supporting him, he shouted "Was ist los?"

"Das Schiff sinkt!" cried someone close.

"Jesus Christ!"

"Ah, Herr Darling." It was the unmistakable voice of Captain Burfeind, as calm as if he was on the Serpentine in Hyde Park. "I am glad you could make it. The ship has been torpedoed and is about to be lost. These idiotic British have done their best to ensure that we all die with their wire but we will show them what Germans can do. Come quickly."

In a column of twos, Burfeind and the rest of his men that he had managed to gather, marched through the gloom and the smoke. Once outside, Pete was shaken rigid. Absolute carnage lay all about him. Two lifeboats were hanging vertically: their davits and falls irredeemably damaged as a result of prisoners trying to effect a launch themselves before the ship's crew could get through the barbed-wire and take charge.

Burfeind continued along the promenade deck followed by his men: some would-be escapees stopping momentarily to watch the procession before resuming their own battles for survival, while others just stood, too terrified to make the jump from those areas that had been already cleared of wire.

At the next lifeboat, members of the crew were desperately trying to clear away some of the barbed-wire so that they could get onto the lifeboat. With the prisoners and internees, as well as the guards, all clambering over each other to get onboard, this was proving impossible. Burfeind barked out orders to his men and twenty or so of them proceeded to muscle their way into the crowd and form a barrier between the crew and the would-be passengers. Amid the howls of protest, the Arandora Star's men were quickly able to release the barbed-wire and get onto the lifeboat. At this point, Burfeind ordered his men to allow an orderly passage into the boat. With that process under way, he marched the rest of his men forward. Once she was fully loaded, the first lifeboat was lowered away. Only when she was in the water and being rowed away, would Burfeind's men allow the ropes to be used by those who so chose to climb down them in their bid to escape.

Burfeind and his men, with Pete still in the column, found exactly the same situation at the next lifeboat station, but this time Pete knew how he could help and he joined the SS Adolf Woermann's crew in effecting the barrier. As the allocation was reached, Burfeind shouted for Pete to join them.

"No, not yet. Let this man go instead" and he grabbed an old man and bodily threw him onto the lifeboat.

In all, Burfeind and his men were instrumental in the launch of four lifeboats and, on each launch, Pete refused a place.

Of the Arandora Star's compliment of twelve lifeboats, one was destroyed when the torpedo hit; another was destroyed by the blind panic of the young soldier thinking he was doing the right thing by shooting dangerous men trying to escape under cover of the chaos; two lifeboats were made unserviceable by the prisoners trying to launch them themselves. Of the remaining eight, only those where Burfeind and his men organised the launch carried the full quantity of men they could have. The others were launched with a very small number of survivors on board; almost all were either part of the Arandora Star's crew or members of the 109th Prisoner of War Unit, the guards.

With all the lifeboats launched, Burfeind ordered his men to abandon ship themselves. He looked at Pete. "And that includes you, Herr Darling." Pete stared into the Captain's eyes – they showed no signs of panic at all, just totally calm and controlled. "Good luck, Sir" he said and he offered his hand which was accepted and then turned to address himself to the problem of getting off the ship, which by now was listing and groaning dramatically.

Towards the rear of the vessel he found a rope ladder which had already been deployed and was gently swaying with the motion of the sea and the stricken ship. The sea still looked an awfully long way down, but he was relieved to see that there were life rafts that he would be able to clamber onto once he had made his descent. Unlike his brothers, Pete was not a good swimmer and he knew he would not survive long without something to hold onto. Taking a deep breath, he climbed over the guard rail and started his descent. It wasn't easy, even for a strong man like Pete – that is he used to be strong before Warth Mill took its toll.

God knows what it must be like if you had to do this in rough weather, he thought. He looked down. He was now no more than ten feet from the thick oil that now covered the surface of the sea. Nearly there.

He heard rather than felt the impact on his head and then everything was black and his hands lost their grip on the ladder.

He knew nothing more: nothing of the two captains – Moulton and Burfeind standing on the Bridge chatting and smoking as the ship keeled over for the last time; nothing of the terror of those still trapped in the bowels of the Arandora Star and who knew their final moments had arrived, some praying, others crying, some pleading with a son or brother to kill them before the waters came. He did not hear the sound of the rifles as a few of the guards turned their weapons on themselves. He could not hear the hoarse screeches of those despairing souls still trapped in the claws of the barbed-wire who realised that they had no hope of survival. He did not hear the cries of the injured or see the eyes of the hopelessly confused old men who had no idea what to do or where to go. He did not hear the sobbing apology of the young Italian who had collided with him whilst making his own bid for freedom and survival. He did not feel the young man hauling him out of the freezing cold water onto a life raft or his searching frantically for a pulse. Nor did he feel the young man reaching into his mouth to ensure that his airway was clear of the thick oil. He did not notice the movement of the raft as the Italian pushed and kicked with his legs to get them away from the ship. He could not see that many of the Welsh regiment had been lined up on the Promenade Deck as if they were on the parade ground or waiting for a number 42 bus. Nor did he see the Arandora Star heel over onto her side, fling her bow vertically into the air and then sink slowly beneath the waves taking hundreds of men with her.

It had been less than forty minutes since Gunther Prien had given the order to fire his only remaining torpedo.

Chapter 13

"Dear Ruby,

Got your letter this morning but I think you should talk to your postman as someone has let a child crayon all over it and some of the words have been crayoned over. I am so glad you are safe your sister Dot and I are also safe and well. The air raids are getting more and more and the other night six houses in Alma Road got a direct hit. You remember old Mr Skinner who used to work in the butchers shop on the high street well he and his wife Edna were killed and there daughter and her kiddies and the dog. No bombs on this side of the high street tho thank god. Have you herd anything from the boys they haven't written at all so I am at a loss to no how they are. Hope this finds you as it leaves me. Got to go to work now

All my love
Mutti"

Ruby had collected the letter, which had "OPENED BY CENSOR" stamped on the back, from the Camp Office that morning after the first teaching session with the children. Although this was the first letter she'd received since being taken by the police six weeks ago, she'd always made a point of sending her Mum one once a week since she'd been on the island – the Camp rules wouldn't allow any more.

She smiled as she read the letter again and again as she walked up The Promenade towards the hotel. Good old Mutti – she never stopped.

Tilly hadn't moved from their room since getting back from the beach the previous day. Ruby had heard her sobbing all through the night but apart from putting her arm round her occasionally, she knew there was little she could do except be there for her friend. She decided that it wouldn't be appropriate to mention her letter so she stuffed it into the pocket of her pinafore dress as she opened the door to their room. Tilly turned, her eyes red and puffy – just slits.

"You alright, love?" asked Ruby.

"Mmm. Just about" said Tilly. "How was your first day at school" she said with as much of a smile as she could manage.

"It was good. A couple of the other mums were there and there were about a dozen kids. We played a sort of charades game, pretending to be cats, dogs and stuff and saying the name in English as well as German. It seemed to work for everyone and it was quite good fun."

"Good. I'm glad."

"How do you feel?"

"Oh, alright…. Well, pretty awful really. Oh Ruby, I just feel so useless. If only I had been there, it might not have happened."

"Don't be daft! How could you have saved them? You know what they say…if a bomb's got your name on it…."

"Yeah, but they might not have been there in the first place."

"You don't know that. You will never know what might have been. Come on, stir your stumps and let's go for a walk."

"No, you go. I don't feel like it."

"Oh come on, Tilly. Just think, if you don't keep your strength up, you'll be no good on the dig and then what will Rico say?" That was the clincher.

"Alright, I suppose you're right" she sighed, getting wearily to her feet.

Ruby smiled to herself. Rico, Rico, Rico. You have a lot to answer for, Mister.

Instead of going into the centre of Port Erin, which Tilly didn't want to do, they turned right and then left onto the track that led along towards Bradda Head – just fields and countryside on either side. At the Head, by the side of the old mine workings, they sat and watched the gannets plunging into the sea after the fish. Tilly talked about her grandparents: what they were like, things they used to say, places they'd taken her to as a child. But gradually, the need to talk waned and after a while they just sat in silence. It seemed to help Tilly as she was much brighter on the way back and even more so when Ruby mentioned that tomorrow was Tuesday and she would be seeing Rico.

"Are you coming?" she asked Ruby.

"No, I don't think I'm going to do it again."

"Oh, why ever not?"

"Well a number of reasons, really" said Ruby, cupping her hands round a butterfly that had just landed on a thistle flower at the side of the road. "Firstly, I don't think my back's up to doing the Dig as well as the stoking that I have to do at the Hotel." She opened her hands and the insect, somewhat reluctantly it seemed, flew away. They idly watched it until it landed again on another thistle flower. "Another reason is that I don't want to play gooseberry with you and lover-boy."

"But you don't" cried Tilly. "It's lovely having both of you. I'm sorry if I've neglected you."

"Don't be daft. You deserve some pleasure, especially now."

This sent both of them back into quiet contemplation and they were back on the main road before Ruby said "But the main reason is that I want to put more time into the school. I really loved seeing the faces of the kids enjoying learning new things. In fact, I was thinking that I might try and become a teacher when all this nonsense is over."

"You mean the War?"

"Mmm."

"Oh, that would be wonderful" said Tilly and then with laughter in her voice she said "You never know, maybe you'll teach mine and Rico's children."

"Christ, you're getting a bit previous, aren't you? You've only known him a couple of days."

"Three days, to be exact" said Tilly, indignantly.

"Oh, I'm sorry. Three days."

"Anyway, he's the one. I just know it" said Tilly dreamily.

"Well, I hope you'll be very happy together" Ruby said, smiling at the change in mood of her friend.

"Have you ever been really in love?" asked Tilly when she'd stopped dreaming of what the future might hold.

Ruby looked out to sea and thought of Dieter but, try as she might, she couldn't even picture his face. "I thought I was once, but now I think it was just a relationship that we both just drifted into. Thinking about it, I know I did." She surprised herself when she suddenly said "I don't think he was a very nice person, to be honest. I think he was just using me. I was very naïve before I came here."

The following day, July 2nd, was Ruby's birthday and, just before she went off to the Dig, Tilly presented her with a card she'd made herself and signed Tilly _and_ Rico. Ruby had to smile. Tilly seemed to get more of a thrill out of giving it to her than she did receiving it. I wonder why that could be, she thought.

After doing her duty in the boiler room, Ruby washed and then walked down to the Church Hall where there were a number of things she wanted to prepare for the next day's school. However, as she walked into the Hall, she was surprised to see she had been beaten to it by two women looking around the room and particularly at the pictures that the children had been using in her first class, the day before.

"Can I help you?" One of the women, who Ruby recognised as being Dame Joanna Cruickshank, strode over to her.

"Eh, I was just going to prepare for tomorrow's lessons. I'm teaching the children."

"Oh I think there's been some mistake" said Cruickshank haughtily. "Are you a qualified teacher?"

"No but..."

"No. I thought not" said the Dame, looking down her nose as if Ruby was something the cat had brought in. "We already have a teacher and a very renowned one at that." She half turned towards the other woman, who was small and bird-like, her hair in braids over the top of her head. "Dr Minna Specht is to be the new teacher at the school. She has been running her own school for many years, both in Germany and in Denmark, before coming to Wales the year before last. I don't expect there will be any need for Dr Specht to call on your services, thank you."

Ruby was dumbfounded. "But I'm the teacher. It's all been agreed with the mothers and the caretaker and everyone."

"No, Fräulein. You are not the teacher and only I have the authority to appoint one. Now if you wouldn't mind shutting the door behind you, Dr Specht and I have important things to discuss." She turned her back on Ruby and walked back to her colleague.

Ruby had felt the tears welling up almost as soon as Cruickshank had started speaking but she had managed to hold them back. Now she couldn't. She just turned and ran out of the Hall, over The Promenade, down the steep bank and onto the beach. She sobbed and sobbed and even when the skies darkened and the light rain started to fall, she just sat and cried at the humiliation; her dreams of becoming a teacher shattered.

"Where have you been?" cried Tilly. "I've been looking for you everywhere. We finished early because of the weather….Oh Ruby, what's wrong? God you're wet through. Come on. Let's get you out of those wet clothes. What's happened?"

Ruby sobbed her heart out to Tilly as she changed out of her wringing wet clothes.

"The bitch!" cried Tilly. "The perfect bitch! I've a good mind to go down and give her a piece of my mind. The cow."

"No don't. Just leave it" said Ruby, blowing her nose.

"But it's not right. You were going to be the teacher."

"I know, but it won't make any difference, you ranting and raving. You'll only get into trouble. Just leave it."

"Well it's not fair. And on your birthday as well."

"Oh, yeah. I'd forgotten. But I'll tell you something I did get for my birthday. I've realised that I really do want to be a teacher when I get out of here."

"So you can teach Vito and Louisa!" Tilly exclaimed, clapping her hands with glee.

"Christ Tilly. After just three days you and Rico have got children and they've even got names. You're mad. Does Rico know what he's letting himself in for?"

"Not yet he doesn't, but he soon will. He's got no chance. He's mine. All mine." Then suddenly the euphoria was gone. "Oh but I wish Grandpa and Grandma could have met him."

After Tilly had finished in the kitchen, there was still time, before the curfew at nine o'clock, to go for a short walk. The rain had given way to warm, late evening sunshine which glistened on their tear-streaked cheeks as they walked, crying and laughing in equal measure, arm in arm, along The Spaldrick and The Promenade, overlooking the bay and the open sea beyond. At the noticeboard, just by the Station, they stopped to see if anything new had been posted.

"This is new" said Tilly, pointing at one of the notices. She read it out loud. "Service Tokens. I have been impressed by the arguments put forward by some of the Internees that good morale can only be achieved by hard work and endeavour. With this in mind, and with the belief that we would all prefer to work rather than to accept charity, we will be introducing a system of tokens which can be exchanged for goods and services available within the Camp. More information will be provided in the next few days. Signed Dame Joanna Cruickshank."

"That sounds like a good idea" said Ruby.

"Mmm, it does, doesn't it?" agreed Tilly. "And look, on the German translation, they've even stuck two of the tokens."

"They're just bits of cardboard, stamped with "Rushen Camp" on them."

"It's got to be better than getting a few pence for the extra jobs we do and then having nothing to spend it on. At least this way it'll get everyone doing more of what they do best. I could use them to buy presents for Rico."

"Oh give it a rest, Tilly. You're becoming quite boring." Ruby laughed and then threw her arms around her friend and hugged her. "I am so glad I met you."

"Me too." Then "Oh Christ! It must be getting on for nine o'clock. We'll have to run otherwise we're going to be in trouble."

Chapter 14

"Southerly or south-easterly 3 or 4, occasionally 5 in west, but variable 3 or 4 in east. Slight or moderate. Fog patches. Moderate or good, occasionally very poor."

Ralph Wood listened to the shipping forecast as he always did at this time of day, sitting in the front room of his little bungalow on the banks of Loch Foyle. The French-made BFR Table Top wireless set, which his wife Rita, their children and his former colleagues at the Bank had bought for him last December as a retirement cum birthday cum Christmas present, was his pride and joy. He thrilled at the seemingly endless number of stations that he could find. When conditions had obviously been just right, he had once even picked up a station in Australia. However, he had recently become fascinated by the broadcasts of Lord Haw-Haw from Germany: not because he had any sympathy for the Nazis, far from it. It was just that this chap seemed to know everything; omniscience somebody had told him it was called. Ralph found this totally compelling. He never ceased to be thrilled by the science of it all as their call-sign "Germany calling. This is Germany calling" came through, loud and clear. But today was different.

Since early this morning, he knew from the wireless traffic that a ship had been sunk somewhere off the north coast of Ireland. By constantly "twiddling", as Rita called it, he had heard the various ships and aircraft co-ordinating their efforts to get to the scene. Now he was riveted to the 500 Hz point on the dial – the emergency frequency. "Poor buggers" he said to the cat which was curled up on his lap. "It might be slight or moderate if you're on a ship, but if you're in the sea, it'll be cold and absolutely bloody terrifying."

If Lino Gallina hadn't covered that last five yards that had taken almost all the strength that he had had left, he, together with the life-raft he was pushing ahead of him and the still-unconscious man laying almost on top of it, would have been sucked into the vortex made by the last journey that the Arandora

Star ever made. Fortuitously, the life-raft was in just the right place to be carried on the crest of the ensuing tsunami-like wave, with Lino hanging on for all he was worth, and they ploughed through the thick oily water like dolphins racing with an ocean-going liner.

In the bitterly cold, oily water a hundred yards away, Charlie and Jonny clung to a collection of discarded suitcases, life-jackets and assorted debris. They were both shivering violently and were finding it increasingly difficult to grip things. Although there was no single piece that was significant, the sum total of all the debris kept them afloat without the need to waste their energy in swimming or paddling. Even so, they knew that they needed to find something more substantial or they would eventually die of cold. So far nothing had presented itself, but that was to change once the Arandora Star had gone.

As the giant wave lost its energy and calmed and the enormous whirlpool disappeared, there was a few seconds of eerie silence, save for the cries of men in fear and despair: the screaming having died along with the lives of hundreds of men when the ship went down.

Bizarrely, less than thirty seconds later, all sorts of debris, anything that had inherent buoyancy and was not securely fastened to the doomed vessel, began to erupt out of the sea; miscellaneous benches, panels, chairs and stools, life-rafts and the like broke the surface. Even the lifeboat that had been shot to pieces surfaced amid the mass of foam and oil.

Seeing all this bounty as their chance, Charlie and Jonny discarded their own collection, save for a lifebelt apiece, and swam as best they could to stake a claim on something that would give them long-term support. Their legs hardly seem to work at all so it was with more of a doggy-paddle that they progressed, agonisingly slowly, through the water. Hardened by what they had already seen, they pushed their way without emotion through the large number of bodies that were floating on the surface– deliberately not looking at faces for fear of recognising someone they had known. But well before they reached the newly surfaced items, they came upon a life-raft with one body half sprawled across it and another, ghostly white and streaked with oil, just hanging on with one death-locked hand.

"This'll do" Charlie said, grasping hold of the raft and using his other hand to reach out for his brother. "Save us swimming any further."

"Don't think I could've gone much further anyway" panted Jonny.

The life-raft, about six feet long and three feet wide, was a slatted-wood construction enveloping large cork blocks. It was intended to hold onto rather than sit on and, with the dead body more or less stretched across it, it sat very low in the water; not a problem if it was being used in the warm Caribbean or the Mediterranean, but in the cold North Atlantic it offered very limited support. They had to lose some of the weight, that much was obvious to both the lads. If the chap half-lying on the raft was indeed dead, then he had to go, plain and simple. They had no choice. While Jonny inched his way round to the man's head, Charlie went to the one that was just hanging on and, as he gripped the ice-cold hand, the man opened his eyes.

"Mama?" he said, feebly.

"This one's alive" shouted Charlie, noticing how difficult it was to shout. "But only just by the looks of it" he added, almost in a whisper.

"I think this one's had it" croaked Jonny as he reached for the man lying prostrate across the raft, and tried to clear some of the thick oil from his face. "Jesus! IT'S PETE. CHARLIE IT'S PETE!"

"Is he dead?" said Charlie, hearing himself saying it almost dispassionately, as if Pete was someone he'd never heard of.

"Hang on, I'm trying to clear the oil away from his face, but my hands are so cold" he shouted. "Looks like he's swallowed gallons of the stuff. His mouth's full of it." Jonny forced open Pete's mouth and felt for his tongue. His fingers were so numb from the cold he couldn't feel anything but then Pete's tongue lolled out the side of his mouth. He suddenly coughed and then vomited over Jonny's face.

"Ergh!" Jonny cried. "He's just thrown up all over my face, but he's alive. He's alive!"

Pete opened his eyes. "Myrna?"

"For Christ's sake, Pete. Don't you think of anything else?" said Jonny, grinning as if he'd just won the Treble Chance on the Pools.

Pete's staring eyes focussed on his brother. "Jonny?"

"Yeah, mate. Sorry to disappoint you. How do you feel?"

"I dunno. Splitting headache and I'm cold, freezing cold. Where are we?"

"In the sea. The ship's gone. Torpedoed. Christ Pete, I'm so glad to see you."

"Rub his shoulders and arms" shouted Charlie, who was doing the same to the young lad. "Get some circulation going."

Between them, they rubbed and pummelled as best they could with their one free hand and gradually it began to have some effect on all of them.

"Christ, Jonny. Not so hard. You'll break my bleedin' arm if you go on like that."

"Sorry Pete, I can't feel much." Then to Charlie "Complaints already he's giving me" but this Jewish idiom instantly brought the sight of Samuel sinking below the surface of the waves flashing through his mind. "I'll bet Myrna wouldn't do it any better" he said, trying to wipe the vision from his mind.

"She bloody well would" said Pete, gripping his younger brother's shoulder and smiling. "But I suppose you'll have to do, in the circumstances."

As Jonny massaged his brother vigorously, Charlie was trying to get through to his charge. "Hang on, mate. We'll soon have you feeling better."

"Mama. Sono così freddo. Tenga la mia mano, mama. Tenga la mia mano. Così freddo."

"This one's Italian" shouted Charlie to his brothers.

"Is he alright?"

"Looks rough. We need to get him onto the raft."

"It'll sink with both of them on it" cried Jonny in alarm.

"I think he's going to die if we don't" replied Charlie.

"But we'll loose both of them, then."

"Pete?" shouted Charlie, ignoring his youngest brother's plea. "Can you move your arms and legs?"

Pete tried. They were numb with cold but, with agonising pain, he managed to lift each of his arms and then his legs. "Hurts like buggery but I don't think anything's broken!"

"Good" shouted Charlie. "Jonny?"

"Yeah."

"Can you come round here and help me lift this guy up onto the raft? Pete?"

"I'm ahead of you. As you get that guy on, I'll slide off enough to compensate. I bloody well hope he's little, though."

"He looks like a kid" replied Charlie.

"Poor little sod. Right, I'm ready. Lift him on. Oh Christ! This water's f..f..freezing."

Between the two of them, Charlie and Jonny lifted the boy onto the raft until only his legs were still in the water. This still left enough buoyancy for Pete to keep his shoulders and upper back clear of the sea.

Massaging the boy with their free hands, the three brothers were soon able to bring some colour back to the young lad's face and hands. He remained unconscious, but occasionally he mumbled incoherently and thrashed his arms and legs about- still fighting the sea even in his dreams.

"Where were you on the ship, Pete?" asked Jonny. "I didn't see you."

"I dunno. One of the upper decks, I think."

"With your Nazi chums, I suppose" said Charlie, with a hard edge to his voice.

"Yeah, I was, as a matter of fact" said Pete, retaliating. "But it's not what you think."

"What do I think?"

"You think I've joined them, the Nazis."

"Well haven't you?"

"No, I bloody well haven't."

"You seemed to want their company rather than your brothers' though. Didn't you?"

"I had to."

"What do you mean, you had to?" sneered Charlie.

"I had to."

"You wanted to, you mean."

"I was told to" said Pete, spitting out some of the foul-taste in his mouth.

"By who?" Jonny joined in, desperately thinking of some way to mend the fences between Charlie and Pete.

Pete looked at both his brothers and then at the ship-less sea around him. "Oh, bugger it. I don't suppose it matters much now, anyway, but you must never, ever say anything to anyone. I was told to by someone I think was in British Intelligence."

"What!" exclaimed both his brothers incredulously.

"You remember when we were first taken from home?"

"Yeah" said Jonny, his imagination already flying.

"Well, when they split us up for the interrogation, I was kept waiting for ages. Then I was shoved in front of an Army officer and two blokes in suits. They told me that Ruby had been spying for the Germans."

"That's bollocks" said Charlie.

"She'd never" said Jonny.

"That's what I said to them, but then they showed me some of the stuff she had hidden under her bed. There were maps and photographs of buildings and that shorthand notebook of hers. They were certain she and Dieter had been identifying buildings for the Luftwaffe. They said she was a Spotter."

"That bloody Dieter" said Jonny. "I never did like him. It's all his fault."

"How could she be so stupid?" said Charlie as he lifted the Italian's head gently. The boy's eyes were still closed but he seemed to be breathing easier, almost as if he was asleep. "No, I don't believe it."

"Well, I didn't at first but they were absolutely certain" said Pete. "Anyway, they said that they had been secretly watching both of them for months and there was no doubt."

"Bloody Hell!" exclaimed Jonny. "She never said anything to me."

"I still don't believe it" said Charlie.

"Let me finish" said Pete. "So they said they had enough evidence to lock her away in Holloway Prison for the rest of the war and years beyond that. She might even be executed for treason. They asked me if I knew anything about it. Well, what could I do? I didn't know what to say just in case it made things worse. So I just said that I knew absolutely nothing about it and that I was sure there must be some innocent explanation why they were doing all that stuff. Then the bloke in the uniform started saying that maybe we were all in on it, the whole family, even Mutti. So I lost it and told him that he must be bloody stupid and if that was the sort of ridiculous ideas that British Intelligence came up with, then God help England. Funnily enough, the two blokes in suits seemed to like that because they just looked at each other and smiled.

"The Major or whatever he was, wasn't having any of it and kept on at me to admit we were all in it together. In the end I told him he was a fucking idiot and that I wasn't going to say another word."

"I bet that went down well" said Charlie, beginning to soften towards his brother as he could imagine Pete giving as good as he got.

"Yeah, well he deserved it" said Pete, looking somewhat indignant. "He was a right pillock – all toffee-nosed and la-di-dah." He paused and looked around. There were definitely fewer cries and shouts now as the cold was beginning to take away some of the survivors' will to hold on. "Christ, it's cold. You'd never believe this was the summer. God knows what it must be like in the middle of winter. I'm sh…ivering like mad, here. Do you think they'll send out ships to rescue us?"

"They've got to" said Jonny. "They can't just leave us out here to die. Can they?" he added and turned to Charlie, imploringly.

"Make things easier for them if they did" said Charlie. "Wouldn't have to bother to send us away again."

"Yeah, but what about all the guards and the ship's crew that survived" said Jonny, almost pleading for reassurance. "There's got to be some of them. They couldn't have all drowned."

"No, you're right, little brother" said Pete seeing that Jonny was beginning to panic. "They'll not let us go just yet. Need to be seen to do everything possible. I'll bet there's ships all over being diverted right now. And we might be in range of some of the RAF boys. Just hang on. We'll be all right."

There was silence for a while as the boys reflected on their situation. "So what happened next?" asked Charlie.

"Well, eventually I think the Suits got fed up with the Army guy and one of them whispered something to him and he huffed and puffed and went all red in the face. Then he just slammed his papers down on the table and walked out. One of the Suits then said that there was a way that I could help Ruby. He said that he and his colleague believed that we weren't involved and would I be prepared to help them. In return they would ensure that Ruby was treated leniently and released as soon as possible."

"Hah! And you believed them?" said a still-sceptical Charlie.

"I didn't have any choice, did I?" cried Pete. "What else could I do but trust that they were telling the truth? I told them that I was sure that they'd made a mistake but that if it helped Ruby then I'd do my bit."

"Well, I think you did the right thing" said Jonny. "Don't you, Charlie?"

"Mmm. Maybe" said Charlie, grudgingly.

"Look!" shouted Pete at his elder brother. "You bloody well weren't there. I was and I thought it was the only thing I could do. So you can snide all you like, Mr High-and-Mighty. I had no choice."

Charlie and Pete stared coldly at each other for a few seconds. Then Charlie softened and said "Well as you say, I wasn't there so I don't know. Maybe it was right. So what did they want you to do?"

Pete was still angry and had half a mind to not answer, but eventually he calmed down enough to say "You know that German Captain you met in the Red Cross tent?"

"The short bloke with the sticky-out ears?" said Jonny.

"Yeah, him."

"I thought he was a smarmy bastard" said Charlie.

"He was actually quite a nice bloke….. for a dyed-in-the-wool Nazi." said Pete. "Anyway, according to the Suits, he's been part of some secret German organization who have been kidnapping scientists and engineers, mostly Jews, and taking them to somewhere in Africa where they're made to work for the Nazis developing some sort of secret weapon that'll blow us all to blazes. And what they wanted me to do was to get close to him and his crew to find out where this place was."

"And did you?" said Jonny excitedly, almost forgetting he was up to his shoulders in numbingly cold water.

"I got close to him alright. We were getting quite pally really. Used to talk about all sorts of stuff; mostly how the Camps were run and stuff like that but also about the outside world and the war. And football – he liked football. Oh yeah" he said, remembering, "the first time I met him I told him about the cure for bed bugs business. He thought that was brilliant."

"That's a point" said Charlie, looking around him. "Where's Manny? I haven't seen him since we were at the Camp."

"Maybe he's still there" said Jonny, optimistically. "You know, maybe he went sick or something."

"I hope so, for his sake" said Charlie, but something deep inside him was dark and fearful. "So did you find out where this place is then?" he said, not allowing himself to dwell on his best friend's fate.

"No" said Pete. "Could never find the right way. I tried all ways I could think of to get him onto the subject of where he went to, but the closest I got to was somewhere in East Africa."

"Do you think they'll make you continue when we get back?" asked Jonny.

"I guess so" said Pete. "Although I suppose it depends on how many of us survive this. Right now I reckon if we don't drown, we'll freeze to death. God, I can't feel anything below my waist. And what I can feel is bloody freezing."

"So you'd be no good to her if Myrna happens to send her private launch out for you then" laughed Charlie.

"Not until she thaws me out first. Mind you, that might be rather nice." Then a thought struck him. Seriously, he said "You mustn't say anything to anyone. Not even Ruby. Promise?"

In the bitter cold, it became more and more difficult to keep rubbing the Italian's back, arms and legs. All of them were finding it increasingly hard to concentrate and Pete gradually lapsed into a sort of sleep, despite Charlie and Jonny doing their best to rouse him. In the end, Jonny was rubbing Pete's shoulders while Charlie patted and pummelled the Italian on one side and then swam round to do the same on the other and even this was becoming spasmodic, with long periods when he simply couldn't summon enough energy. They had found lifebelts for Pete and the Italian by taking them off two dead soldiers and this helped a bit, but Charlie knew in his heart that unless they got some help soon, none of them had a hope in hell.

Despite desperately trying to stay awake, he lapsed into sleep and was soon dreaming that his father was teaching him to kick a football but his legs were in callipers and he kept missing the ball as it rolled towards him. "I can't do it, Vati. I can't do it" he shouted. But his father just kept smiling at him and rolling the ball towards him. "I can't do it" he shouted in frustration.

He was awakened by a hand on his shoulder, shaking him. He opened his eyes and saw the Italian staring at him. "English, you stay wake" he said. "You stay wake."

"Th……thought y…you were d…dead" said Charlie, shivering uncontrollably, but the lad obviously didn't understand and just looked quizzically at him. "You stay wake" was all he could say.

Charlie smiled at him and gave him the thumbs up. The boy smiled back but then suddenly looked up to the sky. Charlie looked up too, but could see nothing. The boy, however, became animated and pushed himself up to a kneeling position. "Aeroplano. Posso sentire un aeroplano. Qui! Qui!" he shouted and waved his arms.

Charlie looked in the direction the boy was waving and at first he could see and hear nothing. Then, a cloud thinned and he saw a spec in the distance, but still could hear nothing. It didn't matter - it was enough. They'd come. They were saved. With renewed energy, he swam round to Jonny, who had tied himself onto the raft with his trouser belt and was asleep with his head resting on one arm while the other was draped over Pete's shoulder, cuddling him.

Charlie shook both of them. "Wake up! Wake up! There's a plane. Wake up. They've come. They've come." But he got no response from either of his brothers. "Dear God, don't let them be dead. Not now. WAKE UP!"

It was Pete who came out of it first. "Not again, Myrna. Let me sleep."

"Wake up, you randy bastard" shouted Charlie in Pete's ear. "There's a plane." By now, he could hear it droning towards them and see that it was a huge Sunderland Flying Boat with its four nacelle-mounted Pegasus engines driving the propellers and its two stabilising floats hanging down from either end of the thick wings. "Pete, there's a plane."

At last, Pete opened his eyes. "There's a plane, Pete. Wave your arms. They must see us."

Jonny, too, opened his eyes to the commotion. "Charlie?"

"It's a plane, mate. It's a flying boat. It's going to land on the sea and pick us up."

But it didn't. In fact Charlie thought they hadn't even been seen until one of the side hatches opened as the plane turned and came back in their direction. Still it didn't land but they could see some of the crew preparing to bundle something out of the aircraft. They kept waving but the crew of the aircraft just waved back as the plane flew off. The package plummeted to the sea and landed not twenty yards away with a huge splash.

Charlie was about to go after it when there was a shadow over him as the Italian boy dived into the water. At first, he swam easily to the package, but his enthusiasm was almost immediately overtaken by the reality that he was still dangerously cold and exhausted. "Help me" he shouted, as he could do no more than paddle to keep himself above the surface. Charlie swam to him as best he could and, with his arm across his chest, dragged the lad back to the raft, leaving Jonny to paddle after the package.

With it securely sitting on the raft, and with numbed fingers making the task almost impossible, they eventually managed to release the straps of the two lifebelts that had been wrapped around the package. They stuffed these under the raft in an attempt to raise it a little more out of the water and then they started on the straps of the waterproof canvas that protected what turned out to be a cardboard box. Inside the box was a first aid kit, some bars of chocolate, cigarettes and matches and something that looked like a hot-water bottle.

"Cor, look at that" cried Pete. "I hope it's hot."

"No chance" said Charlie, twisting the bung and sniffing the contents. He gingerly took a sip. "It's drinking water. Here, pass it round. But don't go mad, it might have to last us a while." Then turning to the Italian boy, he gave him the thumbs up again. "Grazie."

"Prego" said the lad with a weak smile and helped himself to the chocolate that Pete offered him. "Me Lino. Lino Gallina."

Pete did the introductions and then, as they ate and smoked, Lino, in halting English made worse by his chattering teeth, explained that he had come to England with his parents, grandparents and sister to stay with his uncle in Warrington. As Italian Jews, his father believed that there was no place for them in Italy; sooner or later the Jews would be in the same situation as those in Germany and Austria. So, from Warrington, they were all going to go to America but then war was declared. When Italy joined in, they were all interned. He told them that his father, uncle, grandfather and two male cousins were all on the Arandora Star but, with tears in his eyes and a voice that had almost disappeared, he said that he didn't think any of them had survived. He had only managed to get through the barbed-wire himself because his father had deliberately thrown himself onto it so that Lino could use him as a ladder. None of the others would take the risk of jumping. He apologised to Pete for hitting him on the way down.

"So that's why I've got this sodding great lump on my head. You nearly broke my neck, but I thank you for saving my life" and he offered his hand to Lino with a smile.

As they shook hands and grinned at each other, Jonny said "How old are you, Lino."

"Me sixteen."

"Jesus" said Charlie, but apart from that, none of the brothers could think of anything to say so they just concentrated on the best picnic they could ever remember.

For an hour, the Sunderland continued to circle and drop packages where they found signs of life. Judging by the amount of times something was pitched out, it was obvious that there were many groups of survivors spread over the ocean. Then, with a waggle of its wings, the plane flew over them and headed off into the distance.

With the euphoria of the contact with the outside world, the emergency rations and the knowledge that there were indeed other survivors, the boys' spirits lifted. However, by the time another hour had passed, they were all in a bad way again.

Conversation had become impossible: they couldn't concentrate and they began lapsing in and out of consciousness. It was Lino with his sixth sense for knowing that something was different, who spotted it first. On the horizon, the Sunderland was coming back. As he watched, it began to circle the area again, dropping more parcels as it went. Then he thought he saw a ship in the distance, but being so low down, he only saw it for a second before the swell of the sea took away his view. He was beginning to think he had been hallucinating when suddenly it was there again. "Ship!" he cried, pointing. "Ship. Ship."

The Canadian destroyer H.M.C.S. St. Laurent, under the command of Commander Henry "Harry" De Wolf, arrived at more than full speed, but it still seemed to make agonisingly slow progress. Their lifeboats were immediately lowered but then the St Laurent had to move, and stay on the move, for fear of another U-boat attack.

It was to take the seamen a further five hours of exhausting and harrowing toil before they were certain that all the survivors were on board the St. Laurent. Picking up people from the Arandora Star's lifeboats was simple enough; but rescuing small parties and individuals clinging to rafts or wreckage required the most amazing diligence and heroic seamanship from the Canadian crewmen.

By the time it came to the four lads' turn, none of them could help themselves. Barely conscious, they were no longer aware of what was going on around them. Even if they had been, it would have been impossible to grasp a rope because of the cold and the slippery scum of oil that they were covered with. In the end, some of the St. Laurent's crew, already cold, wet and exhausted themselves, had to jump into the water with bowlines round their waists, but eventually all four were hoisted bodily on board.

Wrapped in blankets, they were gently lifted onto the destroyer and, equally as gently, carried below into the comparative warmth where other members of the crew gave them hot, sweet tea via a spoon. Many, however, did not recover: their bodies could take no more and simply shut down during the thawing-out process. Such was the fate of Lino Gallina aged sixteen, who passed away, deep in the bowels of a Canadian destroyer bound for Liverpool; dying on the same day as his father, his grandfather, his uncle and two of his cousins.

Chapter 15

"Guess what?" Tilly cried as she bounded into their room after spending the day at the Dig.

"Your third child's going to be called Aristotle."

"Eh?" Tilly was floored for a second. "Oh. No, silly. I haven't thought that far ahead, yet."

"Oh, you surprise me" said Ruby, who was drying her hair on a towel.

"Anyway, listen" said Tilly, determined that she was not to be distracted. "They're going to have a party where all the married internees can meet their other halves."

"Oh, that's a nice idea. Some of the women here are in such a wretched state; it's probably just what they need."

"Oh, it'll be so wonderful to be able to hold Rico in my arms and dance to the music" swooned Tilly as she danced around their room holding on to a make-believe Rico.

"Eh, excuse me, Ginger Rogers" said Ruby. "I know I've been to sleep since yesterday, but I was under the impression that you and Rico hadn't yet walked down the isle. In fact, I wasn't aware that he'd even *asked* you to marry him. I know you've known him for ages now… what is it, a month?…."

"Thirty-three wonderful, magical days" said Tilly dreamily, continuing to waltz round the room.

"Sorry, thirty-three days. I apologise with all my heart for any hurt I may have caused you in getting it wrong" said Ruby, sarcastically.

"You're apology is accepted."

"You're most kind. But there still remains the fact that you and Rico are not yet married, unless something's happened that you haven't told me about. So how are you two going to go to the party, let alone dance together?"

"We've got it all worked out" said Tilly, plonking herself onto Ruby's bed. "It's like this. One of the men on the Dig mentioned it first thing this morning. He's an internee as well, from somewhere in Poland originally, and his wife's here in Port Erin. Anyway, he said that he had been told about this party for the married internees last week, but he didn't think it was going to happen so he just forgot about. Besides which, his wife's a frightful dragon and he's enjoying being on his own."

"So when is it, then?"

"Day after tomorrow. Three 'til four. They're using somewhere called Derby Castle in Douglas. It's a large entertainment centre and it's got a huge dancehall." Tilly paused, turned over to lay on her back and cuddled one of Ruby's pillows. "So, where was I? Oh, yeah. This Polish chap, Zak's his name, short for Zacharias, said that this morning he'd been told that his name was on the list and he would have to go whether he wanted to or not. He's not best pleased, I'll tell you. I think he's frightened stiff of his wife."

"Look, I know I'm not the sharpest knife in the box, and I don't wish to interrupt this scintillating story, but I still don't understand how you and lover-boy have got an invitation."

"Well, if you didn't keep interrupting, I'd be able to tell you, wouldn't I? So Zak's telling us all about his invitation and why he doesn't want to go, when the Professor wanders over so I asked him if he and Frau Bersu would be going to the party. Well, he just laughed and said what was the point, they see each other every day as it is. So I said I thought it would be wonderful and I wished Rico and I could go. Anyway, this afternoon, the Professor comes over to us, Rico and me, and says he has had an idea. Apparently there are one or two disabled internees, you know, in wheelchairs, and they would need help in getting on and off the trains and through doors and that sort of thing. So he's pulled some strings and Rico is going to help one of the male internees and I'm going to help one of the women. And," and she paused to take a deep breath, "and once they've met up with their partners, Rico and I can dance and kiss and cuddle just like all the others will be doing. Oh, I'm so excited I could burst" and she started dancing round the room holding the pillow as a partner.

"Well, Cinderella, if you are going to the Ball, we'd better make sure your ball-gown is clean and your jewellery is polished. Hadn't we?"

"Oh, my God! What am I going to wear? I've got nothing. And my hair will need doing. Oh, no. It's not my turn for a bath until Friday. That's too late. And I've got no decent shoes. Oh Ruby! What am I going to do? I've got to look wonderful for Rico."

"I don't see why. He's fallen for you when you've been up to you're eyes in mud so I don't think he's going to go off you just because you haven't had chance to wash your hair. Just keep the light behind you and you'll be fine."

"You bugger" cried Tilly and threw the pillow at her with all her might.

The next forty-eight hours in Port Erin was a mixture of excitement, tears, short-tempered frustration and ecstatic joy. And that was just a description of Tilly. The dressmakers and the hairdressers worked non-stop. Jewellery that had been deposited at the Bank when the women had first arrived, was now removed and polished. Shoes were borrowed and Exchange tokens were amalgamated so that their owners could share the purchase of lipsticks and scent bottles. Even those not going were drawn into the thrill of it all and the whole of Rushen Camp became a hive of excited, chattering activity.

Most of the women going to the party were taking small gifts for their men so Tilly decided she was going to cook something for Rico. Unfortunately, after two attempts, all she had to show for her efforts were some "burnt-offerings" and a frayed temper. However, Mrs Mylechreest took pity on her and made a special batch of her renowned Carrot Fudge for Tilly to take to Rico.

On the big day, all the men were marched under military escort from their various Camps. Most had done what they could to spruce themselves up: hair was freshly greased down and chins shaved as closely as the blunt razors would allow, while jackets and ties were top of the list of items borrowed from fellow internees.

As the men arrived at the Derby Castle, many of them clutching pathetic bouquets of fuchsias and other flowers which they had collected from the hedgerows along the route, they were marshalled into small sections on the dance floor and up onto the galleries. Windows were packed with the eager faces of men desperate for a first view of a loved-one not seen for months in some cases. But three o'clock came and went and, as flowers wilted in sweaty palms, many began to fear that the whole thing had been arranged too hastily and that the meeting was not going to happen.

It was nearly four o'clock before the first of the coaches containing nearly two hundred women arrived from the railway station in Douglas. Once all of the coaches had arrived, the women were allowed to disembark, only to be surrounded by armed soldiers. Then one of the Army officers blew his whistle and the group were gently escorted towards the main doors of the complex.

The plan was that once all the women were inside, they would be allowed to join their men, section by section, in an orderly fashion.

It didn't happen.

As soon as the women came into the dance hall, the men started shouting ,waving and whistling to attract their spouse's attention. After the merest of pauses, and barely enough time for the soldiers to run to safety, two hundred women and a wheelchair stampeded across the dance floor in a charge that would have done credit to many a Cavalry Regiment. Nothing and no one was going to stand in their way. With one hand holding onto their hats and the other clutching a bag or two containing little presents and paintings drawn by their children, the women hurtled into the arms of their men folk. As tears flowed freely and unashamedly and gifts exchanged, a little band of musicians struck a chord and began to play as though this was just an ordinary tea-dance.

To the strains of "Some Enchanted Evening" Tilly left the lady she had been helping in the tender care of her rather embarrassed-looking husband and went in search of Rico. As she walked across the dance floor, she saw her friend Zak, from the Dig, standing next to a formidably large woman wearing a brown coat that had its fur collar lifted up so that it covered all of the back of her head. In fact, she reminded Tilly of a great big bear that had raised itself onto its hind legs and was about to attack. The couple had only just met after God-knows how many weeks apart and already Tilly could hear her laying into her husband. The tirade was in Polish so Tilly didn't understand a word, but the vehemence of her delivery left Tilly in no doubt that this woman must be a direct descendent of Attila the Hun. No wonder Zak had been enjoying his freedom.

The get-together had been scheduled to run between three and four o'clock but because the women's arrival had been delayed by a problem with the train, and much to Zak's discomfort, the internees were allowed to continue their meeting until well passed five o'clock. In all that time, Tilly and Rico were not physically separated for more than a few seconds. A bomb could have dropped on the building and neither would have noticed. They talked about their families and friends, what they'd done and where they'd been. But most of the time, they just looked into each other's eyes and giggled and smiled, and, by the time the whistle had been blown and bodies prised apart, the question had been asked, the answer given and a single future planned.

Ruby had spent the first part of the afternoon writing a letter to her Mother but as she wrote she knew that it wasn't her best. More "How are you?" and "What have you been up to?" than "This is what I've been doing." She was doing it out of duty and for something to do. Without Tilly, she was bored. Without Tilly, she had all the time in the world to feel sorry for herself. She thought of Dieter, and what a serious mistake she had made in supporting him - what an idiot she had been. By doing what she did, she had put the lives of her family and friends in danger: not only from the bombs that she had directed but also from the new, oppressive lifestyle that would certainly come if Hitler successfully overcame the Allies. She thought about the interrogations: the first when they all appeared before the Aliens Tribunals. She had been scared stiff about that one because she was convinced that they would know about what she and Dieter had been doing and would take her away for trial as a traitor. But it went fine, just as Dieter said it would. Category "B"; the same as her brothers and the same as all the rest of the people she knew who were foreign or part-foreign. That was why the second interrogation, when the policemen had come for them, had been such a shock. She thought they had got away with it and then suddenly knew they hadn't. But what she couldn't understand was why she was treated as an Internee rather than a traitor. It didn't make sense. She was under no illusion that if the tables had been reversed and she had been living in Berlin and working for the British, she would have been taken out and shot, long before now.

She was so lost in thought that she didn't hear the first knock on her door, but she did hear the second. "Come in" she shouted. The door opened and the face of a young girl about twelve years old peered round it.

"Er, excuse me" said the girl, timidly. "Are you Ruby?"

"That's right. What can I do for you?"

"Mum said it would be alright if I came up here. I'm just so bored and needed someone to talk to, really. I wondered if you were doing anything."

"I'm sorry, I don't understand. Who's your Mum?"

"Mrs Mylechreest. I'm Daphne Mylechreest, her daughter."

"Oh, I see. I'm sorry. I didn't know Mrs M., sorry, your mother, had any family."

"I'm away at boarding school on the other side of the island. Mum thought it safer if I was away from all the prisoners. Oh! I'm so sorry. I didn't mean......"

Ruby laughed at the girl's embarrassment. "Forget it" she said. "We're not all in love with Hitler. And besides, I could really do with some company myself at the minute. But first can we agree on something?"

"What?" said Daphne, knowing she was still blushing.

"Can we both stop keep saying "sorry" to each other?"

"Oh, yes. That would be great. Thank you."

"Good. Now, sit down and tell me all about yourself and what you get up to in that school of yours. My whole world at the moment comprises of just Port Erin. So you can tell me what's happening in the outside world?"

"Well actually Mum was wondering if you'd like to come with me to visit my aunt. I've got some stuff to take to her. Maybe we could even stop for tea. If you'd like to that is."

Daphne turned out to be a lively and outgoing twelve year old who was full of questions along the lines of why Ruby was interned, how long she was going to be on the island, what she would do after the War. Naïve, innocent, non-judgemental questions that forced Ruby to see herself through someone else's eyes. She knew that inside she wasn't a bad person; just someone who had taken a wrong turning and now needed to find the right path back to who she really was.

It was this thought that remained in the back of her mind during their tea with Mrs Mylechreest's sister. She turned out to be much younger than her sister and much less tolerant of the internees being in Port Erin. She made no bones about her belief that all the internees, women included, should be shipped off to Canada and Australia for good – "forced emigration", she called it. But she was polite to Ruby and was at pains to stress several times that "it was nothing personal", although she was not totally sure that Daphne should be "fraternizing with the enemy".

Her Madeira cake, however, was superb and Ruby showed no hesitation in having a second slice when it was offered. Nevertheless, she wasn't sorry when the tea was concluded by Daphne's Aunt saying that she thought it was time for her niece to be going home.

"Did you enjoy yourself?" asked Daphne as they walked back to the hotel.

"Yes, I did" answered Ruby, not totally untruthfully. "Although I'm not sure if your Aunt would be pleased to repeat the event."

"Oh, don't worry about that. She's always been a bit difficult. Something to do with hormones, Mum says. Whatever they are."

Ruby couldn't resist a smile and this remained until she got back to her room to find Tilly had returned with news that seemed about to cause her to explode. As she listened for the umpteenth time to Tilly's re-enactment of the whole afternoon, Ruby knew that she had turned a corner; that her life was now in front of her not behind; that she was exceedingly lucky to be treated as she had been so far. But there still remained the question - why wasn't she still locked up in Holloway Prison with all the rest of the traitors like Mosely and Mittford? As Tilly continued to bubble and bounce, Ruby tried to rationalise the facts surrounding her detention, but there seemed no rational explanation.

Chapter 16

Jonny opened his eyes again. Still above him was the khaki-green canvas of the tent. If he moved his head as far as he could to the right, he could just see Pete out of the corner of his eye: bruises blackened on the side of his head and still lying in exactly the same position as before. Was he dead? Surely they would have drawn a sheet over him if he was. He turned his head to his left. Charlie had his eyes open, staring at the tented ceiling, but seeing nothing.

"Charlie" Jonny croaked, his lips cracked and dry, his throat sore, his voice a stranger. Charlie showed no reaction: maybe he was dead as well? "Charlie!" he shouted as best he could. Still nothing. Jonny closed his eyes. The effort of making any sort of noise at all had left him exhausted. Someone lifted his wrist to feel his pulse. Jonny opened his eyes again. A doctor – white coat and stethoscope. "Where are we?" Jonny whispered.

"You're safe, son. Save your energy."

"Are my brothers alive?"

"Are these chaps your brothers?" said the doctor, who looked as rough as Jonny felt, indicating to the cots either side of Jonny.

"Yes."

The doctor smiled. "As my old professor used to say, they're not dead until they're *warm* and dead. You chaps have been through hell and by rights all three of you should have passed away. But so far, so good. Just take it easy and relax. We're doing everything we can. Would you like a hot drink?"

A Red Cross orderly quickly brought over a mug of something hot. For the life of him, Jonny couldn't tell whether it was tea, coffee or dish-water, but it was hot and welcome. The orderly held the mug as Jonny sipped the liquid. After a few sips, which lubricated his mouth such that talking was a little easier, Jonny was able to ask again where they were.

"Huyton Camp, mate" came the answer.

"Christ, we only just left here."

"I know. There's loads of the survivors in here, although some of them went to other camps."

"What do you mean, survivors? I can't remember a thing apart from getting on a coach out of here."

"Don't you remember the ship you were on was torpedoed? You lads were lucky to survive. Lots of 'em didn't, poor buggers."

Jonny closed his eyes and tried to remember. There was something there, in his head, but he couldn't quite latch onto it. His head seemed muzzy, like it was full of cotton-wool. He couldn't seem to think straight. Ship? Torpedo? And then cold, he remembered being cold. Very, very cold. And in water. Freezing cold water. But nothing else would come to him. He drifted into sleep.

When he opened his eyes sometime later he could tell it was dark outside – the tent fabric was somehow more solid, as if there was nothing beyond it. This was enhanced by the golden, almost ethereal, glow from the flickering oil-lamps that were stationed around the tent. Maybe this is Heaven, he thought. He moved his head to the right: easier than before. Pete was still there and still in the same position, eyes closed. To the left, Charlie had his eyes closed this time. Jonny stared at the roof of the tent and then closed his own eyes. He could remember some things now: the Arandora Star, the explosion, the smoke, the panic, that fucking barbed-wire. Everywhere there was barbed-wire. And the screams. Oh God, the screams. He clenched his eyes tightly, trying to block out the memories he'd tried so hard to regain. He remembered the water: icy cold, oily, sea water. He thought he would remember the taste of that water as long as he lived. But everything else was indistinct, hazy. In the water, holding on to a plank or something. Himself, Pete and Charlie. And someone else? Was there someone else? Manny maybe? It wouldn't come. He thought about his mother; he still hadn't written to her like he'd promised Ruby. Ruby. Something about Ruby. Something dark, unwelcoming, scary. He opened his eyes again and looked at each of his brothers and whispered their names. No response. He stared at the roof of the tent and watched a spider scurrying along the fold at the top. He could move his hands and fingers now. He gripped the side of his army cot and felt pins and needles coursing down his arms and hands as he released his grip. Suddenly he could feel itching all over his body, right down to his toes. He smiled at the thought that it might be the bed bugs again. "Don't think I could charge about naked or otherwise at the moment" he whispered, just so he could hear the sound of his own voice.

"Jonny." It was Pete. "You awake?"

Jonny turned his head and smiled at his brother. "Back in the land of the living, then. Have you both had a good time?"

"Who?"

"You and Myrna."

"Christ, I wish. I don't remember a thing and my head's pounding. Are we dead?" he added, looking around at the celestial glow.

"Don't think so."

"Where's Charlie?"

"He's here. The other side of me. Still asleep, though."

"What happened?"

"I've been trying to remember. I remember us being in the sea after the ship exploded. The cold and the oil. We were hanging on to something. I think there was someone else with us, but I can't seem to grasp…"

"Lino" whispered Pete. "Lino Gallina. Young Italian boy. He fell on me when he jumped off the ship and then saved my life by getting me onto a raft or something."

"Oh, yeah. That's it. Just a kid. Hope he made it."

"Yeah, me too" said Pete, gazing passed Jonny into nothingness. "Me too."

The next time either of them opened their eyes, the sun was boring through the canvas.

"Mornin'". The orderly had come round with mugs of tea and some "bread and scrape" as he called it, for Pete and Jonny. He helped them both but surprisingly neither had much difficulty in grasping the mugs. And they were ravenous.

"Two eggs and crispy bacon, please." It was Charlie. A croaky whisper and a thin smile was all he could manage but he was alive.

"Charlie!" Jonny reached out an arm and touched his brother.

"Glad you're back with us" said Pete. "Thought we might have needed a new full-back, for a moment."

"I could still take you out of the game, any time" whispered Charlie, closing his eyes but smiling now. Pete and Jonny grinned at each other. The three of them were back together; battered, bruised and aching. But they had survived. They were safe.

Over the next two days, they regained much of their strength and mobility. At first they just laid in bed, drinking tea, eating bread and jam, sleeping and talking – putting together all they could remember from the time they entered the water until they found themselves back in Huyton Camp. Between the three of them, they could remember most of what went on right up to the point when the St Laurent was spotted. Then it started going hazy. Charlie could remember Pete beginning to slur his words and talking to Myrna as if she were sitting on the raft in front of him. Jonny was sure he'd seen their mother paddling a canoe towards them, but the more she paddled, the further away she went. Pete couldn't remember a thing until they were being lifted out of the water. Someone was saying they were all dead and he was shouting and screaming that no, they were all alive. But although he was screaming, he knew he made no noise at all and the sailors just ignored him. He remembered no more until he woke up in the cot.

"I don't understand it." The grey-haired doctor was doing his rounds. "You chaps must have anti-freeze for blood; most of the survivors have lost toes and some have even lost a foot or two. You lot – nothing."

"Good, clean living and a dose of castor oil every night. Just the ticket, Doc" said Pete.

"Mmm" said the doctor, smiling over the half-glasses that were perched halfway down his nose. "I think it's about time you lads were up and about. Far too cheeky. Can't be much wrong with you now. And besides, you're causing too much disruption. What little staff I have seem to be spending an inordinate amount of time with you three."

"They like the jokes" said Jonny. "Doc, have you heard the one about Hitler and the three little pigs?"

"I'm sorry" interrupted the doctor. "I'd love to stay and hear it but I've got other patients to see." As he walked away, he turned. "I'm moving you out later this afternoon. Just take it easy on those legs and drink plenty of tea."

By three o'clock that afternoon they were hobbling slowly along the unmade road towards their new home – one of the tents that they'd seen being erected the last time they were at Huyton. One of the soldiers had been detailed to show them which tent they were in, and it was he who was, somewhat reluctantly, carrying the bags of new clothes that the brothers had been given by the Salvation Army.

"Good to be back" chirped Jonny. "Like being home again."

"Mmm" said Charlie through gritted teeth; of all of them, he was the one having the most difficulty walking: his feet were painful and swollen. "Haven't seen anyone we know, though. I wish I knew what happened to Manny and the others from the English class."

"Perhaps they're in one of the other camps" said Jonny, ever the optimist. "That orderly bloke did say that some of the survivors had been taken to other camps."

"Mmm, maybe" said Charlie. "Just wish I knew he was safe. That's all."

"He'll be alright" said Pete. "You know what Manny's like. Always lands on his feet." Then he had a sudden thought. "Unless they've taken him to Warth Mill, of course. If he's gone there, he'll wish he'd gone down with the ship."

The brothers spent the next three days eating and enjoying the warmth of the summer sunshine. At one point Jonny had remarked that it was almost like being on holiday, except for the food, which hadn't improved at all while they'd been away. But, in between eating and sleeping, they spent their time, with increasing concern, searching for news about Manny. They eventually found one of the former students from the English class who could remember seeing him on one of the coaches going to the docks in Liverpool, but he couldn't recall seeing him again.

And then something happened that took their minds completely off Manny and his whereabouts. All the survivors from the Arandora Star who had been discharged from the Medical Hut were called to the Mess Hall to be told that they were to be shipped out early the following morning. Where to? No one was saying.

At dawn on Wednesday July 10th, exactly one week after they had arrived at Huyton Camp for the second time, they were loaded onto transport and taken to Liverpool again.

"I don't think I can manage going in a ship again" said Pete, who had been very quiet since receiving the news that they were to be moved again. "And I certainly don't want to see barbed-wire again. Ever."

"We'll be alright" said Jonny. "We're all together and we'll get through it somehow. Maybe we're going to another camp in England…or maybe even somewhere in Scotland." He put his arm round his brother. "And don't forget, we've got Myrna looking after us."

"You get your own guardian angel. Myrna's mine."

"Christ, this is awful" said Charlie seriously. "Can't they see what they're doing to us? We've done nothing wrong, we've just survived a torpedo attack, we've been half-drowned and frozen to death and still they want more. What more can we give?"

"You'll go where you're told to, do what you're told to and be thankful we don't bloody shoot you like the rest of the bastard traitors." A soldier who, like the rest of his mates, was angry at only being given just two hours notice that he was going to be on escort duties on a ship going to an unidentified destination, aggressively prodded him with his rifle. "Now fucking get on that ship otherwise I'll shoot you here on the gangplank and save us all the bother."

His Majesty's Transport Dunera was a three-year old troopship built in Glasgow by <u>Barclay Curle</u> & Company. She was designed to carry a maximum of one thousand five hundred men, including the crew, but there were already over two thousand scheduled to sail on her when, at the last minute, some nameless individual in an office in Whitehall decided that the four hundred or so survivors of the Arandora Star disaster who were able to walk should also be loaded on board. A total of two thousand five hundred and forty-two men were crammed onto the vessel as it sailed out of Liverpool on that bright, sunny July afternoon.

On the top deck, all suitcases and bags were piled into a heap: for hygiene reasons to make sure there were no perishable goods that would go rotten down below, they were told. From there they were forced down metal stairwells and into the hold of the ship.

"Christ, it's like the slave ships they had in history" said Pete, peering into the gloomy, already-fetid "cabin" that they were evidently going to share with twenty others. It looked as if it had originally been some sort of store-room. On one side, five hammocks had been strung up but, as the prisoners were filing in, these were in the process of being hastily removed by two of the soldiers.

"I hope they don't want us to row this bloody boat" said Jonny.

"Something tells me this isn't going to be nice" said Charlie.

As they put down the thin mattresses that they had been given into a space along one side of the room measuring about forty feet by fifteen, they looked around at their shipmates. Although all were actually aged between sixteen and forty-five, many looked to be nearer their sixties; frail, traumatized old men: German, Italian, Polish, Austrian, Dutch and Russian. Some of them were definitely Jewish: black coats and hats, long beards and curled payot with others just wearing the yarmulke. The majority however, like the Darlings, were not Jewish but there didn't seem to be any animosity amongst the travellers, although the Jews did keep in a group together; everybody seemed to have just a tired acceptance of whatever lay ahead. However, by the shouting that could be heard from some of the other cabins nearby, it was obvious that harmony wasn't universal.

At the end of the room was a small enclosed toilet, with a pan and a single tap over a small sink in the corner. No windows, just a grill covering a ventilation shaft. Along one side of the room, the boys' side, were four portholes, bolted shut. Peering through the filthy glass, Charlie could just distinguish between the sky and the sea. But apart from that, there was nothing.

"Cosy" remarked Pete, to himself more than anything.

"Like ze Black Hole of Calcutta" said the man next to him in an Italian accent.

"Where you from, mate?" asked Pete.

"I come from Ischia, near Napoli. I am sailor. Now Prisoner of the War."

"I met a bloke from Italy last week. Saved my life when our ship got torpedoed. Only a young spit of a lad. God knows what happened to him, poor sod."

The Italian crossed himself and offered his hand, introducing himself as Salvatori Zola. Pete shook it and introduced himself and his brothers.

"D'you know where we're going?"

"Canada they say to me" and he indicated upwards.

Pete just stared at him. God! Not again.

As the Dunera gradually moved out of the flat-calm Irish Sea and the protection of land, the sea quickly changed its mood too: from a gentle swell producing an almost soporific rocking for the prisoners locked below decks to what seasoned mariners might have called "a bit choppy". However, to those incarcerated below, it was a full-frontal assault on senses already battered beyond belief. Very quickly the room turned into a rancid, slimy hell as sea-sickness took first one, then two more and then almost every one of them, including all three of the brothers. Even those who could cope with the Dunera's movements, found it impossible to remain unaffected by the pervading stench of vomit which was soon washing around on the floor and soaking into the mattresses and clothing of the unwary.

For hour after hour the Dunera continued to pitch and roll into the North Atlantic and for hour after hour throughout the ship, the prisoners held below, as well as most of the guards, continued to suffer sea-sickness on a scale beyond anything any of them had ever experienced before. By now, most were dry-heaving and had chests and stomachs that were racked with pain. In the boys' "cell" the vomit sloshing around on the floor had now become diluted with the urine that had missed the toilet pan as soon as it had become a moving target. And they were not even twenty-four hours into their voyage.

However, as suddenly as it had started, so it stopped. The ship resumed its gentle swaying but this did little to improve the predicament of those on board, particularly those being held in the gloomy, airless, dungeon-like holds below. On every level of the ship and in almost every enclosed space, the cloying aroma of vomit and the groans of men wanting to die filled the air. Where the boys were, things were no different except for the small matter of the "added" ingredient in the vomit which made the noxious atmosphere almost unbreathable. Indeed, for five of the men, there was no "almost" about it: they had fainted. Then, without warning, the door was unlocked and four soldiers marched in. All looked as if they had been victims of the sea-sickness themselves for they were pale and sweating. Immediately the stench hit them, one recoiled back into the gangway clutching his mouth while the other three, and without any fuss whatsoever, simply added their own contribution to the floor's decoration. Two more soldiers followed them into the room, holding their berets to their noses. One lifted his rifle one handed and pointed it at the middle of the group of prisoners, none of whom moved a muscle, while the other, a Corporal, looked at the first three soldiers with contempt. "Get out of here, you three. I'll talk to you later." The three didn't need to be asked twice and hurried out of the room and presumably up to the fresh air.

"Bubble, get in here" shouted the Corporal, still holding his beret over his nose. This must have muffled the sound of the order because no one appeared.

"BUBBLE! GET YOUR FUCKING ARSE IN HERE, NOW."

Sheepishly, a lad in his teens poked his head round the door. He held his own beret over his nose so that only his eyes, as large as saucers, could be seen.

"Get in here!" shouted the Corporal, grabbing him by the shoulder and propelling him into the room. "Right lad. Now point your rifle at these dangerous Nazis and if one of them so much as farts, you shoot him. Got that?"

The answer was probably "Yes, Corp" but because it came from behind the beret, it was just an unintelligible mumble. With one trembling hand, the terrified soldier raised his rifle and pointed it in the vague direction of the prisoners. Were these men, who looked to him as if they were incapable of harming anyone, really dangerous? He was shaking so much, any bullet fired could have gone anywhere: floor, roof, walls or bodies and he frantically tried to steady his aim. Every prisoner looked at the hole in the end of the rifle, willing it to point anywhere except at him.

"Now" said the Corporal from behind his beret. "I will pass out these paper bags. One for each of you. Into your bag you will put all your documentation, your false teeth if you still have them, and all of your valuables."

Those of the prisoners who had understood translated for those that hadn't.

"Why?" said Pete, stepping into the empty space in front of the Bubble who gulped, went even paler and looked as if he was about to add his urine to those who had been before. His rifle shook so violently he looked as if he was about to drop it. Pete gave him what he hoped was a reassuring smile and then turned to face the Corporal, waiting for an answer.

"What d'you mean, why?"

"Why have we got to put all our stuff into those bags?"

"Because I fucking well tell you to" said the Corporal who, it was obvious to all who stood before him, was more bark than bite. "And because we don't want them getting lost, do we?"

"Thank you for your concern, but I think mine will be safer if they remain with me." All around the room, many of the prisoners were saying they agreed with Pete.

The Corporal was lost for words and stood, purple faced, staring at Pete. Pete smiled at the Corporal's discomfort but said nothing. Everyone waited for the soldier's next move. "Stand here, Bubble, and guard these men. I'm going to get the Sergeant."

There was a squeak from the young Private: terrified at the thought of being alone with all these dangerous men. He turned to face his Corporal, his eyes pleading for an alternative course of action. As he did so, his rifle pointed in the same direction as his eyes.

"For fuck's sake" said the Corporal, grabbing hold of the end of the rifle and pushing it down so that it was pointing to the floor. "While I go and get the Sergeant, you wait outside the door. And we'll lock it behind you." The last statement directed at Pete as if to warn him that he wasn't going anywhere. The relief on the boy's face was almost palpable.

"You silly sod" said Charlie as soon as the door closed. "You could've been shot."

"Maybe" said Pete. "But I'm sick of being pushed around all the time." Then, looking down at the pungent debris that sloshed around his boots, he said "and I'm sick to death of being treated like an animal."

With that, the door was unlocked and the Corporal came back into the room, no longer with his beret clasped to his nose. This time he was accompanied by two different soldiers, each of whom looked as if they knew what they were doing with the Lee-Enfields that they held in front of them. Each had what looked like candles hanging out of each nostril. Vaseline. The Corporal too had availed himself of the jelly. Not so the fourth man who came into the room. The Sergeant, ramrod straight and with his hands behind his back. No Vaseline candles and not a sign that he needed them. "Now, Corporal, what seems to be the problem?" as if he were sorting out a customer's complaint in a top Knightsbridge store.

"I'll tell you what the problem is…" said Pete furiously.

"SHUT YOUR MOUTH" shouted the Sergeant, the kindly mask disappearing instantly. "I'm asking this soldier. Not you."

Pete was going to shout back but Charlie's gripping of his arm urged him not to. He just stared back at the Sergeant.

"Now, Corporal" said the Sergeant, calm once more. "What's the problem?"

"These men are refusing to hand over their documents and valuables."

"You forgot the false teeth" said Pete, trying to be helpful.

The Sergeant looked witheringly at Pete but said nothing to him directly. Instead he looked around at the other prisoners: coldly, no hint of compassion nor sympathy. "BALL. PHILLIPS." The Sergeant continued to look menacingly at the men. Two burly, unarmed soldiers trotted into the room and grabbed hold of Pete and hurled him into the gangway. He had no chance of defending himself nor getting any assistance from his brothers and the others. It was just too slick. The first blow was a kick in the groin followed immediately by two punches to the stomach and then one to the jaw. From the room, none of this could be seen; just the sickening sound of the blows and the resulting groans could be heard. Charlie made to go and help his brother but the soldiers with the rifles made it absolutely clear that that would be the last help he would ever give, to anyone. And besides, he knew he was in no condition to take on the soldiers in the gangway.

As Pete was carried, barely conscious, back into the room, the Sergeant spoke, to the accompaniment of mumbled translations in the ranks of the prisoners. "There seems to have been a misunderstanding which I am pleased has now been sorted out. These bags are for your documents, valuables and dentures. We need your documents to ensure we know who you are and why you are here. We need your valuables to ensure that they are not the cause of temptation and unrest. And finally, we need your dentures so that you don't choke on them in your sleep. We wouldn't want to loose any of you, now. Would we?" His smile was utterly ice-cold. "All of these items will be returned to you when we arrive at our destination. And before any of you ask, I don't know where we are going. Thank you Corporal, carry on." The Corporal handed out the brown-paper bags and this time there was no dissension. Once he was satisfied that everything would now run smoothly, the Sergeant turned on his heels and marched away, brushing passed an overwhelmed Bubble in the gangway.

Hours later, the door opened. The Corporal didn't come into the room this time but stood at the door. Then he beckoned to someone behind him and Bubble sheepishly came just into the room carrying two galvanized steel mop-buckets with two mops under each arm. "There you are" said the Corporal. "Compliments of the Management." He was just shutting the door when he opened it again and said "You" pointing at Jonny. "With me. Time for a bit of spud bashing."

Jonny had never enjoyed peeling potatoes so much before in his life. The cool breeze washed through his matted hair and across his face, breathing life into him. It was the most wonderful sensation. Even though there were tons of the vegetables packed in the hessian sacks that surrounded him, he would have been quite happy to have stayed there all day. In fact he was quite disappointed when he was told that they only had to peel three sacks: *they* being Jonny and a wizened little man in a green tweed jacket at least two sizes too big for him and grey, stained trousers that finished above his ankles. The man paid Jonny no attention whatsoever: he didn't look at him, nor did he utter a single word despite Jonny's efforts to engage him in both German and English. The man just sat, hunched over his bucket of water into which he hurled each peeled potato with such vehemence that Jonny was certain this was not a man to upset.

By the time they'd finished the first sack, Jonny's hands were already sore and his back ached. After the second, he was cold and his shoulders were screaming at him. His companion, however, showed no signs whatever that he was in any sort of discomfort; he just continued peeling and throwing the potatoes into the bucket with the same monotonous rhythm. Jonny stood up and stretched his arms above his head, shaking the cramp out of his fingers. As he exercised, twisting from the waist with his arms outstretched, he noticed a group of about twenty soldiers marching to the far end of the ship. As he watched, they started opening the mountain of suitcases and bags that the prisoners had been ordered to deposit there when they came on board. Clasps were forced where necessary and the contents sifted through. Some of the soldiers held up clothing and laughed as others donned hats and danced around. This was bad enough, but what horrified Jonny was that once played with, the items were thrown over the side. Then he saw one soldier hold up what looked to be a gold necklace. A number of his colleagues tried to snatch it from him, but he held them off and put it in his jacket pocket. Another soldier found what must have been a pair of ear-rings because he put his hands up to his ears and pranced around effeminately. As the soldiers laughed at him, these too were quickly stashed away. A picture in a frame was given the barest of glances by another soldier before being pitched into the sea. This went on for quite some minutes until Jonny heard someone coming and he quickly sat down on his stool and started peeling again.

"Christ, haven't you finished yet." It was the Corporal. "You should have done this lot ages ago. Trying to get a suntan are we? You idle bastards."

Jonny was half inclined to tell the Corporal what he'd witnessed, but then thought that he was probably in on it anyway. Besides, he could very well find himself going over the side with the discarded possessions. "I keep getting cramp in my fingers" said Jonny.

"Oh, diddums" chided the soldier. "Just pull you finger out, sunshine" and he walked briskly off towards the group of soldiers. There were no admonishing shouts from the Corporal when he got to them so Jonny knew his first thought was right; the Corporal was in on it.

By the time they had finished, Jonny never wanted to see another potato again. Every muscle ached and he was frozen. The Corporal came back, took the knives off them and escorted them back towards the metal stairwell that led to the deck below. Just as they got to the top of the stairs, a stream of prisoners were being led up them: in front was Bubble looking as frightened as ever and Charlie was next.

"You alright?" he said.

"Yeah" said Jonny. "Knackered though. I must have peeled a million spuds."

"Oh is this your lot?" said the Corporal. "Well you might as well stay with them and get some exercise. Up the front, Bubble."

The exercise session, consisting of a series of halfhearted physical jerks led by a soldier wearing just a khaki vest above the waist, lasted exactly fifteen minutes. After a few minutes, Jonny noticed that the Bubble was standing at the back, leaning against a rail and glumly looking at his boots. Continuing with the forward bends and high steps, Jonny maneuvered his way towards him.

"Bubble" he hissed. The boy looked up, startled. Seeing Jonny so close, he raised his rifle warily, but said nothing. "Just want to ask you a couple of questions" said Jonny quietly, smiling reassuringly. The Bubble looked at him, not sure what to do. "First, why do they call you the Bubble?"

The boy looked around him then turned to face Jonny. "My name's Yannacopoulos. Colin Yannacopoulos."

"Oh, I see! Bubble and squeak – Greek." Jonny laughed, but then he became serious. "Look Colin, d'you know about those soldiers down the other end of the ship, going through all the suitcases and stuff?"

The soldier looked around then said "They're looking for perishables, food and that."

"Don't be bloody daft, man" said Jonny. "They're looking for anything valuable and pocketing what they find."

"Rubbish."

"I saw them with my own eyes while I was peeling spuds."

Colin Yannacopoulos looked astonished and was just about to say something when a whistle blew to mark the end of the exercise session. With a quick look at Jonny, he marched the prisoners back down below.

Chapter 17

June 22nd 1940

The Priest looked around at his congregation. So many sun- and wind-burnt faces – salt of the earth, these people. It was a good turn out. Everyone loved a wedding. "Such a pity that it isn't like this for Mass" the Priest whispered to himself. He was looking directly into the eyes of the man kneeling in front of him and he smiled. Composing himself once more, the Priest said "Michael James O'Donnel, Vis accípere Mary Regina Dwyer, hic praeséntem in tuam legítiman uxórem juxta ritum sanctae matris Ecclésiae?"

"Volo" replied Mickey, his mouth dry, his hands clammy.

Then he could hear the Priest again. "Mary Regina Dwyer, Vis accípere Michael James O'Donnel, hic praeséntem in tuum legítimun maritum juxta ritum sanctae matris Ecclésiae?"

"Volo" Mary whispered.

The Priest raised his voice, his sonorous tones filling every part of the church, and said "Ego conjúngo vos in matrimónium. In nominee Patris, et Fílii, et Spíritus Sancti. Amen."

He had been over and over the whole service so many times that he reckoned that if he ever stopped being a fisherman, he could become a priest. Well, just as long as they only wanted him to do weddings. But, come Saturday he would be a married man so they would have to allow him to be a married priest who only did weddings.

"I don't think so" Mickey said to himself.

The engagement had been a long and painful process for Mickey. Mary had insisted that there would be no wedding until they had saved the £400 that was needed to buy her grandmother's cottage from her landlord, Mr Alden White. Although Mr White owned half of the village and the land around it, he had grown up there himself and knew most of the families and many of their children. In fact Mary had once told Mickey that, as a nine year old, she had dreamt that one day she would marry Alden White even though in reality he was all of thirty years her senior. Nevertheless, she remembered with considerable pride the day she cornered him at the Spring Fayre and made him promise (she was sure his enthusiastic consumption of Tommy O'Shaunessy's home brew had nothing to do with it) that if she should ever raise the £400, he would sell the freehold to her. And she never let him forget that promise in all the next four years in which she and Mickey scrimped and saved and did without.

"Four years" Mickey smiled. "Four years …… and in all that time we've never so much as…………..

"Hey Mickey! Will you come and have a look at this?" Lenny Dwyer, Mary's father, called out from the port side of the Lady Elizabeth, the twenty-four foot sailing yawl which Lenny and Mickey's father, John, had bought almost twenty years ago and which Mickey had inherited when his dad had been killed in an accident just three years ago. "There" he pointed, when Mickey had come up to his shoulder. "About half a mile."

Mickey followed Lenny's arm across the flat-calm sea into the slightly misty early morning light. At first he could see nothing but sea and mist but then, for only a second, the mist cleared a little beyond where he had been looking and he could see, against the grey of the mist, a whitish pole sticking up out of the water. The waves no more than lapping around it. "What the …..!" he said. And then "What d'you make of it?"

"To tell you the god's-honest truth" replied Lenny, feeling the hairs on the back of his neck tingle, "I don't know what to make of it. Seems unreal just sticking out like that surrounded in mist."

"Well there's nothing we can do for now" said Mickey. "We've got to get the net in. We'll maybe have a closer look when we've finished."

As if on cue, the winch motor was cranked up and, with a belch of smoke, it spluttered into life. The motor coughed a couple of times as if it was apologising for breaking the silence, and then started to chug away smoothly. The gears were engaged and the drift net was slowly hauled in.

The catch looked pretty good without being spectacular. The precious salmon, together with other fish they would also be able to sell, were held fast in the net and they arched and gasped their last minutes as they were hauled onboard. When the fish and net had been stowed away, Lenny said "Let's go and have a look what that thing was. You never know, we might be able to get something for it back home".

"Fair enough" said Mickey, "but let's not be long doing it. We've got the rehearsal tonight."

They came about and headed for the spot where they had seen the strange shape, reckoning that they were now about a mile away.

After ten minutes, one of the crew members shouted and pointed to a spot some four hundred yards off to starboard where the object could be seen gently wallowing in the slight swell.

"It's a boat" cried Lenny.

A few minutes later, they could see that it was indeed a boat, roughly about the same length as the Lady Elizabeth and, eerily, its mast was fully erect.

"Looks like a lifeboat" said Mickey. "You know, one of those ones you see on the sides of those fancy cruise liners". The boat, which was almost totally submerged, seemed to be defying the power of the sea by not sinking. The sea water, both inside and out, was up to the gunwales. If the swell had been any stronger it would surely have been quickly swamped and lost.

"Let's see if we can bail her out" said Lenny. The rest of the crew just looked at him.

"Have you been at the whiskey?" laughed Mickey. "What are we going to do with her even if we can get her to sit on the water rather than in it? She's at least as long as we are."

"C'mon" Lenny shouted, undaunted. "We're bound to get something for her if we can get her home." So buckets and scoops of all sorts were put into a frantic attempt to raise her in the water. After ten minutes, however, it was obvious to all that the boat was lying just as heavily as she had been when they started.

"She's holed" said Mickey. "Must be." Then added "Let's forget this and get home. We've wasted enough time already." But Lenny wasn't listening. With lengths of stout rope he secured the lifeboat, fore and aft, to the side of the Lady Elizabeth. "You're not serious" chided Mickey, realising what his partner intended.

"Look" said Lenny "we need to get this back. I've got a feeling about it and we're only about four miles out. Something good's going to come of it, you'll see. There might even be a reward! If not, you can at least use it as a roof for a shed in that posh new place of yours."

Mickey knew there was no point in arguing. When Lenny got something into his head, not even the Pope himself could stop him, but it was going to be very hard work to make any headway at all with their newly-acquired anchor. "If the flat-calm holds, fair enough." said Mickey. "But the minute it changes, we get ditch it. Agreed?"

"Fair enough" agreed Lenny.

So, with the two vessels lashed together, they limped their way back to Owey, their island home off the north-west coast of Donegal in Ireland.

With the help of some very intrigued and amused fishermen who were still on the harbour side and a shout of "Are yer going to be doing trips round the harbour then, Lenny?", the crew of the Lady Elizabeth managed to bring the boat to a small landing on the edge of the harbour. They winched her up, stern first, until all but the bow was clear of the water. As they did so, they could see the green-grey sea water spouting from the hull of the lifeboat like cabbage water through a colander. With some extra bailing, the awful truth became apparent.

"Holy Mary" whispered Lenny and a few of the older fishermen crossed themselves.

"It's been shot at. Shot to pieces" said Mickey. And indeed it had for there must have been at least twenty holes in the hull.

"Look" said one of the men, pointing to part of the hull. "You can see where someone's tried to plug the hole with a rag."

"So it does" said another, as he reached inside to tug the rag free. He opened out the rag to reveal part of a man's shirt.

"This looks like blood" said another man, holding up a piece of rag that he had pulled from another gaping hole. It had been rammed in the hole so tight that brown stains could still be clearly seen.

"Poor bastards" said a man.

"I don't understand this at all" said another. "Why shoot at a lifeboat - even if it was full of Englishmen?"

"Let's get her clear of the water" said Lenny. "I want to see if she's got a name on her."

As the lifeboat came clear of the water, Mickey was the first to reach the bow. "Anyone heard of the Arandora Star?" he said, staring at the brass nameplate that was now visible.

Chapter 18

Throughout the summer so far, the weather had been hot and dry, but as July gradually morphed into August, the clouds gathered ominously in the afternoons and these developed into some of the most vicious and spectacular thunderstorms the Island had seen in years. While it had been dry, Ruby found that she was spending more and more time on her own as Tilly found a seemingly endless supply of reasons and excuses why she had to be allowed onto the Dig. But as soon as it started raining cats and dogs, all archaeological work ceased and a miserable Tilly was forced to spend all her time in Port Erin.

"Come on, misery guts" said Ruby as she was changing out of her work clothes after her shift. "Cheer up. It can't be that bad."

Tilly sat staring out of the window as yet another heavy shower pelted down outside. She hadn't even looked at Ruby as she'd come into the room: just waved an unenthusiastic hand vaguely in her direction and said a gloomy "Hello." Ruby thought it pointless to continue with the conversation so she carried on changing her clothes.

"I'm missing him, Rube." The new nickname.

"I know you are. But the Professor will still be there when the rain stops."

"Oh, don't start that again" said Tilly, irritably. "You know what I mean."

"Sorry. I was just trying to cheer you up. That's all."

"Well don't." And then, with a hint of a smile, "I'm quite enjoying being miserable if you must know."

Ruby laughed and came round her bed and put her hands onto Tilly's shoulders, gently massaging them.

"Mmm, that's nice."

"Tell you what, let's go for a walk."

"What, in this?"

"We can put our raincoats and wellies on. It'll be fun."

"Ruby, in case you hadn't noticed, it's pouring."

"I know, but it's better than just moping around in here. What time have you got to be back in the kitchen?"

"Half past four."

"Well there you are then; we've got a couple of hours. We can go along the beach and see what's been washed up."

"Another blinking mine, I expect."

"What d'you think, then? Fancy it?"

"Nah, not the beach. Let's just walk down to the village and see what's in the shops."

"Sounds good to me. Not that I've got enough Service Tokens to buy anything."

Kitted up in their raincoats, galoshes and rain-hats, the pair linked arms and braved the deserted Promenade. As they walked down the hill passed The Snaefell Hotel where Amalia was now staying with her mother and sister, Ruby noticed that her companion was wistfully looking out to sea. "Penny for them" she said.

"Oh, I was just wondering when all this is going to end; when we are going to be allowed to get on with the rest of our lives."

"You mean when you are going to be allowed to get your hands on Rico."

Tilly smiled coyly. "And that."

After a few more yards, "Oh! I forgot to ask you, what did your Mum say in that letter you got the other day?"

"Nothing much really. They're alright, Mutti and Dot. Dot's got this new boyfriend and Mutti says it looks serious."

"She's not old enough, surely?"

"No, I don't think she is, but the trouble is, she's sixteen and any day now the police are going to come for her. Mutti seems to think that Dot maybe looking to marry this chap so that she doesn't get interned."

"Christ, that's a bit drastic."

"Mmm, I know, but you can understand her thinking. Can't you?"

"Well, I suppose so, but it's a bit hard on the boyfriend."

"Oh! Don't get me wrong" said Ruby. "Mutti says she thinks the world of him."

"Good. Let's hope it all works out. What about your brothers? Has she heard from them?"

"No, not a word. I think between you, me and the gatepost, she's worried sick. Apparently there's been a big shipping disaster in the Atlantic somewhere. Hundreds of prisoners of war have been drowned."

"Oh my God! Does she know if any of them were on the ship?"

"No. She doesn't know a thing and I don't know what I can do either."

"Well, let's see if we can find anyone at the Camp Office who can help."

With the rain continuing to hammer down on them, they were like a couple of drowned rats by the time they got down to the centre of Port Erin.

"You're not the first to ask about it." They'd talked to this woman from the Commandant's Office before. She was a kindly and sympathetic soul; born on the Island but had lived most of her life in Düsseldorf. She had been married to a German sailor who had been killed in the First World War and had returned to live on the Island about five years ago. Although not an internee, she had volunteered to help out in the Camp Office. "All I can do is take their details and I'll see what I can find out. But I can't promise anything, you understand. I do know that there were hundreds of survivors, so even if they were on board, there's a good chance they're safe."

"Thank you" said Ruby, conscious that their dripping onto the floor had created quite a puddle. Her hair plastered to her head despite the rain-hat, Ruby looked at Tilly, who was equally drenched, but there was nothing to say – they just had to wait.

"Before you go" said the woman. "You had better have a copy of this and if you want to sign it let me have it back as quickly as you can."

"What is it?" said Ruby.

"It's a repatriation form. Fill it in with all your details and we'll try to get you back to Germany as soon as the opportunity arises."

"But we're both English" said Tilly. "We both live in England."

"Neither of us has ever been to Germany" added Ruby.

"Oh, I'm sorry" said the women, her face colouring as she realised her mistake. "Because we've only ever spoken in German, I automatically assumed you were both German. My mistake. But nevertheless, if you feel that you would like to be included in any repatriation, then fill in the form."

"I don't think we'll be bothering, thank you" was Tilly's immediate response. But something still inside Ruby made her less dogmatic.

"What will happen to those who do sign it?" she said.

"I'm not sure. I do know that they're trying to arrange for all the applicants to be grouped together in one or two hotels. Easier to manage them, I suppose. I've also heard that if they take some sort of oath of allegiance to the Third Reich, then they get a small allowance via the Red Cross. Not that the money comes from the Red Cross, you understand. No, that comes from Herr Hitler. Do you know Sister Jochmann?"

Both girls nodded. Tilly said "She's the one from the German Hospital in London, isn't she?"

"We met her and her nurses when we were catching the boat in Liverpool" added Ruby.

"That's the lady. Anyway, Sister Jochmann is the one who's going to be responsible for giving out this "German Money" and good luck to her is all I can say. All that money to look after and no one will be satisfied, you mark my words. Everyone will want more."

"Well, we won't be troubling her" said Ruby, brusquely "so I think we had better let you get on. Thanks for seeing us and thanks for your help with my brothers."

"Not at all, dear" and then in English for the first time "Toodle pip!"

Tilly and Ruby just giggled as they went back out into the rain.

"Gosh, couldn't she talk" said Tilly.

"I don't suppose she's seen too many people today" said Ruby. "She's probably been storing it up."

"You know, I just had a thought."

"Careful" said Ruby.

"I'll choose to ignore that, thank you. Anyway, as I was saying, I've just had a thought. If they are going to get all the Nazi women together into one or two hotels, they are going to need to be the large ones. I wonder if they've got The Golf Links in mind."

"Let's ask Mrs Mylechreest when we get back" said Ruby, whose mind was churning away on the fact that she wasn't sure whether the idea of all the Nazi women coming to their hotel appalled her or made her excited. She was shocked to realise that it might be the latter, despite the fact that she thought that she had put the past behind her after going to tea with Daphne Mylechreest and her Aunt.

"Yes, I know all about it" said Mrs Mylechreest when they managed to get her alone in her office just before Tilly had to start work on the evening meal. Tonight it was everyone's favourite: Savoury Potato Cakes deep fried in dripping with salad leaves and beetroot followed by Honey Cakes and custard.

"I had the letter this morning and I'm not very happy about it, I can tell you. The thought of the Golf Links being full of those evil women, makes my blood boil." Ruby thought she might be blushing and turned away to look out of the window as the dark clouds continued to roll in off the sea.

"Anyway" Mrs Mylechreest continued, "there's nothing I can do about it. Just have to make the best of a bad job, won't we?"

"Well, I don't suppose we will be allowed to stay here" said Tilly. "We haven't signed the repatriation form, so I suppose we'll have to go somewhere else."

"Oh, my dears!" exclaimed the hotelier, "We can't have that. You two girls are my rocks. I rely on you two to make sure this place runs smoothly. Of course, you've got to stay and help me. I'll sort it out with the Camp Office tomorrow. Now off you go, both of you. Oh my god, is that the time?"

"Well, that's that settled" said Tilly as they closed Mrs Mylechreest's office door. "Right, I'd better get into the kitchen, else I'll be in trouble. See you later." And she was gone, running up the corridor towards the kitchens.

Ruby stared at the old picture of some long-lost landscape somewhere which was hanging on the opposite wall as her mind mulled everything over. She was certain she wasn't a "Nazi woman" in her head: she didn't feel any allegiance towards the Third Reich, she didn't like their racist intolerance towards the Jews and she definitely didn't want Herr Hitler and Germany to rule the world. So why was she getting so stressed about the impending rearrangements? Why couldn't she just accept in her mind that she'd made a mistake by falling in love with the wrong man and, as a result, had done some things that she shouldn't have? That didn't make her a Nazi, did it? Wasn't she just a naïve young girl who had thought she knew everything and, when it came down to it, knew nothing? Now that she'd met Tilly and talked to Jewish women who were really just ordinary, decent, hard-working people, hadn't her eyes been opened? Absolutely. Hadn't she changed in the last three months? Most certainly. So, was she now being honest with herself? Yes, she thought she was. So where was the problem? There wasn't one, was there? No, there wasn't. Right then.

"Ruby? Is everything alright?" It was Mrs Mylechreest coming out of her office.

Ruby smiled the biggest smile for a long time. "You know Mrs M, I do believe it is" and she walked briskly down the corridor, back to her room.

Mrs Mylechreest watched her go in puzzlement, then after Ruby had long disappeared she said with smile "and don't call me Mrs M."

During the next week, Tilly was away most days as the weather had improved significantly: the ever-present breeze on the Island becoming a godsend as the sun beat down out of a cloudless, blue sky. In the Golf Links Hotel, those that had not signed the repatriation form were given new accommodation addresses and soon hundreds of women could be seen lugging suitcases and bags up and down The Promenade as they sought out their new abodes.

While Tilly continued to juggle her duties in the kitchen with her more physical and emotional needs that only a certain Italian gentleman could satisfy, Ruby was given total responsibility for the boiler-room. In addition to her regular stoking duties, she now had to compile the staffing roster as well as liaising with Mrs Mylechreest when fresh supplies of coal were required. The task of staffing was solved with the arrival of three German sisters: Dagmar, Brunhilde and Heidi Schwarzenberger. All three, together with their father, had been rescued by a Royal Naval frigate when the family fishing boat had begun sinking in the North Sea just two days before the War was declared.

Unfortunately for them, by the time they had been taken back to port in Portsmouth, they had been classed as Prisoners of War and therefore had to be incarcerated. They were big, jolly women with thick muscular arms and strong backs and Ruby was delighted to learn that one of their main jobs on the boat was to stoke the boiler. To them there was no better way of passing the time until they got back home to Büsum in northern Germany than to shovel huge amounts of coal. Indeed, when they hadn't got anything to do, they had competitions between themselves, and anyone else who cared to try their luck, as to who could shovel a given amount of coal from one pile to another in the quickest possible time. Hundreds of tons must have been shovelled needlessly by the women, but they seemed to like nothing better and Ruby never had any need to find others to stoke the boiler.

One of the other newcomers to the Golf Links Hotel was Annalise Braun, who Ruby literally bumped into one morning on her way out of the front door. It was a genuine accident, two people going round a corner at the same time, but Annalise's reaction was unexpectedly hostile and aggressive. "Look, I'm sorry, Annalise" apologised Ruby. "I didn't see you coming."

But Annalise immediately rounded on Ruby. "Don't patronise me. You're all the same. You think I can be intimidated but you're not going to beat me. I know what I know and it stays in here" and she tapped her forehead.

"I don't know what you're talking about" said Ruby, absolutely flabbergasted.

"I don't trust you. You're nasty" spat Annalise. "I've heard things about you. You're just like the others. I'll show you, just you see." With that she pushed passed Ruby and went into the Hotel.

Ruby stood, looking after her: astonished. What had she done to her? "She's bonkers" she said out loud. "Totally raving."

The encounter continued to play on Ruby's mind throughout the day and eventually she decided to talk to Mrs Mylechreest about it. However, after numerous visits to her office only to find her in one meeting or another, it wasn't until nine o'clock that evening when they met up.

"Hello Ruby. Something wrong with the boilers? Don't usually see you at this time of night."

"Look I'm sorry to bother you when you must be shattered but I bumped into Annalise Braun this morning."

"Yes, she's one of the new arrivals. Is there a problem between you two?"

"No, nothing like that. I literally bumped into her by the front door and she reacted so very strangely and aggressively I was actually quite frightened. Look I don't like to say this, but I don't think she's very well."

"Well, there does seem to be something going around. My sister's had a nasty cough for weeks now."

"No, I didn't mean that sort of unwell. I meant... well...I think she might be going a bit mental."

"Oh, my dear. I'm sure you just caught her at a bad time. With all that's happened to you women, the moving into the Golf Links might just have been the last straw for her. Just give her time and I'm sure she'll settle down. You'll see."

"But you didn't see her eyes. They were weird, staring."

"Look, we'll both keep an eye on her. Let's see how she is in a couple of days."

But they didn't have to wait a couple of days.

The following day, being Sunday, was the day when those who were so inclined went off to St Catherine's Church immediately after breakfast. Their numbers always included the three Schwarzenberger sisters, which meant that Ruby had to do the stoking duties first thing. With the new girls now taking the brunt of the physical work, Ruby found stoking the boiler really hard work and she was really looking forward to getting cleaned up and going back to bed when she'd finished.

Once everything in the boiler-room had been done that needed doing, she walked up the stairs, removing her head-scarf as she went, and went to open their bedroom door. But it was locked from the inside. Strange, the doors were never locked. "Tilly. Wake up" she shouted as she knocked on the door.

No answer.

"TILLY!" She shouted and knocked the door again, even louder. Then she thought she heard a sound from inside the room.

"C'mon Tilly. Open the door! I'm knackered. Don't mess about."
Again a noise from inside the room. "TILLY!"

"Go away."

"Who's that? Tilly is that you? Are you alright?"

"I said go away. This is my room now. They won't be listening to this room."

With horror, Ruby realised who it was: Annalise. "Annalise, where's Tilly? Is she alright?"

"Go away. I need to be quiet. Too much noise."

"Annalise, open the door. There's no one else here – it's just me. Just please open the door."

"You're not coming in. This is my room now. Go away."

By now some of the other residents had come to find out what all the commotion was about, and Ruby asked one of them to go and get Mrs Mylechreest. A few minutes later she arrived, drying her hands on her large pinafore.

"What's going on?" she said as she pushed her way through crowd standing in the corridor. "Ruby, what is all this?" Ruby explained and then Mrs Mylechreest hammered on the door. "Fräulein Braun, open the door, please. It's Mrs Mylechreest here. We must get into the room."

"Go away. This is my room now. Mine. Mine. MINE."

"Annalise" said Mrs Mylechreest, softer this time. "You must open the door, dear. Is Tilly with you?"

"You must be quiet" came Annalise's voice, barely a whisper now, from inside the room. "She's asleep."

"Oh my God!" cried Ruby.

"Annalise dear, please open the door" said Mrs Mylechreest, her calm voice belying her grave concern for Tilly's safety.

"GO AWAY! GO AWAY! GO AWAY! GO AWAY!" Annalise screamed hysterically and hammered on the other side of the door.

Fearing that any further attempts to get Annalise to open the door would only make matters worse, the hotelier moved everyone down the corridor and then told one of the girls to run down to the Camp Office and get them to telephone for the Police.

It was thirty excruciatingly-long minutes later when a young constable burst into the hotel followed, some minutes later, by a puffing Sergeant Pike, her chest heaving with the exertion of peddling her bicycle up from the village. Having leant against the pillars by the front door for a minute to regain her breath and her voice, she took charge by taking Mrs Mylechreest into her office, leaving the young constable to stand quietly outside the bedroom door to make sure nothing else happened to inflame the situation.

Ruby was left standing at the bottom of the stairs, apparently not required by Sergeant Pike to give her side of the story. Just then, the hotel's front door opened and in marched the Schwarzenberger sisters returning from church. Ruby was able to quickly explain what had happened and why they couldn't go passed the room but was completely taken aback when the eldest, Dagmar, just looked at her sisters, nodded and then led the three of them up the stairs on tiptoe.

The young constable never had a chance as Brunhilde wrapped her huge arms round him and whispered "Shh" into his ear. Dagmar and Heidi simply mimed a count of three and then charged at the door, which came off its hinges and toppled down onto a praying Annalise, who was kneeling on a rug behind it.

As Sergeant Pike went to race up the stairs, hearing the noise, she was confronted by the three sisters walking down the stairs: Dagmar with an unconscious Annalise in her arms, Heidi similarly carrying Tilly who was bound hand and foot and gagged with a pillow-case tied tightly around her mouth, and Brunhilde carrying the young constable, who had fainted.

Everyone applauded as the procession descended. Everyone, that is, except the Police Sergeant who was fuming: not so much at the action of the sisters for she was planning a similar assault, but at the embarrassment caused by the lack of fortitude of her young colleague.

As a straitjacketed Annalise was taken off in an ambulance and the shame-faced policeman was led away by his berating sergeant, Tilly was given a strong, sweet cup of tea as she explained what had happened. She'd been only half-awake and was aware that the bedroom door had been opened and shut. Thinking it was Ruby coming back, she continued to doze until a hand was suddenly put over her mouth. It was Annalise: her eyes huge and staring. Quickly Tilly had been bound up with the cord from her dressing gown and gagged by this woman who seemed to be possessed with enormous strength. "There was nothing I could do. She was just too strong."

"Well I'm glad you're alright" said Ruby.

"Yes, thanks for what you did."

"Thank the girls; they're the ones who rescued you."

Tilly turned her head and there were the three sisters, standing at the door and beaming back at her, their red cheeks glowing with pride and exertion.

Chapter 19

They'd lost all track of time, but the general consensus was that they'd been on the ship for just about four weeks. In that time only one thing had improved: very few of them were still being sea-sick, apart from during the storm. Everything else was worse: the weather was hot and the holds, where the prisoners were kept, were stifling; the now-warm and stale drinking water was being rationed; the potatoes were too as the remaining supplies were beginning to go mouldy; the prisoners were still allowed their fifteen minutes exercise per day but now the soldiers had devised a new form of entertainment by smashing empty beer bottles on the deck and making the prisoners walk over them in bare feet; and, of course, there was the ever-present threat of torpedoes.

There had been one alarm already, with shouts from the soldiers and the crew to go to their stations, unheeded screams from the prisoners to be unlocked from their potential communal coffins, prayers from the resigned and anger from the frustrated. But whether the incoming torpedo had malfunctioned or was outmanoeuvred by those controlling the Dunera, the upshot was that the ship continued on its way unmolested. For those who had already survived the sinking of the Arandora Star, the attack was a cruel reminder that once-in-a-lifetime horrors could still be repeated; that survival so far was no guarantee of safe passage in the future.

With no way out of their incarceration, some of the prisoners tried to lose themselves in games of cards or a last reading of a hidden letter from a loved one whose words were already known by heart. Some joined in prayers given in a form that they had never known nor in words they understood. And yet others just looked at friends and relatives: unsaid words seeking whatever comfort could be had in this shared nightmare.

There were footsteps on the stairs outside – running down to them. Then a voice through the door, the Bubble's, almost whispering that the torpedo had missed. Gasps and hugs of relief from the prisoners; joy at their continued good luck replacing the despair and humiliation brought about by their squalid conditions and by the daily abuse they suffered at the hands of some of the guards.

Jonny had told everyone what he had seen happening to the prisoners' suitcases and personal belongings and this had brought fury and tears in equal amounts from their owners. Two days after his session, one of their number was "volunteered" for spud-bashing duties and on return to the hold, he had confirmed that there were no longer any suitcases piled up at the back of the ship. Everything had been either re-distributed among the guards, and possibly members of the crew, or been thrown overboard.

With all of the prisoners now suffering with painful and sometimes infected feet as a result of the almost-daily broken glass routine, the Sergeant had insisted that they be given time to soak them in sea-water every day. "We don't want any feet dropping off, do we Corporal? And I think you'd better get your dustpan and brush out and sweep all that glass away otherwise someone might get into serious trouble." A statement that could be taken in many ways, but the Sergeant knew his message had got home. Within an hour, all of the glass was in the sea. In fact, many of the prisoners had taken the opportunity of washing their feet in the salty water to have a bit of a wash-and-brush-up of the rest of their body at the same time, although this was not encouraged by some of the soldiers who used the buts of their rifles to show any miscreant the error of his ways.

Unsolicited beatings were common-place and many of those held below suffered from a variety of cuts, contusions and small-bone fractures. None was spared: the old and/or sick were too slow, the young and relatively fit were too threatening and the scared and retiring were too cunning and must be up to something. Fortunately, there were a considerable number of medical doctors among the prisoners and they were called into action, tending the various needs of their fellows, as well as the guards and crew, throughout the ship. It was this free passage that allowed news of how others were coping, as well as messages for specific people, to be passed around the Dunera.

From what the boys could determine, they were all being treated pretty much the same: abominably.

The most consuming question of all concerned their destination. In the initial stages, everyone had assumed that they were bound for Canada and talk below decks had been about friends and relatives who were already there and how they had succeeded in building new lives for themselves. Promises had been made to new bosom friends that help would be provided once they landed in this new world. But this "new world" obviously wasn't where most thought it was because the journey there was becoming noticeably hotter. After they'd been at sea for ten days, the temperature on the deck was blistering and in the holds it was unbearable. It was then that the first mentions of Australia were heard. According to the Bubble, who was beginning to enter into snatched conversations with Jonny, the guards were none the wiser. The young soldier had had them all roaring with laughter when he told them that the Corporal was pissed off because news of their imminent departure from the UK came while his wife was away shopping with her mother in Liverpool, leaving him at home minding the kids. He'd had to dump them on a neighbour and run. No note, nothing. Although none of the soldiers had ever met the Corporal's wife, they were all convinced that it was she who ruled the roost in the Corporal's house and he was certainly going to be in for it when he eventually got home. What a shame!

They'd had only the one storm: lightning, huge claps of thunder, waves that crashed over the ship, more prayers, more fear, more vomit. But afterwards there came a sudden stillness. Peace amid the moans. Pete, his bruises from that first beating just about faded, lay on his mattress watching a beetle negotiate its way out of the stream of vomit and urine that washed lazily across the floor with the motion of the ship. Every time it succeeded in scrambling to safety, Pete nudged it back into the rank liquid. Time after time this happened and eventually it was Pete who gave up, not the beetle. All of the prisoners were listless, hot and bored. The stench in the hold was no longer something that concerned them. The only time they noticed it was when they returned from their daily "treat" on deck. For a few minutes, breathing was done in small pants through the mouth, but after that they just breathed normally. You just got used to it.

With little energy to do anything else, sleep was the universal refuge from time that had all but stood still, but even Pete, despite his well-earned reputation, found it tedious to sleep twenty hours a day. He turned onto his back and listened to Charlie's snores. Jesus, what would Myrna think if she could see this now? As he counted the rivets in the steel beam above him, as he had done many, many times before, he reviewed their journey so far: the policemen coming to their house, Ruby telling them to look after each other and write to their mother – some chance they'd had of doing that, the interrogation when he was told about Ruby's spying and how he could help her by spying on Burfeind and his crew, Ascot Racecourse and Manny's cure for bed-bugs – where was Manny? – that bastard sergeant who was just looking to be thumped, Warth Mill – just the thought of it made Pete shudder, Huyton Camp which seemed to be so luxurious by comparison, the Arandora Star with all that fucking barbed wire – someone should be shot for that, the explosion, the sea, the cold, Lino Gallina – poor little sod. And then this bag of worms. Christ Almighty.

He thought about Ruby again and what might be happening to her – were they honouring the bargain? He hadn't seen Burfeind since the Arandora Star – did he escape? If he did, had the Intelligence bods put someone else in place to watch him? Perhaps Burfeind was on board the Dunera. Nah!.... Maybe? If he was, would they want him to carry on spying on him once they'd arrived in Australia or Timbuktu or wherever it was they were heading? If he wasn't, did the deal about Ruby getting special treatment still stand? Who knows?

He thought about his mother. Mutti. She must be frantic with worry although Ruby at least would have written – if she was allowed to. Bombs! Had there been any on that part of London? Was Mutti safe? Was Dot safe? Christ, this bastard war. He turned over onto his side again. The beetle had gone but the yellow-brown stream hadn't, it was still gently sloshing down a gully in the steel-plated floor inches from Pete's mattress. He turned onto his back again and recounted the rivets for the millionth time but then gave up and closed his eyes. No sooner were they shut than there was a knock on the door. No one in the room seemed to have heard it so he got up and walked to the door. He tried the handle. It wasn't locked. He opened the door and there was Myrna Loy, standing in the corridor wearing a long, silver evening gown which was possibly about the thickness of a coat of paint. She had nothing underneath it. The neck-line plunged to her navel and Pete could make out a small mole on the underside of her left breast. As he looked at it, the mole changed shape: it became two tiny smiling lips. Well, I'd be smiling too if I was in their position, he thought.

"Well, aren't you going to invite me in?" Myrna purred.

Pete panicked. He couldn't let her see the squalor of this place. He looked back at the room. All the men there, including his brothers were naked; their filthy bodies grotesque in the gloom; their toothless grins urging him to show her in so that.....he didn't want to think what they would do.

"No, I can't" he said, turning back to face her. But she was now his mother in her Sunday pinny. "Mutti. What are you doing here?"

His mother just smiled, knowingly. Pete turned back to the room to tell Charlie and Jonny that their mother was here, but his brothers had obviously heard because they were frantically trying to get their clothes back on. "You'll have to wait" said Pete as he turned back, but he was speaking to Myrna again.

"Why are you being like this, Pete? Why won't you let me in? Have you got a girl in there? You have, haven't you?" and she pushed passed Pete and came into the room. "Oh, God!" she cried. "This is disgusting. Is this how you live? In this filth? With these awful men? I won't stay in this wretched place for another second. We're finished." She turned and walked back to the door.

"No, wait" cried Pete. "It's not what you think. They make us live like this. They treat us like animals."

Myrna just looked into his eyes with contempt and disbelief. What she said next absolutely floored Pete. "I always like looking at the oak trees in May."

"What?" said Pete, even though his jaw felt like it had dropped through the floor.

"Especially when the sun shines on them in the late afternoon." It was the Corporal who answered, appearing behind her. He kissed her bare shoulder and then smiled smugly at Pete.

"You bastard" shouted Pete and lunged at him. But the door closed before he could land a punch. "Corporal! CORPORAL. YOU BASTARD. MYRNA, COME BACK. MYRNA."

"Pete, give it a rest, will you." It was Charlie, shaking him awake.

"Oh" said Pete, apologetically. "I must have been dreaming."

"Mmm" said Charlie. "Now there's a surprise."

Suddenly there was the sound of running down the corridor outside. "ALL HANDS ON DECK" someone shouted. Someone else shouted the word "TORPEDO."

Oh God, not again. The men in the hold just looked at each other and collectively held their breath for a few seconds as if that would make the threat more discernable. The running soon ceased. Apart from the sound of the ship's turbines, there was no sound. Then there was silence. The engines had been stopped. Someone fainted and the noise caused everyone to turn and look at the culprit, an old man, crumpled in a heap in a stream of urine. Someone knelt down and moved his mouth out of the brew. Everyone else remained motionless. Everyone else thought that if the torpedo struck this time they had no chance of survival whatever. They were locked in. This was to be their tomb, their shared coffin.

Then gentle footsteps could just be heard coming down the stairs outside. The lock was turned in the door. It opened just enough for a head to appear. Big eyes searching. The Bubble. He just looked for Jonny and, having found him, motioned for him, and therefore all of them, to stay still and quiet. Then he closed the door, but he didn't lock it. He was giving them a chance to survive and they all knew it.

The silence seemed endless. No one dared to move, or even cough, sneeze or fart. It seemed that the whole ship was holding its breath now.

Then, ages later they heard laughing and footsteps on the deck above. Men were shouting orders. Whistles were blowing.

Another escape! How many chances did they have? They heard the key turning in the lock. They were safe: at least for the moment.

Chapter 20

Some of the young German women were naked and lying on towels which they'd put down on patches of the small beach that they had cleared of rocks. Others, with bathing costumes or without, threw a tennis ball back and forward to each other: laughing and screaming. All were totally unconcerned that, although they were hidden from the main road and the track that ran round the north side of the bay between the Spaldrick and Bradda Head, they could still be seen by some of the local menfolk who seemed to find themselves in the undergrowth further down the slope. Accidentally, of course.

Ruby sat on a rock and watched the women. Once, as the result of a dare by Tilly, she'd agreed to take all her clothes off and had been surprised that she had quite enjoyed the strange sense of freedom of swimming naked, but she'd felt too self-conscious when she came out of the water and hadn't tried it again, much to Tilly's amusement.

The day was hot: very hot. Even the Island's constant breeze seemed like it was coming from the Sahara. The mid-August sunshine was so fierce that the tar in the road surface outside the railway station was melting. Small children were prodding it with sticks and flinging the gooey, black treacle into the air: their mothers' not best pleased with the ensuing mess they made of themselves.

Sitting by the sea was the only place that was comfortable and, with Tilly away yet again on the Dig, Ruby was free to enjoy her time away from the Golf Links Hotel in whatever way she chose. The Schwarzenberger girls were a godsend and, even though the temperature in the boiler-room must have been a hundred degrees or more this morning, they just loved every minute there. It was their dedication to duty which enabled Ruby to finish her chores and be away before lunchtime. Today, she'd walked along the track that led up to the old mine workings above the cliff and watched the gannets diving into the sea for fish. Then she'd walked back along the lower path and down to the tiny rocky beach where the girls were. Now she planned to go across the rocks and round to the main beach and then along towards "Cheer ny Yindyssyn" where Tuppence, now universally known as Hannah, still lived with George. From there, she'd make her way back up to the Hotel along The Promenade. It was a walk that she'd done many times and it had always lifted her spirits by the time she'd got back: the wind in her hair and the salt spray on her face seemed to release her somehow. But not today.

Today she couldn't put her finger on it but something was different. Nothing to do with the weather, which suited Ruby just fine, and the gannets had put on a spectacular display. No, today there was something else, but she just couldn't work out what it was. At one point she thought that she was being followed, but could see no one. She took to singing at the top of her voice: "Sing as we go and let the world go by", the Gracie Fields song. It didn't matter that she couldn't hit the high notes. No one could hear her, could they? She scrambled across the rocks and then back onto a path which led up through a small spinney before descending back on itself to the beach. Coming from the glare of the open seashore, Ruby found the shade of the trees made everything dark and cool, but it was so refreshing.

She was about ten yards in when it came. "Not much of a singer, are you?" A voice from the trees to Ruby's right.

"Who's there?" said Ruby, the hairs on the back of her neck instantly erect.

"I hate that song and I could never understand what people saw in that singer, what's-her-name. Sounds like a cat being strangled. Have you ever heard a cat being strangled?"

"Who are you?" Ruby was scared; the voice had unnerved her and she began to edge back towards the entrance to the spinney where she'd come in but the voice now came from somewhere in that direction.

"Don't you know? I'm disappointed you have forgotten me so soon."

"Tilly, if that's you, stop messing about. This isn't funny. You're scaring me."

"Oh, we're scared are we? Well, I'm afraid your little friend, the blonde whore, is not here to save you this time." The voice had a definite viciousness about it.

Ruby looked to where the track disappeared into the trees up ahead. Could she outrun whoever was behind her?

"Think you can make it? Why don't you try?" The voice had moved. It was now coming from Ruby's right again.

"Look, stop this" said Ruby, trying to sound assured and brave and feeling anything but. "Come out where I can see you."

"Is that what you'd like? To see me." The voice was now coming from somewhere up ahead.

"Look, you've had your fun, but enough's enough."

"Am I scaring you really? I thought you wouldn't be scared of anything. I'm quite surprised."

There was something about the voice that was familiar, but Ruby couldn't put her finger on it. "Well now you know. So if you don't mind, I'm going to resume my walk." Ruby turned to go back the way she had come; back towards the small beach where the German girls were.

"I don't think you should be going back that way, my dear. It's not safe and besides those whores are not nice girls. You're better off coming with me."

"I don't want to go with you."

"But, my dear, you don't have a choice. You see, if you don't come with me, you'll stay here……..for ever."

"Look, unless you come out here where I can see you, I'm going to count to three and then I'm going to scream so loudly they'll hear me in London. And there's bound to be some of the peeping toms around here somewhere."

"Hah! Do you think they'll come to help you? Those perverts will be out of here the moment you open your mouth."

Ruby knew she was right. The men wouldn't want their wives finding out they were over this way. But she had no choice. "One!" Ruby looked around her. Nothing, just trees and sunshine shafting through their leaves. "Two!" Again she looked around but again, nothing. She took a deep breath. "Th…"

"Hello, my dear." Annalise Braun was standing right in front of her, her eyes wild and wide.

"You. But you're in hospital."

"Oh that dreadful place. As soon as they found there was nothing wrong with me, they discharged me."

Could that be true? Could they have done their tests and found she was alright. Ruby doubted both assumptions. There was no way she could have been released so quickly. There was only one other alternative: she must have escaped. Oh, Jesus. "Eh, how about we have a nice stroll back up to the road, Annalise? You can tell me all about your bookshop in Croydon" Ruby said, trying with all her might to sound calm and unthreatening. "Maybe we can have an ice-cream."

"Oh, that sounds nice, dear. Let's go this way." Annalise was indicating a narrow path which led up the slope through the trees.

"But the path to the road is that way" Ruby said, pointing in another direction.

"I said we'll go this way. When we get to the top of the slope, we'll turn back onto the main path. You go first, my dear." Annalise smiled, but it was only with her mouth, her eyes were cold and piercing.

The slope was so steep, Ruby had to work her way up on all fours. Then she realised that if she was struggling to get up the slope, then so would Annalise be. If she could make the ground fast enough, she might be able to make a run for it.

"Wait" said Annalise, as if she could read Ruby's mind. "You're going too fast. Stop still."

Ruby carried on faster. Now was her chance.

"STOP. BITCH."

Panic overtook Ruby but there was only five yards to go before she got to the path at the top of the slope. She was out of breath but there wasn't a snowball's chance in hell that she was going to stop. Then she heard Annalise coming up behind her like a gazelle. It was as if she was flying. Suddenly Ruby felt an excruciating pain in the back of her right calf. She screamed and fell back into the ferns that covered the slope on either side of the path.

"Now that should slow you down, my dear. Naughty of you to try and run away from Mummy."

Ruby turned to face Annalise who was wide-eyed and panting with the exertion. In her hand was a small kitchen paring knife, its blade covered in blood. Ruby's blood. Ruby clenched the stinging wound. God it hurt. "You stabbed me" she cried.

"It was for your own good, my dear. Mustn't have you running away again. You might get knocked over by the traffic on the main road. Now, Mummy will take you somewhere nice and quiet and we can have a lovely little chat, just the two of us. Won't that be nice, Veronica dear?"

"But I'm not Veronica. I'm Ruby. Don't you remember? And I'm bleeding badly."

"Nonsense, my dear. You've just scratched yourself on a thorn. Shall Mummy spit on it to make it better like she did when you were a little girl?"

"No" gasped Ruby. "Leave me alone." But Annalise grasped her by the arm and bodily lifted her out of the ferns and pushed her up the slope; using the same raw strength that she showed when she had taken Tilly hostage at the Hotel.

Every step that Ruby took on her right leg was like the knife going in again and again. She could feel the blood running down her leg into her ankle-socks. Her foot was now squelching in its shoe. "It hurts. Annalise, don't do this." Annalise rushed up to Ruby's side.

"What did you say? How dare you call your mother by her name? MUMMY! Do you hear? Say it. SAY IT!" and she held the knife an inch from the end of Ruby's nose. "SAY IT!"

"Mummy" said Ruby, instantly deciding that playing along was her only option while she waited for a better chance.

"That's better. Now let's get on. Your father will be home soon and wanting his tea, no doubt, before he goes down the pub" she added with a sneer.

Once they reached the top of the slope, Ruby made to go to her right, back towards the main road, but Annalise stopped her. "Not that way, Veronica dear. This way" and she grabbed Ruby's hand and dragged her to the left. As they stumbled along the path, Ruby could hear the sounds of the German women in the bay below. She thought about screaming for help, but what if their sounds and the noise of the waves drowned her out. Worth a try if it wasn't for the knife. The presence of the knife had changed everything and Annalise looked as if she was capable of anything. God her leg hurt.

Annalise dragged Ruby around the headland and eventually Ruby could see that they seemed to be heading back to the old mine workings. The only remnant of the past was the tall, brick-built tower that Ruby presumed had once held the winding gear. On the side away from the sea, what looked like a chimney had been incorporated into the towering wall, its bricks beginning to show the signs of crumbling. On the north side was a heavy door but this was barred and padlocked.

"Oh, bother. Mummy's locked herself out. Silly me. Well, we'll just have to wait 'til Daddy gets home, won't we, Veronica dear?" But Ruby was concentrating on staunching the flow of blood from her calf. She pressed her handkerchief tightly against the cut, but the crimson liquid was soon oozing through her fingers.

She knew from when she used to go to the St. John's Ambulance Brigade meetings that the only thing she could do was to lift it up to stop the flow, so she sat down and raised her leg up, resting it against the tower.

"That's it, Veronica dear. We might as well be comfortable while we wait."

"Look An…..Look, I'm really not Veronica. I'm Ruby. Don't you remember?"

"You always did play funny little games: pretending you were someone else."

"But I'm not pretending. I'm Ruby Becker from Islington."

"Yes dear, of course you are. Now try and be quiet so that I can think about what we can have for tea."

Although the pain in her leg was still very sharp and stinging, Ruby thought it didn't seem to be bleeding quite so much now that it was raised and supported by the wall. Annalise seemed to be calmer too. In fact she looked as if she might have fallen asleep, but there was no way Ruby was going to try and escape. She knew that she wasn't going to be able to move fast, certainly not as fast as Annalise seemed to be able to move. Her only hope was that someone would come along and that they would scare Annalise off. But no one came.

"I need to go to the toilet" said Ruby after trying to ignore the messages she'd been getting from her bladder for the last hour at least. She gingerly got to her feet; her head throbbed from the stress and the lack of water to drink, her leg throbbed with the pain from the wound, but it did seem to have stopped bleeding.

"Shall Mummy hold your dress out of the way, then?"

Ruby was mortified. "No" she shouted. "I don't need your help. I just want some privacy."

"Oh don't be silly, my dear. I've watched you go hundreds of times."

"Well, not this time. Can you please go round the other side of the tower?"

"You must think I'm stupid, my dear. Mummy's not going to let you run away from her again…ever."

"I promise I won't run away" but Annalise just stared coldly at her. Ruby was getting desperate in more ways than one. "Well at least turn your back."

"Alright, my dear, but I really can't see why you're making such a fuss." Annalise turned her back and Ruby pulled her knickers down and crouched as best she could. The pain in her calf was excruciating but she couldn't hold back any more. It was when she was mid-flow that she looked up to see that Annalise was watching her; her face having taken on a twisted, perverted leer.

"You're sick" said Ruby, feeling Annalise's eyes devouring her.

"Not at all, my dear. I feel on top of the world, but I do wish your father would get home. We need to get inside and get the tea on the go. And a nice cup of tea would be good, too."

It was nearly two hot and thirsty hours later that Ruby thought she glimpsed a face in one of the bushes on the top of the slope away to her left. She blinked and looked again but there was nothing there. The thirst is making me hallucinate, she thought. Perhaps I'm as mad as she is. By keeping her leg propped up against the wall, she had managed to stop the bleeding, although as soon as she tried lowering it to the ground, it started again. She knew that if she was going to escape it would have to be sudden and decisive. There was absolutely no chance she would be able to overwhelm Annalise physically: she was just too strong. She could try disabling her: hitting her over the head with a rock or lump of wood, but the area was clear of any likely weapons. Still, if they moved to somewhere else there might be that possibility. Certainly outrunning her would be impossible. She turned to Annalise who was crouched with her arms around her legs and rocking rhythmically back and forwards. "How long are you going to keep me here?"

Annalise turned to face her, a vacant expression on her face as if she had been brought back suddenly from a place far, far away. "Why, Veronica, this is your home. Where else should you be?"

As Ruby looked at her captor, she noticed a movement in the bushes about a hundred yards beyond Annalise. A dog maybe?

"Why are you doing this?" said Ruby.

"Doing what, my dear?"

"Keeping me here. I need to see a doctor. This cut has got to be stitched"

"Don't be silly. It's only a scratch. You've only snagged yourself on a bush. Anyway, Daddy will be home soon. You know what will happen if we're not here when he comes home from work."

"No, what will happen?"

"You know very well you'll have to calm him down by doing all those special, nasty things he likes you to do to him."

Oh my God, thought Ruby. What sort of life did Veronica have? If she existed at all, that is. She stared at Annalise, who had lain on her back and closed her eyes. She's insane, thought Ruby, I know that. But what made her go like it? Was her husband abusing their daughter? Her as well, probably. God there's some sick people in this world. As she stared at Annalise, there was a movement behind a gorse bush fifty yards away to her right. Definite this time. A man. A man in a navy-coloured jacket and white stripes on his arm. A policeman. He was coming out from behind the bush and trying desperately to do it silently. Two other policemen were coming into view further round to her right. She looked over her shoulder and saw four soldiers coming over the edge of the slope that ran down to the rocks.

Now they were all running .

Annalise heard them and leapt to her feet. She glared at Ruby, snarling like a cornered tiger. "You bitch! You whore!" She spat as she spoke. The knife was raised. Ruby was convinced she was about to attack her. She, too, was on her feet now. She could feel the blood begin to trickle down her leg again. She braced herself for the inevitable lunge and wondered if the men could get to them before Annalise had cut her to pieces. Visions of Mutti and Dot and the boys all together at Christmas flashed through her brain. But Annalise's expression suddenly changed: from tiger to kitten in nought seconds flat. She smiled at Ruby: warmly, apologetically and then she took a quick glance at the policemen and soldiers rushing towards her.

To Ruby, everything from then on went into slow motion as she watched Annalise turn and sprint towards the cliff. There was no sound whatsoever; the raw animal agility of Annalise easily evading the arms of two of the soldiers who were running up from the direction of the cliff. She didn't jump from the cliff, she ran over it; deliberately, silently.

Ruby gasped but it was done. She hadn't screamed or shouted. She didn't feel any sudden sense of sorrow for Annalise; she was safe now, that was all she could think of. All she felt was an overwhelming sense of relief that the nightmare was over and she collapsed to the ground.

Chapter 21

(Diary entry for September 5th 1940 by Alan Frost, Medical Officer, The Royal Australian Army Medical Corps)

Jesus, what a bloody awful day. Rupert went sick, the lucky bugger, so at last minute yours truly "volunteered" to inspect ship arriving from England, HMT Dunera. According to info from British authorities, she was supposed to be transporting hardened German and Italian fascists.

On August 27th, 500 prisoners offloaded at Melbourne and taken to Tatura Camp. Apparently no personnel available to inspect there.

Early start. Arrived 0600 at Sydney Harbour. Dunera had come in sometime during night. Even at that hour, hundreds of spectators – booing, shouting, almost made me blush to hear some of the things they were saying they'd like to do to these blokes. Right bloody pantomime.

First on board. Christ the smell. Didn't have to go below to smell it. Thought someone had died.

Pommy soldiers were a right bunch – no discipline, uncouth lot – where did they get them from?

Dunera apparently built to take about 1500 passengers and crew. According to the paperwork, there was over 2500 shipped from Liverpool, England. Thought it must be a mistake. I was wrong.

Went below decks to where prisoners held. Nearly threw up. Christ I wouldn't keep a dog in those conditions. Boy, did they cram them in. Drinking water foul – warm, stale. Portholes battened down – no air, stifling, God knows what it was like going through the Tropics.

If these are what the English call "a considerable risk to National security", they must be really paranoid. The poor sods on this ship were emaciated, exhausted – both physically and psychologically, and suffering signs of physical abuse [see below].

Couldn't understand why so many of the prisoners spoke with English accents. Also Jews everywhere. I don't know what I was expecting by "Nazis", but this wasn't it.

Guards kept trying to stop me getting anywhere near them: telling me it was for my own good. Soon realised it was because they didn't want me talking to them. Had to order their Sergeant out of the way. Thought he was going to burst blood vessel.

In one cell spoke to three brothers, English with German father, non-Nazis. Told me that they were only allowed on deck fifteen minutes per day. Showed me their mattresses – urine soaked, due to toilet overflowing onto deck and nowhere for it to go.

Told by everyone they'd been abused by guards – regular beatings, made to walk barefoot through broken beer bottles, <u>all</u> called "Jewish bastards."

Asked for their papers. No one had any – taken by guards along with all valuables. Asked guards where they were kept – apparently all lost overboard in storm. Not convinced. Brothers say saw guards taking valuables for themselves.

Saw the food store – most of it rotten.

Over 50 men sick – no wonder. Surprised it's not more.

Have to do report tomorrow. I know these men shipped under difficult circumstances but no need for this. Someone's going to cop for it. Appalling.

About an hour after the Australian Inspection personnel had disembarked, the door to their cell was unlocked and the Corporal, with two of his squaddies plus the Bubble, came in. Although all of them had rifles, none of them pointed them at the prisoners this time. "Well, Gentlemen" the Corporal needlessly shouted to attract their attention because everyone was already silent and looking at him. "Time for you to leave us, I'm afraid. You're about to become the responsibility of the Royal Australian Army. Gather you're personal possessions and follow the Bubble up on deck."

That's a joke, thought Charlie, nobody's got any personal possessions, you nicked them all.

In single file, they went up to the deck and joined the queue waiting to file on to the gangway that had been positioned at the side of the ship. Once on deck everyone could get their first look around.

"So this is Australia" said Charlie.

"Don't look any different to Liverpool, if you ask me" replied Pete. "Just another dock."

"And it's raining" said Jonny, raising his face to the sky and feeling the refreshing drizzle.

As they shuffled towards the gangway they got their first sight of the crowds below. "Jesus" said Jonny, "There's hundreds of them."

"Nice of 'em to turn out in such rotten weather" Pete said with a grin.

"I don't think the natives are too pleased to see us, though" said Charlie. "Look!" And with that, some in the crowd started hurling eggs and tomatoes at those already going down the gangway.

"Nah, they're just being friendly" said Pete. "They know we haven't 'ad a square meal for ages." Despite the aggression that was clearly being directed at them, the brothers laughed, the thought of being on dry land again making them almost hysterical.

At the top of the gangway stood the Bubble. He nodded to some of the men that he recognised and sometimes received a nod in return.

"Cheerio, Bubble" said Pete, when it was his turn. The Bubble half-smiled, almost embarrassed.

Then came Jonny and the boy said "Sorry" quietly. Jonny just looked back at him, trying to think of something appropriate to say. In the end he just winked and smiled at him. "Take care, Colin."

Having run the gauntlet of the crowds, the prisoners were escorted along the dock towards a variety of waiting army trucks and coaches.

"I feel pissed" said Jonny.

"Yeah, me too" said Pete.

"I think everyone does" said Charlie. "Look at the way everyone's staggering. We've just been on that fucking ship so long, that's all."

It was true, every one of the prisoners looked like he'd had a skinful.

For the rest of that day and the next, the prisoners were billeted in various places around Sydney. By comparison with the deprivations of the Dunera, it was luxury: halfway-decent food, showers, and beds. So, by the time it came for them to move again, they were all feeling considerably better.

On the morning of September 7th, four trains, loaded with two thousand prisoners of war and internees plus a new set of guards, Australian this time, set off to journey westward, arriving at the town of Hay in the late afternoon. Railway stations bearing strange and exotic names such as Cootamundra, Wagga Wagga, Coolamon and Narrandera just seemed to rise out of the scrubby countryside as if they had been dropped there by a spaceship. Kangaroos, the first they had seen outside London Zoo, seemed to revel in trying to outrun the train.

So this was Australia!

From the quaint Hay Railway Station they were taken, under the guard of the16th Garrison Battalion of the Australian Army to a purpose-built Internment Camp which had been set up on the site of Hay's showground and racecourse. In many ways it was remarkably similar to Ascot Racecourse where the boys had started their nightmare all those weeks ago. The accommodation was in wooden huts and it had roads, a water supply and electric lights.

Yet, within hours of arriving, classrooms were operating again just like they had been in Huyton. "Fancy giving it another try, Jonny?" asked Charlie.

"D'you know" said Jonny, "I've actually quite missed it." Then his smile vanished. "Poor old Samuel. I still see his face disappearing under the waves."

"Yeah, so do I" said Charlie, sombrely, "and we still don't know what's happened to Manny."

After several minutes of quiet contemplation, Pete said "Right, now's the time to get those letters to Mutti written, otherwise we'll be in even more trouble." So, four months after Ruby had told them to make sure they wrote regularly to their mother, the boys had their first opportunity to write a letter home.

The boys were to stay together in Camp 7 at Hay for another six months at which point they were moved, along with hundreds of others, to the Internment Camp at Tatura, about a hundred miles north of Melbourne.

On the morning of Sunday, December 7, 1941, the Japanese Navy mounted a surprise military strike against the United States' naval base at Pearl Harbor in Hawaii. Fearing an imminent invasion, the Australian authorities ordered the internment of all Japanese residents in Australia. As a result, many of the internees, the Darling brothers included, were moved out of Hay to make space for the influx of Japanese. They were taken to Loveday Internment Camp, some three hundred miles to the west and here they would spend most of 1942, alongside Germans, Italians, Japanese and Chinese, growing all sorts of vegetables, tobacco and pharmaceutical crops as well as woodcutting and charcoal burning.

In September 1942 all three brothers were given the opportunity to join the Royal Australian Army rather than continue to be detained at Loveday. On October 16th, at Royal Park, Victoria, Charlie, Pete and Jonny joined up.

Chapter 22

"How are you this fine and wonderful morning?" Tilly had bounced into the room just as Heidi Schwarzenberger was helping Ruby to get out of bed. "Here, let me help you."

"I wish you two would stop fussing over me like I was eighty. I'm alright."

"But you've been through a nasty ordeal" said Tilly. "You've got to take it easy."

"Look" said Ruby, tetchily "I need to move about. The Doctor said so." Tilly looked hurt and frustrated.

"Oh, Tilly. Don't look like that. It's just that between the four of you….Oh I just need some time on my own. Please!"

Tilly knew it was true. In the week since the attack, she and the three Schwarzenbergers had been at Ruby's side round the clock: fetching and carrying, washing and feeding. "Alright, we'll leave you in peace if you're sure. C'mon Heidi, let's go and find somewhere where we're appreciated." Heidi beamed at Tilly and then at Ruby and then they were gone.

Ruby smiled to herself. She really did understand that she was so fortunate to have friends that cared for her. She closed her eyes and lay back on her bed but immediately the cut on her leg started itching. She propped herself up and rubbed in some more cream that the doctor had given her. She'd had to have seven stitches in the wound and although she still felt tired, the pain in her leg had gone after three days. Now all she had was this infuriating itching as it knitted together.

For the umpteenth time, she thought over the events of the past week. Annalise hadn't died. Her attempt at flying off the cliff had ended in a crumpled heap on the slope which was just twenty feet below her take-off point. She suffered a broken ankle and a broken arm as well as cracking a couple of ribs and a collarbone and covering herself in cuts and bruises. But these would mend in time. It was her mental state that was likely to keep her hospitalised for a much longer period.

It turned out that Annalise, originally from Regensburg in southern Germany, had never been married and had never had a child. Veronica was a figment of her imagination or maybe a throwback to something in her own childhood. She had, according to Sergeant Pike when she'd come round to take Ruby's statement a couple of days later, been running a bookshop in Croydon which was suspected of being the centre of some "subversive doings". The stress of the investigation, whether the allegations were true or not, together with the internment on the Island, had been too much for Annalise and she had suffered a complete nervous breakdown. She would now be recovering from her injuries in a secure unit at Braddan Mental Hospital at Ballamona.

Despite what had happened, Ruby couldn't help feeling sorry for her assailant. If she hadn't found Tilly, maybe she would be in the same state. She lifted out the cardboard shoebox that she used to keep her letter forms and pencils in and looked at what she'd written so far to her mother. No mention of the attack, of course, just the usual stuff about how they were keeping and what they had been doing. She'd also asked if anything had been heard from the boys yet. She'd murder them when she got hold of them for not writing.

Ruby finished off her letter and put it on the dressing table which to anyone but Ruby and Tilly it would look just like an orange box stood on its end with a table-cloth over it, but to them it was a dressing table.

She walked round the room feeling the tightness in her damaged calf, but was only too aware that she had got away so lightly. Halfway across the room, she jumped as Tilly burst through the door.

"Look. Look." Tilly screamed and waved an official-looking letter in front of her startled friend. Ruby took the letter and started to read it but gave up almost immediately as Tilly saved her the bother.

"They're going to start Release Tribunals" she said, gleefully clapping her hands "and apparently I'm the first one to be called."

Ruby didn't know whether to laugh or cry. All she could say was "When?"

"Day after tomorrow. Isn't it wonderful?"

"Of course it is, love. I'm very pleased for you. It's terrific news." But she didn't look pleased and Tilly picked up on it straight-away.

"Oh, Ruby, please don't be miserable. We'll still see each other 'cos I'm not leaving the Island. I've got nothing to go back home for now. Everything I've come to love is right here on this Island. And anyway, I might not be successful."

"You will be" said Ruby seriously but managing a smile. "Why would you not be?"

"Oh! I can't wait until tomorrow to tell Rico" and she danced round the room with her pillow.

Ruby spent the rest of the day trying to be happy for Tilly but not succeeding very well. She really was pleased for Tilly; she hadn't deserved to be interned in the first place, but the thought of living here without her was just unbearable. She had no appetite for food, despite all the encouragement from Tilly, the sisters and even Mrs Mylechreest, who came in to see if she was alright. "Just not hungry at the moment. Perhaps I'll get something a bit later" she would say.

Her misery continued through into the night. It took ages before she could get off to sleep and then only to fall into a dream in which she was lying on the top of a cliff desperately hanging on to Tilly who had fallen over the edge. Tilly was screaming "Don't let me go! Don't let me go!" Then the hold broke and Tilly fell away into the black void below her. Ruby woke up with a start, sweat covering her neck and chest. It was dark in the room but she could make out the shape of Tilly in the dim light; she was snoring contentedly.

The following day began with Ruby trying not to feel selfish that at least half of her wanted Tilly to be rejected by the Release Tribunal. To compensate, she spent the couple of hours until Tilly had to go to the Dig, going through all the questions they could think she might be asked and rehearsing appropriate answers. In the late afternoon, with Tilly on one arm and Brunhilde Schwarzenberger on the other, Ruby managed to walk to the edge of the golf course where they sat for a while before gently making their way back to the Hotel. As they opened the door, they saw that the kind woman from the Commandant's office was talking to Mrs Mylechreest.

"Ah, here they are now" Mrs Mylechreest said when the door opened and the three girls came in. "Mrs Schiller has brought a letter for you, Ruby."

"For me? Thank you." She reached out to take it from the smiling Mrs Schiller who said "It came this morning and I knew you wouldn't be able to get down to pick it up, so I brought it up on my way home."

"That's kind of you. Thank you" said Ruby, looking at the envelope. It was identical to the one Tilly had received, from the Release Tribunal.

"Go on, open it" said Tilly.

"I'm too nervous" said Ruby, never once taking her eyes off the envelope.

"Do you want me to do it?" Tilly said, excitedly.

"No" she said sharply and then, realising she'd overreacted, she said softly "No. Thank you. I can do it." She was puzzled. This couldn't mean she was going before the Tribunal because the authorities knew she had been spying for the Germans. There was no chance she was going to be released so this must be to tell her that she was going to be on the Island until the war ended or maybe that she was to be sent to a prison somewhere.

"Come on, Ruby. Open it!" cried Tilly. "I'm going to wet myself in a minute."

Somewhat reluctantly, Ruby opened the envelope:

To Ruby Becker
The Release Tribunal of the State of the Isle of Man has been authorised by the Home Office to investigate the circumstances surrounding the detention of all those Prisoners of War and Internees who are currently held at Rushen Camp.

Therefore we require you to attend a meeting which has been arranged for you at 2.30pm on Wednesday 11th September 1940 at St Catherine's Church Hall, Port Erin.

Signed Magnus Whittaker, JP.
Chairman of the Release Tribunal

"Oh" gasped Ruby and burst into tears. Mrs Mylechreest wrapped her arms round her as Ruby sobbed into her neck.

Tilly took the letter and read it for herself. "It's exactly the same as mine except for your name and the time of the appointment. That's wonderful. Oh I'm so glad. Now both of us has a chance of being released together."

Ruby abruptly stopped crying and pulled away from Mrs Mylechreest, embarrassed that she had left a wet patch on her shoulder. She reached for her hanky and blew her nose. "Don't you see? It's their way of saying that they're going to review my situation and that maybe they're going to send me back to Holloway or some other prison."

All the smiles and joy that the others were feeling for her suddenly evaporated.

"Why?" cried Tilly. "I don't understand."

"Oh I'm sure that's not going to happen" soothed Mrs Schiller. "Perhaps I shouldn't say so, but I've not heard anyone suggest such a thing."

"I'm sure it'll be fine, dear" said Mrs Mylechreest. "I have a feeling that it'll be good for you."

"No it won't. You don't know…" Ruby was in tears again and turned to go up the stairs aided by Brunhilde's arm around her waist.

Tilly looked at Mrs Mylechreest and Mrs Schiller, quizzically and then followed them up the stairs. When Brunhilde had made sure Ruby was settled on her bed, she tactfully left her with Tilly. "I don't understand why you're so sure that they'll send you to prison."

"Because they will! Alright! Now please leave me alone."

"But why?"

"Because I want to be on my own for a bit."

"No, why are you so sure they'll send you to prison?"

"BECAUSE I'M A SPY. There, are you satisfied now?"

"I don't understand. You're not a spy. If you were, you'd still be in Holloway. They would never have let you out to come here if they thought you were a spy. Don't you see that?"

"I am a spy. I know it and they know it."

"Well I don't, so you'd better explain. Now" Tilly had taken on a role that Ruby had never seen in her before: serious, hard and in control.

Tilly sat on the side of her own bed. "Well. I'm waiting."

"I don't know how to explain."

"Well you'd better start at the beginning and tell me everything because you are in danger of loosing the best friend you've possibly ever had. I don't like it when people lie to me, and certainly not people I thought were my friends. So…."

So Ruby started at the beginning: how she'd first met Dieter, how she'd fallen in love with him or thought she had, how they'd gone for walks around London with him taking photographs of boring buildings and how he'd talked to her about the damage the Jews were doing as they were taking over all the businesses in London.

"I thought I knew it all after what he told me" said Ruby. "I was stupid. I know that now. Since I've met you and Amalia and all the others, I've realised just how wrong he was; how wrong I was. Oh Tilly, I'm so sorry."

"What I don't understand is why you didn't tell me. We've become like sisters, you and me. I didn't think there was anything that we didn't share. Now I find out that's not true. You've been lying to me all along."

"No it wasn't like that. Honest it wasn't. The thought of being without you in my life is just horrible. You became so dear to me that I just felt that if I told you everything you might not want anything to do with me again. And I couldn't bear that" and she burst into tears again.

Tilly watched her for a few minutes, not making any attempt to comfort her. Then she jumped to her feet and said "I'm going for a walk." With that she walked straight out of the room with the sound of Ruby sobbing in her ears.

It was almost curfew time, nine o'clock, when Tilly came back into the bedroom. Ruby still lay on the bed, her eyes red and swollen. "Hello" she said, sheepishly.

Tilly sat on the side of Ruby's bed. "I've made a decision" she said ominously. Ruby looked at her, scared to death that she was going to say she was moving to another room. Tilly continued, gravely. "I've decided that I'm going to stay here sharing with you until we find out what the Release Tribunals say about each of us." Ruby let out an audible sigh of relief. "But, and I'm going to say this only once: if I ever find out that you've lied to me again, that's it. Finished. Do you understand?"

"Yes" sobbed Ruby, tears streaming down her cheeks. "I'm so sorry."

"I know you were so much younger then, and naïve. You were in love and we all feel differently when we're in love. I know you've learnt a lot about what's happening in the world; that it's not all black and white like you thought. But I mean what I said. We mustn't have any secrets from each other. Is that alright with you?"

"Yes" said Ruby, throwing her arms round her friend's neck and sobbing uncontrollably with relief while Tilly patted her back.

Tilly's attendance in front of the Release Tribunal was a straightforward affair. She sat in front of a large table in the Church Hall, which had been cleared for the occasion. On the other side sat Mr Whittaker, the Chairman, together with Dame Johanna Cruickshank, and a Colonel something-or-other. Mr Whittaker had a thin manilla file open in front of him. He confirmed some of the personal details with Tilly, such as date of birth, former address and next-of-kin. Tilly told them about her grandparents' deaths and that she therefore had no idea who her next of kin was. The committee in front of her didn't seem to be that bothered and Mr Whittaker just made a note on the file and then he cleared his throat.

"Well, Miss Nussbaum, we have looked at all the relevant notes on this case, and together with the information that Dame Johanna has received about you, we consider that there is no longer any requirement for you to be detained under the Emergency regulations. You are free to go. Dame Johanna will arrange all the details. Would you close the door on your way out."

Tilly sat there, dumbfounded. "Is that it?"

"Yes" said Whittaker, "You can go."

"They've released me" screamed Tilly as she burst out of the Hall to find Ruby sitting on the wall with the Schwarzenberger sisters, Amalia and her mother and sister, Hannah and George, and Mrs Mylechreest together with about fifty other women, some of whom Tilly knew at least by sight, in a crowd beside her. Ruby hobbled immediately to Tilly and threw her arms around her neck.

"I'm so, so pleased. I told you they'd let you go, didn't I?"

Tilly beamed at her friend and then around at the rest of the crowd who started clapping. Even Sergeant Pike, standing by the gate, was clapping, having come round the corner to find what was going on.

Over the next few days, all sorts of things changed for Tilly: her Release documentation came through; she was appointed Assistant Manager of the Golf Links Hotel to help Mrs Mylechreest deal with the Nazi-sympathizing women occupants and their documentation, much of which was in German; and she was appointed to the unpaid position of Archaeological Liaison Officer, which basically meant that on her time-off from the Hotel she could still meet Rico at the Dig. This was Professor Bersu's idea; "Eet is the early vedding present, Ja?"

At the same time, Ruby was feeling increasingly nervous about her impending visit to the Release Tribunal, despite Mrs Schiller saying to her quietly one morning that everyone who had appeared before it so far had been released. "Someone's got to be first" Ruby had said.

When the day actually arrived, Ruby was at her lowest ebb, ever. She was short-tempered with Brunhilde over where a new delivery of coal was going to be put. She shouted at one of the other women who was running a minute over her allotted bathroom time. And she felt sick, as if she'd swallowed a football and it was stuck in her stomach. It wasn't that she was frightened that she wouldn't be successful: she already knew she wouldn't be. It was the anticipated humiliation of it all: being told she was like something that had crawled from under a stone, a criminal, worse, a traitor. She wondered how her mother would feel when she found out that her daughter was in prison for spying. She thought seriously about suicide: ways that she could do it; when it would be the right time. But, she knew that she would never have the guts.

Tilly was going to come with her to the hearing, but this meant that she had to work right through until two o'clock without a break. So it was nearly ten minutes past two when Tilly raced up the stairs.

"Are you ready? Sorry I'm late."

"That's alright. I was just wondering if I'd bother going anyway."

"Enough of that. Put you're mac on, looks like it might rain." Tilly held up the raincoat and Ruby reached backwards with her arms. "I'm scared, Tilly."

"You'll be alright. I'll be with you."

The walk down the road to the Church Hall was taken at a gentle pace because Ruby's leg, although healing nicely, was still quite tender. At spot on the dot of two-thirty, they entered the Hall. Ruby gave her name to a woman sitting by the door and was directed to an empty bench-seat at the side of the room. Tilly was told she must wait outside and, despite trying to argue that Ruby needed help in walking, was unceremoniously shown the door after blowing Ruby a kiss Good Luck. After five agonisingly long minutes, Ruby was ushered into the main Hall, which had been partitioned off by dark-green examination screens on castors. She was shown to the same chair that Tilly had sat in and introduced to Mr Whittaker and then to Dame Johanna and Colonel Jordan.

The initial procedure was the same for all and she was asked to confirm her date of birth, her address in London and next-of-kin.

"Thank you, Miss Becker" said Whittaker. "I have to say straight-away that I am exceedingly disappointed that it has been necessary to call you to this hearing. I can honestly say................"

As he continued to speak, Ruby thought "I knew it. They're going to tell me I'm a worthless traitor and that I'm going to be sent to prison."

".......sad duty................"

Ruby suddenly had visions of what it must be like to spend years in a locked cell in Holloway Prison and shivered.

"….so in view of that we have no option but to release you."

For ten seconds, Ruby just sat staring at Mr Whittaker, lost in her thoughts, then something forced her into reality. "Pardon" said Ruby, trying to unscramble her brain.

"Mr Whittaker has just informed you that a higher authority has ordered your release" said Dame Johanna. "In my opinion you are lucky not to have been hanged for treason. As it is, my office will let you have the necessary documentation within the next day or two. Now get out."

The door to the Church Hall opened and Ruby just stood there, her face drained of all colour. She looked stunned and just stared at the nothingness ahead of her. Tilly rushed over and put her arms round her.

"Oh love, I'm so, so sorry. Was it awful?"

Ruby raised her head and looked at her friend. "I…." Her mouth was dry and her voice sounded more like a frog's croak.

"Don't worry, love. We'll all look after you. Maybe there's some way we can appeal."

"No. You don't understand."

Tilly wasn't listening. She was already working out who she could contact to try and get Ruby's case looked at again. "I'll have a chat with Professor Bersu. He might know someone."

"They released me."

"And then there's Sergeant Pike and Mrs Mylechreest. Oh Ruby, I'm sure they'll be loads of people who will help us."

Ruby grabbed Tilly's shoulders and forced her friend to face her. "They released me. Tilly…. They released me. They released me and I don't know why."

"What? Oh that's wonderful. I told you it'd be alright, didn't I?"

"But why?"

"What did they say?"

"I don't know. It was all a blur. One minute he was saying how disappointed he was and the next I'm being released."

"I can't believe it. Both of us are free. Freeeeeeeeeeeee!" The sight of Tilly whirling around in front of the Church Hall stopped a couple of elderly locals in their tracks. They tutted, disapprovingly, to each other and then, muttering something about foreigners, they carried on walking, shaking their heads as they went.

"I still don't understand why they let me go. I'm guilty. I shouldn't be here, let alone free."

"You said that they told you it was because of orders from above" Mrs Mylechreest said as she handed Ruby a cup of Camp coffee, with a drop of "something special" in it.

Ruby took a sip of the hot liquid and felt the kick of the alcohol after a second or two: the first time she'd had any alcohol since the glass of port and lemon she'd had at Christmas. "Yes. That's what they said."

"So presumably that would be the Home Office or the War Office. Very strange. You obviously have friends in high places, my dear."

"Mmm" said Ruby. "Can't think who."

After a few minutes pondering who on earth could have authorised her release, Ruby's musings were interrupted by Mrs Mylechreest saying "Well, my dear, what are you going to do now? I'm afraid I can't take you on the books as well as Tilly."

"Oh, no, that's alright. I'm going to go home. With the boys God knows where and Dot getting wilder by the minute according to Mutti, I think I'd better get home and help her cope. Thanks anyway."

Two days later, Ruby had all her documentation, together with her ferry ticket and rail warrant to get her back to London. Her suitcase was packed and she'd said goodbye to the Schwarzenberger sisters, who's copious tears threatened to flood the floor of the lounge where they'd found her. They'd given her a posy of wild flowers and made her promise to come and visit them in Büsum after the war. She'd made the promise but they all knew it would never happen. She'd endured a hug from each of them that had left her with sore ribs and bruises on the tops of her arms which would last for weeks, but she'd miss them very much.

As the sisters walked sadly back to the boiler-room where, no doubt, they would have a coal-moving competition to raise their spirits, Amalia came into the Hotel with her mother and sister. The mother gave Ruby a small white handkerchief on which she'd embroidered "Thank you for saving my Amalia." This had set Ruby off again and, with tears flowing unrestrained down her cheeks, she hugged each in turn.

Saying goodbye to Mrs Mylechreest was altogether easier because each was determined that they wouldn't cry. "Take care of yourself, my dear. Have a safe journey home and give my regards to your mother. And if you ever decide to come over to the Island again, you will be welcome to stay here as my guest."

"Oh thank you, Mrs M."

The hotelier opened her mouth and was about to say "And don't call me Mrs M." but she just smiled and enveloped Ruby in her arms.

Saying goodbye to Tilly was strangely easy. Both the girls had cried and cried the night before as they discussed how often they would write to each other and what they would do with the rest of their lives. In a lull between tears, Tilly had said "Oh, by the way, we've decided our first daughter is going to be called Ruby." That had sent Ruby reaching for yet another hanky.

Now, standing on the pier watching the last crates being loaded onto the Princess Josephine Charlotte before the passengers were allowed to board, the girls just looked at each other with nothing to say and yet with so much to say. Then as the shouts from the crew for the passengers to get on board came from the ship, the girls hugged one last time. "Take care, love" whispered Tilly.

"You too."

Then standing at the stern of the ferry as it manoeuvred away from the pier, Ruby blew Tilly a kiss and shouted "I love you!"

Tilly smiled, blew the kiss back and mouthed "Me too."

Chapter 23

On August 14th 1940, the body of Emmanuel Goldfarb of Islington, London was found by a local fisherman, washed onto rocks near Glenlossera in County Mayo, Ireland. The body, however, was never identified and was buried in an unmarked grave in the grounds of St Muredach's Cathedral at Ballina on August 20th. It would have been Manny's twenty-second birthday.

Four days later, a couple walking their dog on a beach near Ardalanish on the Isle of Mull, Scotland discovered the body of Samuel Weiss, formerly of Linz, Austria. In his pocket were the remains of a letter and this provided sufficient identification to allow him to be buried in the Jewish Cemetery in Tobermory. He was fifty-eight.

Chapter 24

March 1952

"Alright, I'm coming."

The child, a girl, had just woken up and was crying for her mother who wiped her wet hands on the tea-towel and ran up the stairs to her daughter.

"Well, what's all this noise about, young lady? Did you have a nasty dream again?"

"There's a fox under the bed, Mummy. It was going to eat me."

This was the third time in as many nights that Shirley had woken to the same nightmare and Ruby was pretty sure why. She had just started at Meadowlark Primary School, which was not far from their home on a brand-new housing estate just off the Canterbury Road in the Surrey Hills area of Melbourne. It was the first time they had been separated from each other since Shirley was born and both had cried that first day. It wasn't that the five-year old didn't like being at the school, she loved it. It was just the going in the morning and saying goodbye that both mother and child found difficult.

Ruby crouched on all-fours and made a play of pulling out everything that was under the bed: shoes, toys, books and the old suitcase that she'd had all those years ago on the Isle of Man and which Shirley now used to keep her dolls' clothes in. "There's nothing here, darling. D'you want to have a look?"

Shirley cautiously lay on her stomach and lowered her head over the edge of the bed so that she could see that her mother was right. "You must have scared it away, Mummy."

"No pet, it was just a nasty dream. There wasn't a fox here – never was. You just try and get back to sleep now. Tomorrow's going to be a busy day at school. Didn't you say you've got to paint a picture of your hand?"

The child nodded.

"Well, that's going to be very difficult so you'll need all the sleep you can get, won't you?"

Again Shirley nodded and then she said "Mummy, can you sing that song for me?"

Ruby knew the one, Brahms' Lullaby: it was Shirley's favourite just like it had been Ruby's when her step-father had sung it to her and her brothers when they was a small.

Guten Abend, gut'Nacht,

mit Rosen bedacht,

mit Näglein besteckt,

schlüpf unter die Deck.

Morgen früh, wenn Gott will,

wirst du wieder geweckt.

Morgen früh, wenn Gott will,

wirst du wieder geweckt.

Guten Abend, gut' Nacht,

von Englein bewacht,

die zeigen im Traum

dir Christkindleins Baum.

Schlaf nun selig und süß,

schau im Traum's Paradies.

Schlaf nun selig und süß,

schau im Traum's Paradies.

Shirley was asleep before the end of the first verse but Ruby carried on singing for her own enjoyment while she thought of how her mother and step-father would have been so proud of Shirley had they both lived to see her. While her step-father had been dead for many, many years, Ruby's mother, Lily, had been killed in one of the last bombing raids that the Luftwaffe had mounted on London before the end of the War. So, with Dot living in North Carolina having married a GI, and Ruby's husband, Eric, having been lost at sea in a storm somewhere off Spain in 1946, she had decided that once the war was over she would emigrate to Australia where her three brothers had started new lives for themselves.

Shirley had slept soundly after that and went off to school happily, eager for the lesson in hand painting. Ruby cleaned the dishes and finished the housework chores that she'd earmarked for the morning and then sat down with a cup of tea. She picked up the latest letter from Tilly; she loved reading Tilly's letters, almost like having her in the room with her.

Dearest Ruby,

How are things in Oz? I'll bet Shirley's grown a bit since the photos you sent us. She's so adorable! And I loved the painting she did for us. We've put it on the wall in the kitchen. Rico says it reminds him of the pictures he used to send to his grandparents in Italy, only better.

Oh Ruby, I've got some great news! I told you last time I wrote that Mrs M was thinking about retiring, didn't I. Poor love, she's just finding it so difficult with her arthritis. Anyway, out of the blue she called me into the office the other day. I thought she was going to say that she was selling up and that we'd have to find somewhere else to live.

"Now, my dear," she said. "You know things have been getting difficult for me these last few years, so I've come to a decision."

Here it comes, I thought.

"I've decided that I'm going to retire and live with Daphne." You remember Daphne, Mrs M's daughter. She's now living in Liverpool and working as a Veterinary Nurse.

"But I don't want to sell the Hotel. It's been part of my life for so long I couldn't bear to just walk away from it. So what I've decided to do is to take a partner and get them to manage it."

"Oh" I said, thinking she meant that she was getting someone new to take over.

Then she said "Do you think you would like to be my partner?"

I didn't know what to say. Apart from yes please.

So I'm now a partner in the Golf Links Hotel and Rico keeps calling me "Boss". It's great. Business is coming on a treat with loads of people coming for their holidays, especially from the Liverpool and Manchester and we've been surprised by the number of ex-internees that have come back with their families. Oh that reminds me, guess who came in the other day. Heidi Schwarzenberger... with her husband. Yes, she's got married to this huge great fisherman named Otto. The pair of them have got a fishing boat and they'd moored it at Castletown and caught the bus over. I'd forgotten just how big she was, but a fantastic nature. She just smiles at everything. Not a bad way to get through life, is it? She sends you her love and best wishes, by the way.

So what have you been up to? Last time you wrote you said that you thought Jonny and Pete were going to come out of the Army soon. What are they going to do? Join up with Charlie in his coach business? I hear that the sky's the limit in Australia these days. Everyone keeps telling me it's the place where anything can happen if you work hard enough.

Maybe some day Rico and I will be able to make enough money so that we can come over to see you for a holiday. It could be our honeymoon because we never did get one, apart from that weekend in London when it rained non-stop.

Talking of weather, we've just had the wettest winter ever. I think if we ever do have a baby, it'll be born with webbed feet. We're still trying. Rico calls it "practising."

Heard anything from Dot? Is she still in America? Do you have any more nephews or nieces? She certainly seems to be doing her bit to repopulate the world, doesn't she? How many is it? Four or five now?

Anyway, love. Got to go now. It's just gone midnight and I've got to be in Douglas by seven o'clock in the morning. Oh well, as the Americans would say – another day, another dollar.

Take care of yourself and do write soon. Love to Shirley.
Tilly XXXXXXXXXX
PS, please send some more photos of you and Shirley. You both look really well. The climate obviously suits you.

Ruby put down the letter and reached for her hanky. "Oh Tilly. I do miss you so much." She took her empty cup through to the kitchen and filled the kettle for another cup of tea, thinking she'd just about have enough time to drink it before she had to go to fetch Shirley home for her lunch. As the kettle was clattering away on the gas hob, Ruby walked into the front room to tidy some of Shirley's toys away. How can one little child make so much mess so quickly, she thought.

It was when she was reaching down behind the settee to pick up Shirley's favourite doll, that she saw a man in army uniform standing by her garden gate. Seeing who it was, she dashed to the front door and threw it open. "Pete!" she cried. "Oh it's so lovely to see you. I didn't know you were home."

"Hello Sis. I'm on my way now. Ten days leave, so I thought I'd surprise Molly."

"Have you got time to stay for lunch? I've got to go and pick Shirley up but it'll only take five minutes. The kettle's just boiled."

"Yeah, alright. That would be nice. Molly won't be home from work until three."

So while Ruby ran off to get Shirley, Pete made the tea. He was sitting in the kitchen when his niece burst through the front door.

"Uncle Pete! Uncle Pete! Have you brought me anything?"

"Shirley!" admonished her mother. "That's not the way to greet people. Just because they come to see us, it doesn't mean they will always have presents for you."

"Sorry Mummy. Well did you get me a present, Uncle Pete?"

"Oh I give up" said Ruby.

"Well, as it happens I do have something that you might like to have." Pete reached into his khaki rucksack and pulled out a little package wrapped in brown paper. He gave it to Shirley and, with a beaming smile, she gently opened it. Inside was a wooden doll that had movable arms attached with string. It had been painted black and had a skirt and headband made of string.

"Shirley, I'd like you to say hello to Suki. Suki was given to me by a very good friend of mine. He's an aboriginal tracker. He said she will always bring you good luck if you shake hands with her every morning. Would you like to look after her?"

"Yes, please Uncle Pete. Hello Suki" Shirley said and gently grasped the little doll's hand.

"You didn't have to do that" Ruby said when Shirley had gone to play with her new friend while her mother prepared some sandwiches.

"I know, but I like spoiling my niece."

"Well, thanks anyway."

Over lunch, Shirley chattered away ten to the dozen telling her uncle all about her school, her teacher, her three boyfriends and her best friend Juliette. By the time she was due to go back for the afternoon session, Pete felt he knew everything he could possibly want to know about Shirley's class and more.

"Right, young lady. Time to go back."

"I'll walk with you if that's alright. I can catch the bus opposite the school."

"It's a shame you can't stay longer" said Ruby, as she buttoned Shirley's coat.

"I'll see what Molly's got planned for the next week or so. Maybe we can all go out together somewhere."

"That sounds nice. I'll give you the phone number of Mrs Murphy, next door but one. You can always leave a message with her." As they started walking back to the school, Ruby asked "Where are you based at the moment?"

"Up near Darwin. Jeez, it's hot up there. And so humid you can cut the air with a knife sometimes."

"I see you're a Sergeant now. Congratulations. Do you like it?"

"Yeah I do. I've had some run ins with sergeants over the years who were nothing short of a disgrace and I'm determined to make up for them. What have you been up to?"

"Nothing much. I don't seem to get time to do much besides seeing to that little madam and the housework and the cooking and the garden. Oh I nearly forgot, and my job."

"Oh, you've got a job now. Doing what?"

"I work in the florist shop on the main road three mornings a week."

"Like it?"

"It's smashing. It gets me out of the house, I meet people and of course the money helps. Oh, and I'm studying in the evenings. I want to become a teacher."

"Crikey? What made you decide that?"

"I've wanted to be a teacher ever since I was on the Isle of Man. I nearly became one then but some qualified teachers were interned just at that same time and they took over everything."

"Do you think about those times much?"

"Sometimes. I get regular letters from Tilly, you know my friend who shared with me then, and now she part-owns the Hotel we lived in."

There were a few seconds silence and then Pete said seriously "You were lucky."

"I know. I could have been made to share with someone awful. Tilly and I hit it off straight-away.

"I didn't mean that."

"What did you mean?" asked Ruby, flummoxed by Pete's sudden change of tone.

"All that spying business that Dieter got you into."

Ruby felt herself blushing. "How do you know?"

"I've always known. Well, perhaps not always, but I've known for a long time."

"But how?"

"Chap from British Intelligence told me."

"I don't understand. Why would he tell you?"

"Because he wanted me to do something for him."

"What?"

"Can't tell you. Maybe some day." He look round behind him, hearing the unmistakable sound of a diesel engine and saw the bus coming along the road. "Look love, I've gotta go. Thanks for the lunch and the tea."

Having kissed his niece, and Suki, Pete turned to his sister. "Look after yourself, Sis. See you soon." He kissed her on the cheek and then turned and ran over to the bus-stop.

"Take care" shouted Ruby, her head spinning as she tried to make some sense out of what Pete had said.

Despite checking with Mrs Murphy everyday for the next fortnight, Pete never rang. Had he had second thoughts about meeting up? Did he feel too embarrassed about her past to want to talk about it? Ruby tried to write several letters to him but every time she sat down in front of a blank piece of paper, she just couldn't get the words to sound right. It would just have to wait until she saw him next.

But it was the best part of two years before they met again and then it was by accident, at a mutual friend's barbecue, and despite trying to get her brother alone, Pete avoided her and wouldn't even make eye contact with her. She knew he didn't want to talk about it and eventually gave up trying……for years.

Chapter 25

May 31st 1987

As the bearers smoothly lowered the coffin to the sounds of the muted sobbing of the dead man's four daughters, the Vicar of All Saints Church began to speak:

"Unto Almighty God we commend the soul of our brother Karl, and we commit his body to the ground; earth to earth, ashes to ashes, dust to dust; in sure and certain hope of the Resurrection unto eternal life, through our Lord Jesus Christ, at whose coming in glorious majesty to judge the world, the earth and the sea shall give up their dead; and the corruptible bodies of those who sleep in him shall be changed, and made like unto his own glorious body; according to the mighty working whereby he is able to subdue all things unto himself."

As he continued with the service, Ruby looked around at the host of mourners who had come to pay their respects to Charlie who had died, suddenly, of a heart attack a fortnight before. All his drivers were there, smartly turned out in their navy jackets with the firm's name, Emanuel Coaches, emblazoned in gold on their breast pockets. Ruby knew that Charlie's best friend Manny had never been found after the Arandora Star had gone down and naming his Company after him was Charlie's way of honouring his memory.

Jonny was there, leaning on his walking-stick. He'd been one of the firm's Directors, but had retired some three years ago, leaving the running of the Company in the hands of his son, Sam and Charlie's eldest daughter, Lily. At his side, with one arm supporting him, was Jonny's wife, Madge. She was dabbing her nose under the little black veil that hung from the front of her wide-brimmed hat which Ruby had thought was totally over the top. The two women had never taken to each other: Ruby always found her sister-in-law to be too full of airs and graces while Madge just couldn't get on with what she had once described as Ruby's "superiority complex." The truth was that both women were very similar.

Sam, tall and bronzed, stood next to his mother whilst clutching the hand of his wife, Lillian. In front of them stood their teenaged son and daughter: twins, but you'd never guess by looking at them; the boy had long curly black hair tied back into a pony-tail, while his sister was blonde. Uncannily, she was the spitting image of Tilly – it always unnerved Ruby every time she saw her. Ruby had forgotten their names and made a mental note to look in the address book when she got home to remind herself.

The Vicar was saying "O God, whose mercies cannot be numbered, accept our prayers on behalf of the soul of thy servant departed, and grant him an entrance into the land of light and joy, in the fellowship of thy saints; through Jesus Christ our Lord. Amen."

And then there was Pete; stooping a little now. His white hair parted precisely, just like it had been for all these years. His hand rested lightly on Shirley's shoulder as she stood next to her children, Martin, James and Juliette, who since birth had always been called Tilly. Shirley had been divorced soon after Juliette had been born and life had been a struggle for her. But Ruby was proud of what Shirley had achieved: the children had grown up to be smashing kids and she was now the local MP. How she found the time, Ruby could only wonder.

She looked to Pete again and found him staring back at her. This time there was no breaking away as the Vicar said "O Lord Jesus Christ, who by thy death didst take away the sting of death; grant unto us thy servants so to follow in faith where thou hast led the way, that we may at length fall asleep peacefully in thee, and wake up after thy likeness; through thy mercy, who livest with the Father and the Holy Ghost, one God, world without end. Amen."

And it was over. The last handful of dusty soil was sprinkled onto the coffin that now bore a red and gold wreath in the shape of a steering-wheel and the mourners moved away to the cars that would take them to Charlie's golf club where the wake would be held. As if by the tacit approval of the other mourners, Ruby, Jonny and Pete were left to say goodbye to their brother privately.

For a minute or two, the siblings, elderly now, stood in silent contemplation and then Jonny said "I kept telling him to pack it in before it killed him. He just wouldn't stop. Work, work, work."

"It was for Manny" said Pete, abruptly.

Ruby and Jonny looked up from the grave at their brother, not sure what he meant.

"It was as if by making the business a success, he could somehow bring Manny back to life."

"Grandad!" It was the Tilly look-alike speaking to Jonny. "Daddy says to tell you we're going now."

"Ok, pet. I'm coming." And then, with a glance at Pete and Ruby, he walked carefully between the other graves assisted by his grand-daughter.

"How times change, eh?" said Pete.

"Old age has nothing to recommend it, does it?" replied his sister.

"I'm sorry."

"What for?"

"For not having the guts to finish our conversation. I just wanted to put the whole of that time behind me: the war, the Arandora Star, the Dunera, the camps, Mutti dying, everything. I used to say life's too short to live in the past, but recently I've realised that that's exactly what I've been doing by not confronting it."

"You remember you told me that a man from British Intelligence had told you about what Dieter and I had been doing?"

Pete nodded.

"What did he tell you?"

"He said that they had evidence that you had been spotting for the Luftwaffe. He accepted that you were being led by Dieter, but nevertheless you were a traitor and a spy."

"What did you say?"

"What could I say? I told him I didn't believe it. Then he showed me the code book that you used and some of the translations that they'd done. I was shocked, confused and embarrassed."

"So what happened?"

"This chap said that it was certain that you would spend the next twenty years in prison and that you might even be hanged as Dieter certainly would be if they ever caught him. I didn't know what to think. I was numb. Then he said there was a way that I could help you to get a lighter sentence – "a significantly lighter sentence" he said. I asked him what he had in mind and he told me about this captured German naval captain who was part of a plan to kidnap prominent engineers and scientists and take them to Africa to work on a secret weapon that Germany was developing. Trouble was, they didn't know whereabouts in Africa so they wanted me to get close to him and his crew and find out. That meant splitting away from Charlie and Jonny and going with Burfeind and his crew."

"Oh Pete. I'm so sorry. I always knew that I was being treated more leniently than I should have been, but I just couldn't understand why. Someone once said that I must have friends in high places, but I didn't believe it." She leant across and gave her brother a kiss on the cheek. "Thank you."

"You'd have done it for me if things were reversed."

"Mm-mm. You know I would."

"Well then. That's what families are for."

"So what happened to this captain. Did you get the information?"

"No. He went down with the Arandora Star. Funny really, he saved my life in the end by making me get off the ship before it went down, otherwise I'd have stayed with him and probably drowned. He was a nice bloke. I liked him."

"Are you two coming?" shouted one of the car drivers.

"I suppose we'd better make a move" said Ruby. As they supported each other across the uneven grass strip between the graves, Ruby said "But why couldn't you tell me?"

"Mixture of things really. Firstly, I couldn't believe that you would really do something like that and then I happened to meet Dieter. Total accident. Bumped into him in Sydney in the sixties. Arrogant little shit. Couldn't help telling me how successful he was. I asked him about what you both had been doing and although he was a bit reluctant at first, I persuaded him to tell me the truth."

"Persuaded him, how?"

Pete just held up his fist and grinned. "I always thought his nose was too big anyway."

Ruby smiled.

"So, he told me that he was just using you and that was all. He didn't love you but needed you as a cover. He admitted feeding you with all sorts of Nazi propaganda and making sure you believed it. Then when he heard from someone on the inside that he was going to be arrested, he fled across the Channel leaving you holding the baby."

They were now back to the car that had remained to take them to the Golf Club. Sitting on the back seat, Ruby said "What else?"

"Sorry?" Pete said, turning away from his gaze out of the window.

"You said there was a mixture of things."

"Oh yeah. Well, one other, really. They made me sign the Official Secrets Act. If I'd have said anything to you and they had found out, I'd have been put in jail."

"What, even after you came out of the Army?"

"As far as I know, there's no statute of limitation on the OSA. I think it applies for ever."

"So you could still go to prison if they found out you'd told me?"

"Yep. But I don't think it's likely. I'm too old."

"We both are" laughed Ruby. "It's strange, but none of it seems to matter much any more."

Pete reached for his sister's hand and pointed with the other outside the car. "That's what matters. All that out there. All the people that can live their lives without tyranny, bigotry and oppression. That's what's important. They might not do it right, but at least they've got the chance to make their own mistakes."

"You know, Peter Darling, you're quite something" said Ruby as she leant across and kissed her brother on the cheek.

THE END

www.ingramcontent.com/pod-product-compliance
Lightning Source LLC
Chambersburg PA
CBHW071612030726
47598CB00001B/241